Praise for *The Kendc*

"*The Kendal Sparrow* takes us on an enthralling journey of risky early ministry with a young Friend in the days when the term was barely coined. Debut novelist Barbara Luetke weaves a fictionalized tale of the real Elizabeth Fletcher, one of the 'Valiant Sixty' in mid-sixteen-hundreds England and Ireland. Readers will appreciate the deeply researched historic detail as they experience the setting and times of the first Friends of Truth."

— *Edith Maxwell, author of the* Quaker Midwife Mysteries

"Carefully researched, this novel captures the excitement and risk that Quakerism offered its early converts, how outcasts could find meaning in a life of ministry and preaching, and how loving friendship bound the Quaker network together. Deftly paced and very moving."

— *Ben Pink Dandelion, Director of the Centre for Research in Quaker Studies at Woodbrooke Quaker Study Centre*

"Growing up in the Religious Society of Friends, the stories of those who founded our faith were plentiful — but the young age of George Fox and those he convinced were noticeably absent. Here the experiences of Elizabeth Fletcher and her companions, alongside so many well-known Quaker names, retell the history of Quakerism's founding through the teenagers who brought it to life. Complete with the true biographies of these young Friends at the book's conclusion, *The Kendal Sparrow* provides generations to come with an invaluable resource. Let us reclaim our history."

— *Breeze Richardson, member of Oread Friends Meeting*

"Early Quakers opposed novels, but it's no fiction that as the subject of a skilled writer such as Barbara Luetke, they make for intriguing reading! *The Kendal Sparrow* lets the life of Elizabeth Fletcher tell the story of how young men and women of the 17th century sought to transform the world, addressing issues as relevant today as they were then."

— *Max L. Carter, emeritus William R. Rogers Director of Friends Center and Quaker Studies at Guilford College*

"I learned so much reading *The Kendal Sparrow*. Ideas lingered long after I put the book down. I am amazed at the writing . . . the lovely little details, the way of telling the story through conversation, the vivid description that let me feel and see the scenes, and the carefully constructed characters. How surprising to find a deaf child and the little that was known about deaf education among the pages."

— *Peggy Mayer, retired Head of School, Northwest School for Deaf and Hard-of-Hearing Children (Seattle)*

"In *The Kendal Sparrow*, Barbara Luetke gives us a thoughtful account of the life of Elizabeth Fletcher, one of the first Publishers of Truth. In Luetke, she has found a sympathetic and readable biographical novelist."

— *Thomas Hamm, Professor of History, Curator of the Quaker Collection, and Director of Special Collections at Earlham College*

"*The Kendal Sparrow* takes us back in time to the dynamic, revolutionary birth of Quakerism — when the world turned upside down. We see how the charismatic founder, George Fox, galvanized this religious movement, inspiring his followers of all ages to follow their spiritual leadings and spread the Word courageously throughout the world. With excellent description and characterization, Barbara Luetke brings to life the intensity and power of the earliest Friends, giving flesh and bone to Elizabeth Fletcher and twenty other young adult Quaker women and men who risked everything in the name of Truth. Through this compelling and moving story, we are able to understand and appreciate the sacrifices made for the freedom of religious expression."

— *Michele Lise Tarter, editor of* New Critical Studies on Early Quaker Women, 1650–1800 *(co-edited with Catie Gill)*

"I was delighted to hear of the publication of this novel focusing on Elizabeth Fletcher and other early Quakers with whom she may have had contact. This will be of special interest to Friends in Ireland, where Elizabeth was among the very first to spread the Quaker message. It is a reminder of the equal roles played by men and women, young and old, in the early Quaker movement. The dedication and tenacity of this young woman are inspiring and remind us of the fresh hope brought by our own contemporary spiritual 'revolutionaries' working for a more peaceful, just and sustainable world."

— *Denise C. Gabuzda, Clerk, Ireland Yearly Meeting*

The Kendal Sparrow

A NOVEL OF
ELIZABETH FLETCHER

Barbara Schell Luetke

PHILADELPHIA, PA

To Gus, Iggy, Tripp, and grandchildren to come: may you work for peace and social justice in all the ways that you know will make our world a better place.

QuakerPress of Friends General Conference
1216 Arch Street, 2B, Philadelphia, PA 19107

Printed in the United States of America

Composition and design by David Botwinik

Back cover photograph of Barbara Schell Luetke by Andrea Vanni

The cover is a detail from the 1998 oil painting "Pendle Waters" by Lancashire artist John Corcoran. It is used by permission of the artist. To see more of John Corcoran's work visit The Corcoran Gallery at http://www.corcorangallery.co.uk/Corcoran_Gallery/Welcome.html

ISBN 978-1-7334126-0-5 (paperback)
978-1-7334126-1-2 (digital)

Library of Congress Cataloging-in-Publication Data
Luetke, Barbara Schell, 1950–
The Kendal sparrow: a novel of Elizabeth Fletcher / by Barbara Schell Luetke
pages cm
ISBN 978-1-7334126-0-5 (paperback) / ISBN 978-1-7334126-1-2 (digital)
1. Society of Friends. 2. Fiction — Society of Friends. 3. Quaker authors. I. Title.
BKR803-76 1-6482010641 2018

To order more copies of this publication or other Quaker titles call 1-800-966-4556 or see the online catalog at www.quakerbooks.org.

Contents

This is Guillaume Blaeu's 1631 map of the British Isles. Cartographically, this map is based upon the plates of Jodocus Hondius, which Blaeu acquired in 1629. This map would become Blaeu's standard representation of the British Isles and was published in most subsequent Blaeu atlases issued between 1634 and 1672. The five most populated cities of the seventeenth century are highlighted here: London, Norwich, York, Bristol, and Newcastle. (Source: https://nl.wikipedia.org/wiki/Bestand:1631_Blaeu_Map_of_the_British_Isles_(England,_Scotland,_Ireland)_-_Geographicus_-_BritanniaeHiberniae-blaeu-1631.jpg)

Part I

Northwest England

1653

Chapter 1

Elizabeth Fletcher sat on the back step of her aunt's cottage north of Kendal, following the antics of a flock of sparrows as they darted about the garden. Elbows on knees, she watched them flit about, happy to flirt and fly, until they followed one another to places she could only imagine. As she untied her work bonnet, the swift-flowing River Kent caught her attention. She considered how the blue of the summer sky reflected in the water, pretending to move the azure swath of color into the places in her body that ached from the bending and twisting of her chores. She unfolded her hands from under her chin and rubbed at her warm cheeks. She was unhappy and restless, and she wished she felt more eager about the days ahead.

Every story Elizabeth had ever been told of her family and neighbors on the farmstead had centered on working the land and herding the sheep, the dignity of it found in how neighbors treated each other. It'd be the expected way of things, wouldn't it? That she'd marry a man strong enough to work the animals and crops, one who'd permit her to walk alone into Kendal for market and church. That they'd have children, lots of children, and grow old together.

This kind of life had been enough for her ancestors, hadn't it? Given the choice, would those people, those women, have chosen something else? Elizabeth wrapped her arms around her knees, enclosing them like the rams and ewes she eyed in the fieldstone walls out beyond the cow barn. The sheep seemed perfectly satisfied with the routine of their lives, oblivious to the monotony of it. They could lie for days without alarm in a pelting rain or under a blanket of snow, apathetic heads tucked down. In the heat of the summer, they stood as they did now, each in its own little spot on the hillside, grazing contentedly on clover.

Just then, across the lane, Lizzie Leavens bounced out the door of the family privy, blond pigtails flying, headed for her cottage. Packed with impatience and full of giggles, she'd been born only a month before Elizabeth, and her Da and Ma, Kelsey and Hannah Leavens, were like second parents to Elizabeth. In fact, although the Leavenses had claimed the name of "Elizabeth," they began to call their daughter "Lizzie" when Elizabeth's Da wanted it, too. The only girls on the farmstead, the two of them had grown up like sisters. They'd played the same games, loved the same dollies, and often ate and slept at each other's cottages.

Elizabeth kept her stare on the whole of the Leavens' home as Lizzie vanished inside it. The cottage was connected with a low roof to the barn, the design allowing for the doing of chores despite the rain and cold. Her home, Jane Fletcher's place, wasn't all that different, a two-room cottage and a cow barn. A privy nearby. The Leavenses rented their property from Lord Wold, but Elizabeth's aunt owned hers. The thought of it caused Elizabeth to bring her shoulders back and sit up a little straighter, proud that Auntie's cottage and the plot of land it sat on had been bequeathed to her by a dead uncle. There was a comfort in the dull, familiar limestone buildings, as much as there was a longing to leave them and live a different life.

Elizabeth slumped forward again and considered the tumble of conflicting futures. Part of her appreciated the life she lived with her aunt and the routine of their days together. But another part of her was lonely, dissatisfied, and wanting something more.

Lizzie'll marry Thomas, she decided. She looked back across the lane to the Leavens' place. Lizzie was certainly ready for it. A full head taller than Elizabeth and almost fully formed, Lizzie's chest was budding out and her monthlies had started. And it was no secret that she loved Thomas Holme. The Holme cottage was but a stone's throw from the Leavens', across the lane from the Fletchers, too, and a bit closer to Kendal. Lizzie already spent most of her free time lingering around the work shed of Thomas' family's woolen business, which made Elizabeth jealous.

There'd been a time when she and Lizzie would both sit at Thomas' knee for hours in the evenings. He'd been like an older brother then, a gifted teller of tales. They'd huddled at his feet as he told stories about witches or ghosts. Back then, Elizabeth had wanted to believe his stories, that spirits lived in the dark corners of the Holme's workroom behind the huge looms. Once, Thomas had taken the girls through the wool shop gardens, gathering the woad plants. Then they'd gone back to the workroom where he'd put them in a huge, black pot that held some unknown mixture. He'd taken a scrap of finished fabric, put it in the pot, and stirred the concoction with a giant paddle, his eyes blinking and winking, as he'd added what he claimed were his Da's secret ingredients — a combination of salt, vinegar, and ammonia from stale urine. Elizabeth and Lizzie had held their noses in mock disgust until a lime green color magically transferred onto the cloth. Thomas claimed the color was the same worn by Robin Hood and his Merry Men.

Elizabeth closed her eyes tight. She didn't know anymore how she felt about Lizzie and Thomas. She'd once been so happy to share Lizzie's glad ways and Thomas' silly stories. Of late, the two seemed to have little time for her. She longed to discuss the news that Thomas brought home from his selling, but she was left out of their conversations, ignored.

"Time to help with sup," Elizabeth's Aunt Jane called

from inside the Fletcher cottage. "Bring in some flowers, would you now?"

Elizabeth rose and went into the knee-high grass to pick a bouquet from among the poppies, bachelor buttons, Queen Anne's Lace, bluebells, and dandelions. Some thought dandelions were weeds, but not Elizabeth. She gathered them into her bouquet, imagining the bobbing heads of the flowers to be her neighbors — Kelsey, Hannah and Lizzie Leavens, Charles, Jennifer, and Thomas Holme — and returned up the step to pull the latch on the wobbly cottage door. "Auntie . . ." she began, her tone a bit whiny as she came into the front room.

"Hmm?" Jane Fletcher asked absent-mindedly. Her back was to Elizabeth as she bent at the fire pit, the whole of it taking up most of the one side of the sparsely furnished room. She arched back in a stretch before standing and stepping to their only table, fixing on Elizabeth as she retied the strings of the apron that covered her mouse-brown skirts.

Elizabeth considered her graying hair and lightly wrinkled face. "I'm, I'm at odds with myself lately. So unsettled . . ." she mumbled. "I, I don't know what's wrong with me . . ." she tried. She went to fetch a container for the flowers, unable to find the words to convey her discontent in a manner that wouldn't insult her aunt.

Auntie turned back to the fire and stirred the large pot of lentil, acorn, and herb pottage that was their sup. "I imagine you're puzzled and wondering these days," she countered carelessly. "It's the age for it."

Elizabeth repeated the words to herself. *It's the age for it.* She didn't think so. Her discontent came from a deep place. "It's not my age," she said aloud, with an edge. "It's that I have no say over it."

"Over what?" Auntie asked softly, cocking her head.

"Over my *life*," Elizabeth replied stiffly, the last word louder than she meant it to be. "I feel left out . . . from Thomas and Lizzie . . . from the sermons at church. Unsure about my life." She worked to tame the barrage of thoughts.

"Don't suppose a person ever stops wondering about their purpose," sighed Auntie, not fully realizing Elizabeth's discontent. "If they can be of better use to their family and neighbors?"

Elizabeth paused in her watering of the flowers. *To be of use,* she repeated to herself. She pulled at the stems to rearrange them. Then she went to the sideboard where she'd left the rye bread she'd made that morning, wishing Auntie would say more. There was no sense trying to rush the woman. She knew that much. She'd talk when she was ready.

Elizabeth walked her fingers on the edge of the cupboard beside the sideboard, the piece crafted by her Da years ago. It held two plates, two forks, two spoons, and a single knife. She pulled out a plate, ripped two hunks from the cooled bread loaf, and set them nicely on it. "Was my Da unhappy here? Is that why he left us?" she asked, unable to wait any longer. Auntie liked to talk about her baby brother, Elizabeth's papa. Perhaps if she got her started, there'd be something new this time, an insight that would justify her own dissatisfaction. She brought the bread to the table and then went back to bring the crockery bowls and wooden spoons to the hearth.

"You know, Elizabeth . . ." Auntie lifted the pot from the chimney crane and set it on the blacken bricks that rimmed the ash of the pit. "He was very much in love with your Ma . . . and I was happy to share him with her . . . and you, too, when you came along." She smiled warmly at Elizabeth as she said this. "Never doubt that he loved you, dearest. You were like a precious stone to the man." She pushed her cap back from her lined brow. "It's, it's just that he was lost after . . . after your Ma died." Auntie tucked her head down, Elizabeth unable to see her expression. "Her death shattered him," Auntie sighed, staring into the fire. "He tried to make a go of it here, with the crops and the sheep, but every flower and songbird reminded him of her. He just couldn't be here any longer."

"And you were here to raise me," Elizabeth added, grateful for it. Still, her aunt's grief worsened her own melancholy. She ducked under the sprig of herbs that hung from the rafters near the fire pit. Maybe her Da hadn't thought she'd miss him, that she'd want a family like Thomas and Lizzie had.

"Oh, goodness, child, you've been the joy of my life," sang Auntie. Elizabeth could hear the resolve in the strong, sure tone and she took refuge in it. She moved beside Auntie to take the filled bowls and set them on the oak table. It'd been hewed by her Da as well. When she sat down, the legs of her chair marked the dirt floor. "A chance I'd have missed if your Da hadn't allowed it. Besides." She stood up with exaggerated slowness and pretended to come feebly to the little table. "What would I do if you weren't learning to make the beer, cure the meats, preserve the vegetables?" She raised an eyebrow to hint at the hoax.

"Form the candles, make the soaps, sweep, and milk the cow. . . ." Elizabeth snickered, playing along. A smile crept up her cheeks. She filled their mugs with the light, malty beer that Kelsey had made recently. He didn't let it age so they could drink it throughout the day, safer than water.

"And this whole last year you've been going to Kendal on your own. When I'm all crippled up and can't go myself, I'll have you." She plopped into her chair.

The idea of it made Elizabeth worry again. *Trapped*, she thought, looking down at her pottage. *Trapped here forever to help Auntie.*

She felt Auntie's fingers catch hers and she stretched her hands out to her across the table for a better grip. For as long as Elizabeth could remember the two had begun their meals with silence. She wasn't certain why they didn't recite prayers as happened at the Holme cottage, but she was pretty sure that even if the Fletchers owned a Bible, they wouldn't have read from it before meals. When she opened her eyes and lifted her head, Auntie was staring at her. "What?" she asked. There was a long pause. "Auntie," she coaxed, "if I'm old enough to marry, I'm old enough to know whatever it is you're wanting to tell me."

"The quiet took me to memories of your Ma dying," Auntie replied wistfully. She bowed her head into her clasped hands, Elizabeth taking note of the neat stitching of the sleeves that modestly covered her wrists. "Of wondering if she'd have lived if we'd sent for help sooner. . . ." She hoisted the pitcher to fill their mugs, hiding her face. Elizabeth waited, her spoon untouched. Thirteen years since her birth, thirteen years since her Ma had died, but the pain was still there, floating in the room.

"We women out here were in our prime back then," Auntie started up again. "Hannah and your Ma so young and full of life, the best of friends . . . telling each other their secrets." Auntie rested her sad eyes on Elizabeth. "Seemed like twins at times, the two of them, with the same auburn hair down their backs, same pleasing faces, and both with such kind hearts. Their giggles made them fun to be around, made the work go easier, and the worries lessen. The two of them like daughters to me." The words came pouring out.

"You know the two of them argued about who could claim the name 'Elizabeth' for their babies, should you both be girls."

Elizabeth nodded. She knew this part of the telling.

"That when Lizzie was birthed, Hannah kindly told everyone to call her Lizzie." Elizabeth nodded again.

"Of course, I was there for that birth, Lizzie just sliding out like a pour of beer — but when your Ma's time came, her labors went on and on and Hannah and I, we, we didn't know what to do." Auntie looked up at the rafters, hunting for a reason. "Hannah and I had never seen such troubles." She blinked back tears. "But yours, yours was a challenge and a worry that we didn't expect — and weren't prepared for. . . . Like a summer sky turned suddenly dark with storm. We were trapped in the thick of it almost before we knew it."

Guilt stung Elizabeth. She'd been the cause of her mother dying and because of that, her Da had left them. Perhaps Auntie's life would've been different, better altogether, if she hadn't been born.

"We could see she was slipping from us," Auntie was saying. "We called for the midwife, but it took her a long time to get here. We never really knew why. Hannah thought it was because we'd talk so publicly about our disagreements with the baptizing of babies. . . ." Auntie stared intensely at Elizabeth for a moment as if she was deciding how much to explain. "There was a man, you see, a Thomas Taylor, who was against it . . . and Hannah, your Ma . . . me . . . we heard him talking in the Kendal market. We took to his thinking, that people should wait until they were old enough to know what they were deciding, and then make the pledge. We liked what he had to say, us ripe for it . . . and we told others about his ideas, expressing our opinions on the matter and wanting to discuss them. . . ."

Ah, thought Elizabeth. *Same as me.*

"Not as careful as we are these days with our saying things against the Church." Auntie swallowed and Elizabeth could hear the gulp. "It might have been that that kept the woman

. . . but it could've been that some thought us witches — because of our herbal brews, salves, potions, and such." She glanced over her shoulder as if she could see the Holme cottage through the cottage wall. "There's some truth to those stories Thomas used to tell you girls. He's older than you. He remembers more." Her shoulder slumped. "How people shunned us out here . . . still do. . . ."

"So, the midwife came late?" nudged Elizabeth, trying to steer Auntie back on track.

Auntie got up and went to the window. "At the end," she sighed, drawing back a curtain the two had soaked in linseed oil and fashioned, "we could but sit and wait with her. Useless." She looked back at Elizabeth. "She didn't fear death, child, only hoped you'd live, you so tiny."

"And was she in pain?" asked Elizabeth softly.

"No, no," Auntie faced her. "She was peaceful in her passing. I've told you that before, yes? Called you her little sparrow, not knowing if you'd be a boy or a girl. Whispered her hopes and dreams for you to us, that you'd be happy with your life. She wanted to write it down for you — for you to read, I suppose, on days like this one."

"She did?" None of the farmstead women could read or write.

"Troubled her, yes." Auntie came back to the table. "And her dying left its mark. The Leavenses stopped going to church, Hannah saying she'd always got her strength anyway from the beauty of the trees and plantings. We'd heard about holding hands in silence before meals by then and we adopted it, the Leavens and I. A time to think of your Ma, of how she'd want us to behave." Auntie skipped ahead. "When the war started up again, your Da saw his chance, a way to leave this knot of farms and his memories. To take up with the troops against King Charles." Auntie's lips trembled. "You remember your Da, don't you? You were so young when he enlisted."

"Riding on his shoulders out in the garden. Playing hide and seek in the cow barn." Elizabeth recounted. They were the vague memories of a four year old.

"You're so like your Da, Elizabeth," bragged Auntie. "The two of you had a strong bond, twisted together like the braids of rope." She stretched her hands to take Elizabeth's again. "You have his goodness, his common sense." She gently squeezed Elizabeth's fingers to affirm it. "His soldiering paid the levied taxes for at least those few years . . . Wold collecting from my uncle, him freeholding it and then passing it to me."

Elizabeth saw the stubbornness in Auntie's expression, her refusing to use Lord Wold's title. She'd only noticed the omission of late but when she'd asked about it, Auntie had answered with a query. "Aren't all men equals, the nobility and landowners no better than the clergy and the commoners?"

"I think it irks the man that a woman owns a part of all that is otherwise his." Auntie was supposing now. "Which Kelsey claims is half of Westmorland. Cares not a bit, that I can see, about those of us who work it for him." She batted at a wisp of gray hair at her forehead. "Don't know for sure. I've heard the wartime taxes grow higher and higher. . . ."

Had he been the one to send the soldiers? Lord Wold? Elizabeth wondered, the thought not occurring to her before. It'd been the night of her seventh birthday, an occasion that should've been marked by the surprise of new stockings under her pillow or the making of a mince pie, but the King had put a halt to all that. Celebrating was no longer permitted.

When Elizabeth heard the loud barrage of knocks, she'd expected to see an excited Lizzie, allowed to cross the lane alone to wish her a special birthday greeting. She saw herself now as that little girl, dressed in her simple sleep shift, the shawl her mother had knit hanging off her shoulders. It'd been Auntie's present to her earlier in the day.

It hadn't been Lizzie standing at the door when she'd pulled the rope to open the latch. Instead, a foul-smelling soldier shoved her back and he and his chum came barging into the room. "You Jane Fletcher?" one had demanded, staring over her head.

Auntie had risen in confusion, her knitting dropping to the floor, to confront the ragged men in their torn breeches and dirty coats. There'd been a quick exchange, the accents unfamiliar. Her father was dead.

Elizabeth hadn't had time to digest the idea before one of the men was in front of her, blocking her from running to Auntie. "An orphan now, huh?" he'd growled. She'd pressed herself back flat against the door casing, her gaze level with his belt. "No papa to protect you." A shiver had moved so completely through her body that she'd clenched herself tightly not wanting her pee to color the floor.

Even now, the memories of that night sent Elizabeth shaking. It had marked the beginning of everything changing. The following year, King Charles was beheaded, and some said England would never see another king or queen. The days were tainted by unrest and uncertainty, everyone fretting about everything. Even now it was a rare event when Elizabeth heard Auntie laugh.

Chapter 2

A couple of days later Elizabeth eagerly strolled the rutted way south into Kendal for market day. She hoped she'd be able to find Thomas and have him to herself for a change. Agilely she hopped over the brushwood that'd been kicked across the deepest holes and listened to the hiss of the wind as it moved through the trees. She followed the path through the Serpentine Woods, thinking about a ragged little girl she hoped to see today. Maybe four or five years old. She'd met her some months back, the child so fleeting, it'd been hard to tell that she was a girl. Elizabeth had pointed to herself. "E-liz-a-beth." She'd enunciated the syllables, stretching out the parts and repeated them several times. The girl had watched her astutely but hadn't said anything.

"What's *your* name?" Elizabeth had pushed. She'd pointed to the girl and nodded encouragingly into the solemn little eyes.

The response was something like a cat in heat. "Mmmmm . . . oe," the tone of it odd, higher than expected.

"M . . . oe? Moe?" Elizabeth had repeated.

Just then, a cart had bumped loudly past. The girl hadn't reacted at all but only reached a rope-thin arm out towards Elizabeth's basket. *She doesn't hear*, thought Elizabeth, unsure. Her concern deepened. She stepped around the girl and called her name. No response. Elizabeth gave her an apple and considered her as the child held it in two hands and bit into it. Such easy prey to the dangers of Kendal, Elizabeth worried. *Who feeds her? Where does she sleep?*

Out of nowhere, a constable had suddenly grabbed the child up, yelling loudly for her to drop the apple. Moe's hands had flown quickly over her grimy face as he shook her.

Without thinking, Elizabeth had intervened. "Oh, no. 'Tis quite all right, sir," she'd told him calmly and with feigned respect. "'Tis why I brought it. 'Tis extra from our orchard," she'd added with a firmness and authority she hadn't realized she possessed. To her surprise, the constable had released the dangling girl, then grabbed an apple for himself.

"See that she doesn't steal from anyone else," he'd muttered as he'd left them. Quick as a wink, the little one had grabbed up what remained of the dirty apple and scurried off in the opposite direction.

Elizabeth thought back on the altercation. Something strong had risen up in her, the courage of it not her usual way. She'd liked the feeling; was sure she could find it again if it was needed. A month or so ago, she'd been able to get Moe to follow her to see Minister Blake. He seemed elated that someone from the north farmstead had come to him for assistance and promised he'd try to find someone who would take responsibility for Moe. He'd listened to Elizabeth and been more understanding of her concern than she'd expected, said he'd see what he could do. When she checked back with him a week or so later, he seemed to have forgotten all about her, about Moe. The child was just one of the many orphans living in the Kendal alleyways, just one of the nippers who'd lost their parents to the plague or for some other reason. He'd played nervously with the tassels of his robe and offered no solution — no place where Moe might eat more regularly or sleep safely.

If the stench of the communal privy wasn't signal enough that Elizabeth was coming into Kendal proper, the sight of the Fleece Inn was. Men on the routes between Scotland, Yorkshire, and Lancashire stopped at the tavern to rest and exchange news. Today the Inn flag, displaying a mug of beer, was flapping loudly in the summer breeze to attract travelers.

Elizabeth crept cautiously to an open window, wanting to overhear the conversations. Lurking there, she heard a man boasting of his plans to confiscate the crops of some poor chap who hadn't paid a debt. She supposed him to be a soldier, one given land for his service, as he complained on and on that all hell had broken loose since the end of the War, laborers thinking they didn't have to abide by the laws. He was interrupted by a burst of jovial banter about the Lord Protector's anger when farmers paid fines with bad beer or country folks cut too much forest wood or ran their sheep and cattle herds free on unfenced land.

Elizabeth heard the word "Quaker" and peeked closer to the opening. It was a derogatory term and she wanted to hear what was being said about them. "Renegades," charged a loud man. "Maggots," agreed another. Before she could figure out the whole of the talk, the front door of the inn banged open and she instinctively dropped to the ground. She held her breath, hunched back from the corner, and prayed she wouldn't be found out. When she heard the gallop of a horse fading away, she peeked slowly around the edge of the inn to see if she could safely get to the market.

Elizabeth arrived at the livestock pens on the north side of town and made her first stop at the large wooden cross that marked the center of town. She stood reverently before it, saying a quick prayer that she might see Moe, and went closer to the town crier. Proud in his white regalia, he was screaming out his announcements above the din of the vendor cries and the noise of the children playing nearby. Elizabeth gave the expected nod and curtsy and listened for any information that was new or different. She moved off when his shouts of reminders and punishments became repetitive, passing the pottery and scullery sellers, then the dairy and vegetables vendors. Thomas' stall would be somewhere ahead if she kept walking south.

CHAPTER 2

Some ten years older than Elizabeth and Lizzie, Thomas Holme was secure in his trade. He came from a long tradition of weavers. The family had their workshop on the farmstead, near to the River Kent, and neighbors to the Fletchers and Leavenses, long before Elizabeth had been born. It was a rare occasion when Thomas wasn't either at the massive looms with his Da or off with his cart — not only to Kendal, the largest town in Westmorland, the largest county in the northwest of England — but down the pack horse trails, south to Lancaster or east to Sedbergh and Durham. He didn't like to go these days, preferring to spend his time with Lizzie when they got the chance. They'd go off and away from the rest of them, wandering the hillsides, talking about who knew what. It perplexed Elizabeth that Lizzie's parents didn't seem to object. Probably, they figured, as she did, that Thomas was working up his courage to propose.

Elizabeth passed a puppet show and two lads in bright tunics tossing clubs in the air. Folding to the crowd, she found herself behind a group of higher-class women gossiping about a man who'd lost his arm in some horrible accident. Their casual chatter, void of any sympathy, put her off. She dodged around them, coming face to face with an even more privileged gentleman. He was elegantly dressed in a belted suit and wore a broad, stylish plumed hat.

"To the other side," the lady he held on his arm commanded. She flounced her colorful, embroidered skirts and pointed with a gloved hand.

Elizabeth dipped before the couple. Nobility of such class were an unusual sight in Kendal and could easily cause her trouble if she didn't adhere to the expected way of things. Working to leave them behind, she merged in with a mob of country folks. They wore ill-fitting hats and were dressed in mis-matched clothes and worthless shoes. Suddenly pushed from behind, her face was jammed in the back of a poor fellow who was fiercely scratching about his head as he limped along. She ducked into a stall selling shoes for relief from his pungent odor and pretended to consider an artistically crafted pair of ankle high, round-toed buckle shoes. *Not very practical*, she decided, although she appreciated the beauty in the workmanship. She tucked her own battered tips self-consciously under her skirts and admired a pair of knee-high stockings. Hers were coarse knit from Holme's wool that she'd spun herself.

"Might I help you, girl?" the vendor asked. He sounded annoyed.

Elizabeth shook her head, keeping her eyes hidden from the man. She exited the stall and stopped to buy a hunk of goat cheese and a small fish. Then she moved on to the section of stalls where soaps and baked goods were sold. Auntie had sent her with a request to buy a raisin loaf topped with icing and only from her friend, Miss Kabian.

With relief, Elizabeth found the old woman and selected the nicest of the breads on display. As she handed over the coins for it, her eye caught on a display of diaries and journals nearby and she went to them for a closer look. She put a finger on the symbols on one of the covers and began to trace the form.

"Can you read?" asked the seller from over her shoulder.

"Thank you, no sir." Elizabeth dipped slightly. She exited the booth, moving out into the stream of shoppers again. *Read. I wish*, she pouted.

Goods beckoned at each stall, a million items that the Fletchers could ill-afford, had they any use for them. The embroidery on some of the fancier items made her think of Lizzie. She had a passion for such stitching. Elizabeth tried to memorize some of the detail of the designs that decorated most of the tunics, long and short gowns, and cloaks should she talk with Lizzie any time soon. Needing a rest and hoping to see Moe, she found a bench out of the way of the shoppers and pulled her basket snug beside her. She put an apple she'd rescued from the root cellar in plain sight atop of her other things.

Ah, there, she thought, catching a glimpse of the girl. *Maybe she was following me. Waiting her chance.*

"Hey, there!" she heard just then. "Auntie freed you, did she?"

Elizabeth turned away from where she thought she'd seen Moe and in the direction of Thomas' shrill voice. She found his face, towering above those moving around him, and met his grin. "I'm right this way," he yelled. A lock of his neatly cut hair jutted out at an odd angle from under his cap and offset his lopsided smile. "There." He pointed the way she should follow, it improper for him to take her hand.

Elizabeth followed his swaying height as he maneuvered through the crowd just ahead of her.

"Have a sit." Thomas waved at her, when they got to the Holmes' stall. He looked clean and ready for the selling, his sparse mustache and short beard trimmed neatly, his clean shirt tucked into his least-patched breeches.

Elizabeth could see that he'd come early enough that he was set up in a good location. She was grateful that she hadn't had to go searching for him in the alleyway with its workshops and stables as sometimes happened. She saw with pride that he'd decorated his booth with the lime cloth for which his family was known.

Thomas waved a pamphlet he held to indicate the little bench at the back of the stall and the two of them pressed together into the tiny space. Thomas purposely tapped a leg of his into Elizabeth's skirt-covered knee and bounced it off again. "Been missing our talks," he offered awkwardly. Elizabeth was pleased to hear it. She hoped he felt guilty enough to share some juicy news. "There's such a stir of ideas about the market. I've been thinking you'd be wanting to know. . . ." He glanced on either side of them for the approach of potential customers.

"You have?" she poked, leaning closer to him. "Well, tell. What are they saying?"

Thomas ran a finger back and forth across his lips. "Changing," he blurted and then checked himself. "It's all about wanting different ways to go about things. That the Presbyterians here in the North are lax in their ways, maybe interested in a new kind of worship. . . ."

"Who, who says such things?" she wondered. "Not Mister Blake, not in our Presbyterian church?" Elizabeth's brow furrowed.

"No, no." Thomas wagged a finger. "And it's not our church, not mine anywa. . . ."

Elizabeth jumped in before he could finish. "Is it why, do you suppose, he leaves us alone at the farmstead, that he doesn't pester the Leavens for their lack of church attendance? I've been wondering about that. . . ." She caught herself and stopped to let Thomas continue. After all, he was the one with the newest information.

"I think so," Thomas agreed quickly. "Though my Da stews about it constantly. He thinks Blake or Wold will fine the whole lot of us out there for Kelsey and Hannah not going. Badgers me, too, about my own failed attending. Thinks it'd protect the business if I were more regular."

"Oh, Thomas," moaned Elizabeth quietly. "I worry for you, too." She adjusted herself so she could see more of his face. "You and Lizzie. Hannah and Kelsey. . . ."

"I'm twenty-six years old, Elizabeth," Thomas retorted

sternly. "I suspect I can make my own decisions." He huffed and then softened. "It's that Lizzie and I are wanting something, something different . . . and we don't find it standing in that church and listening to Blake's dull sermons."

"'Tis dangerous is all," Elizabeth muttered.

"Oh, Elizabeth, 'tis *attractive*!" He pushed against her and laughed. "These parts are aswarm with Independents and Baptists, Seekers and Quakers, rising up with fresh and fair ways."

Bleak wisps of clouds moved past the sun and brought a welcomed warmth to the market. "Tell me more," Elizabeth begged.

"It gets complicated," Thomas admitted, floating his gaze cautiously out beyond the stall. "I'm not sure I understand it all, but what's important, important to me at least, is that so many of the folks I talk to here — and when I travel — say that just because we're baptized as infants, we're not shackled for life to the way of the Church. . . ." He brought the pamphlet up low between them.

"What's it say?"

"Seekers passed me this," replied Thomas, squinting at her. "*Seekers*," he repeated, as if the group of them held great promise.

"And what are they seeking?" Elizabeth asked innocently.

"A revelation from God as to how to worship, what to worship." Thomas bit his lip. "It's not that they hold anything against the likes of my Ma and Da, those who find comfort in the prayers and ceremonies at Church. It's that the ministers and their cronies are corrupt . . . do *nothing* for us. Take the offering for themselves and make a living from it."

"And these Seekers, you've met some then?"

"I have," Thomas replied, sitting tall. "Two young lads,

Edward Burroughs and John Audland. Talked with them at some length. They worship mostly in people's homes or outside if the weather is good. John sometimes preaches in a chapel not far from here." He bumped her knee again. "And everyone is allowed to sit."

Elizabeth ignored the tap; Thomas' annoying ways could irritate her if she let them and today she wanted to hear him out. "Is he ordained? Legal in the work?"

"Was once," said Thomas, "but wears no collar now. And others in the congregation who preach are not. Edward Burroughs says that all who attend their meetings for worship are led by the power of the Lord, that the Messiah is *all* people. And get this, they decide as a whole how to distribute the collection back to those in need of it."

"They *do*?" In her mind's eye Elizabeth saw a door crack open. Before she could ask more, a man came toward the stall, admiring the goods as he did so. Thomas saw him, too.

Are things really changing? Elizabeth wondered as she gave her goodbye. The talk with Thomas excited her. She passed Moot Hall, the courthouse, and found a new location to sit. Digging into her basket, she unwrapped some of the things she'd brought from home just in case she saw Moe — an apple from the root cellar — she seemed to like those — and a buttered hunk of fresh bread. She'd made a little bundle for her to keep — more of the bread, a wedge of Fletcher cheese, and two eggs she'd hard-boiled. Things Auntie wouldn't notice.

Elizabeth wished the child would come. It was like waiting for a butterfly to light. She surveyed the market and suddenly saw her peeking out from a corner of Moot Hall. When the orphan saw Elizabeth watching her, she came bravely forward with a wide, impish grin, until she stood a few feet away. Elizabeth handed over an apple and watched the child chump into it, the juice trickling down her chin and dampening the collar of her filthy smock. When she was finished, she came nearer to the bench and let Elizabeth comb through the tangles of dirty, blonde hair so she could better see the dark, sad eyes. There were so many in Kendal in need. Elizabeth wished she could help at least this one.

Chapter 3

On Sunday, Elizabeth woke to the crow of the cocks and forced herself out of bed earlier than usual. She hoped Auntie would be pleased she was getting their breakfast started — and would keep a good mood as they went into town for the service. She wanted to tell her about Moe, wanted her to know of her concern for her welfare, of her growing love for the child.

Once things were going as expected at the fire pit, Elizabeth tiptoed into the back room to dress in her cleanest homespun. She tied the better of her two sets of sleeves onto the gray bodice and slipped on a top skirt she tried not to wear for heavy farm work. It had been dyed reddish-brown from the roots of the madder plant by the Holme men, who could produce a range of colors. For church, Jennifer Holme preferred this shade and Auntie went along with it.

Things didn't work out the way Elizabeth had planned. Once they'd started off, Auntie was grousing about this and that and the other, and Elizabeth decided it wasn't the right time to bring up Moe. Then, when they neared the church, rumors were flying that Lord Wold would be in attendance, and the news sent Auntie into a fit of more grumbling. Elizabeth kept quiet as they made their way inside.

The interior of the church was divided by sex. Auntie and Elizabeth went to stand behind the pew at the front of the women's side. It was reserved for the wealthy women of Kendal, the rent of a seat rumored to cost as much as the Holme men made in a good month. Once in their spots, Elizabeth shifted from side to side, impatient for things to start and be finished so she'd again have a chance to talk with

Auntie. She let her eyes drift to the cherubs and lettering near a top edge of one of the side walls. The décor was the work of a Lancashire artisan who'd been hired to disguise the poor state of the building. He'd painted the woodwork green and added text as a border.

As she stared at the shapes of the bold, black forms, Elizabeth wondered how it was that they made words. She tried to find a pattern but eventually, her neck sore from craning up to the ceiling, she turned to the noise of the others who were entering the two wide church doors. Just after the last bell she spied Thomas' parents and followed them with her eyes as they hurried across the room, separated, and went to the back of their proper section. After that, the noble Kendal families paraded in, men and women dividing, and sat in the pews.

When the sanctuary was almost completely quiet, the tall and stately Lord Wold promenaded across the front of it to the stairs leading up to a platform above them. He wore a white curled wig and a plain black suit of high quality. Elizabeth couldn't see his expression but she didn't suppose he was smiling. Lord Wold was a man to be feared. He was well positioned to influence the hopes and desires of nobility and commoners alike. As he dipped his chin ever so slightly to those sitting in the front row, Elizabeth tapped her fingers on her chin, imagining the reasons why they eagerly acknowledged him.

Tap one. Lord Wold oversaw the workings of all the churches in the diocese and had decision-making power over the collection baskets of the congregations.

Tap two. He'd sway the ordination of Minister Blake as well as the church deacons, coveted positions of local power.

Tap three. He owned the land on which the Kendal Church stood, as well as many of the surrounding acres. This gave him influence over what the nobility were able — and not able — to do on their estates.

Lord Wold came to the base of the stairs at the center front of the room, stopped, and turned to face those in attendance. At his command, two deacons brought a red-faced fellow forward who was covered from shoulders to boots in a white sheet, his hands tied behind his back. As they did so, Lord Wold announced that this was the first of three Sundays that "the alleged witch" was to stand for the entire service to face them. Should anyone have tellings of how he'd spoiled their crops or caused anyone of them any other harm, they were to inform Minister Blake.

Elizabeth found it hard to watch the humiliation or keep her eyes on Lord Wold as he turned abruptly from the poor man to ascend the stairs. She followed Minister Blake instead, the short, stout local minister who was dressed as he always was in his dull, brown robe, belted with a cord below his ample gut. She hoped he was relieved to see the sanctuary full. With Lord Wold in attendance, it was important that the town folk had packed it as they had.

Minister Blake walked hesitantly to the stairway and waited there until Lord Wold had reached the protruding platform where the lectern was positioned. Then he plodded up the stairs, too, and took a seat adjacent to where the landlord was staring out at them. He bowed his bald head as Lord Wold stepped closer to the podium and loudly cleared his throat to begin to make announcements, issuing reminders of the importance of regular attendance at services, dwelling on the expectation to tithe, and giving lengthy descriptions of the punishments for not doing so. He interjected a Bible verse here and there to support his expectations and to confirm that, as Presbyterians, they were to hold to the Church beliefs and not stray from the teachings of his interpretation of the Bible or the laws of the authorities. The whole of it got Elizabeth to yawning. She discretely covered her mouth, her mind beginning to wander as Lord Wold described Lord Protector Cromwell, sitting in a golden chair to conduct his affairs. It was fashioned after those the holy trinity supposedly sat on in Heaven.

In her mind's eye Elizabeth saw angels fluttering around God and Jesus and the Virgin Mary, their faces turned down to earth to see the Lord Protector acting in their stead to ensure there was no rebellious or disloyal behavior. *He's not my God*, she thought, giving a subtle shake of her neatly combed hair, loose at her shoulders instead of tied back as it was when she was working. She saw herself then, a young woman dressed in her church clothes, hands folded piously in front of her waist, staring up into the clouds to the only heaven she'd ever known. *Can't be so*, she frowned.

Minister Blake and Lord Wold exchanged places, the stutter of nervousness in the minister's voice causing Elizabeth to wonder if what Thomas had recently told her was true. Was the man softening his stance on some of the church expectations, supportive of the changes that other groups in the region were espousing? If so, she knew she wouldn't hear any hint of it today in his disjointed, rambling sermon. His job was to repeat the gist of what Lord Wold had said, emphasizing obedience and making a case for plentiful tithing. After all, his salary depended on the coins in the offering basket.

It was early afternoon by the time the benediction was given, and aunt and niece were on their way back to the farmstead. Elizabeth ached from the hours of standing and she could see from Auntie's bent frame that she was stiff and sore, too. It didn't seem a good time to try to begin a conversation about Moe. "I get so nervous when Wold is at

Church," she finally started, not sure as to how she was going to make her way around to what was really on her mind.

"Keep your voice lower, child," Auntie shushed, her eyes darting about.

Elizabeth stopped talking, hoping to appease her. She suspected Auntie was thinking about Lord Wold's intimidating threats, but no one of any rank was near them. Just commoners moving off and going home.

"You know, don't you," asked Auntie, finding her hand, "that we're only able to keep our holdings because we have the sale of sheep and goods from the garden to pay the taxes? Not just to Lord Wold but for the stiff cost that the High Sheriff adds when he's riding about collecting?"

Elizabeth gave the soft hand a gentle squeeze. She knew that raising funds was a constant worry. Even with the two of them working all day long, and the Leavenses to occasionally help with chores when she or Auntie was ill, it was a constant strain to end the harvest and sheep shearing with enough profit to pay what was owed. And the amount seemed to increase every season.

"What's important for you to understand . . ." said Auntie as she continued to scan the area, " is that we're women, *unmarried* women who don't read, and well he knows it." She wrung her hands.

Elizabeth was reminded of a pompous nobleman she'd overheard recently in the market cross. "Women are no smarter than a goose," he'd declared. She shook her head now as she recalled the man's demeanor. Surely, he'd never worked as they did or witnessed the ingenious ways women like Auntie and Hannah and Jennifer thought to solve a multitude of daily challenges at the farmstead.

"We'd have little chance with the sheriff and magistrates, and that Wold," Auntie was saying now. "They've got spies all around — and each other's backs. . . ." She gave Elizabeth an uncertain glance, a scowl on her face. "Wold could challenge my papers and force us off our land, Elizabeth."

"And yet you don't use his title," Elizabeth fretted.

"'Tis a matter of respect. He's owed little from me."

Elizabeth bit her lip. "Weasel Wold," some called him. The greedy man seemed to be doing whatever he could to claim as many Kendal farms as possible. It was common talk at the Fleece Inn. "We're trapped," Elizabeth sighed. "Snared."

"We are that," agreed Auntie. She put a comforting arm around Elizabeth's shoulder and hugged her to her side.

"And I've no chance to escape it — to find myself a place in heaven — unless I add a heap of coins in the offering basket."

"Not without marrying nobility," sniggered Auntie. She stepped over a twig on the path.

"Thomas says we shouldn't put up with the services, that there are other choices. All kinds of groups popping up. . . ."

"Oh, Thomas," Auntie scoffed. "That one needs to be careful." She let loose her arm and slapped her hands together on her cheeks. "Charles and Jennifer are worried sick for the fines that can be levied for Thomas' absences. . . ." She stopped short. Auntie wasn't one to gossip.

"What'd Jennifer say?" Elizabeth urged, despite herself.

Auntie let out a sigh. "That Thomas is wanting something that he can't name. That he respects their loyalty to the Church — not trying to be hurtful — just honest in his searching. Thomas is that, honest. Jennifer says he has some new friends and is attracted to their silent worship." She locked eyes with Elizabeth. "He hasn't told you of them, these Seekers then?"

"Some," Elizabeth admitted, torn between allegiance to

Thomas and not wanting to lie. "Sometimes we talk a bit if I see him on market days and he doesn't have customers. He's only recently mentioned the Seekers. . . ."

"Well then, it's good he tells you about his wonderings himself. It's his story to tell. Must be important to him," Auntie acquiesced. She was quiet for a bit and then took Elizabeth's hand again. "These are the strangest times, indeed," she said, shaking her head. "Never lived through anything like them."

"But why don't we talk more about it?" Elizabeth blurted, her heart thumping.

Auntie stopped in her walking and turned to her. "I don't know. I see that you're ready for it. I think we — me and Kelsey and Hannah — have maybe been waiting for you and Lizzie to get a little older. There's a burden in the knowing . . . if you're asked by Blake, or a constable, or, heaven forbid, Wold and his cronies. . . ."

Elizabeth thought about the stocks and the women she'd seen in them, the constables purposely spreading their legs and making sure every passerby knew of their offenses. *Surely it won't come to anything like that*, she thought. "I'm 13, Auntie, and you *do* trust me. . . ." She said aloud. It wasn't a question.

"I do — and it's a relief to be talking with you about things." She started them walking again. "We aren't well-formed on our habits, she mumbled, looking to the Holmes' cottage as they passed it. "Things have come to be over time. . . . We've tried to stay open to our own thoughts and behave accordingly."

It was an invitation, a nudge. Elizabeth met the sweet face. "I'm ready, Auntie. I want to know, know what you really think about things." She swallowed, deciding she should offer the same. "There's a part of me that's excited about the things Thomas tells me. I, I like to hear about them, talking about them. . . ." She held her gaze firm on Auntie. "It's that I'm not sure of the parts I'm wanting. . . ."

"A Seeker?" Auntie raised an eyebrow. "Perhaps we're not all that different from those people then, do you think? The two of us?"

Us? thought Elizabeth. "I'd welcome talking about that, Auntie," she offered, an unexpected tremor in her voice and tears found their way to the backs of her eyes. She'd been waiting for this moment. She felt almost commanded to take it. "I, I have something I've been wanting to tell you, to share. . . ." Elizabeth started, finding her courage. She ran her nervous hands down the worn fabric of her skirts and took in a sharp breath. "Something important to me. It's about a child . . . a little girl I've befriended in the market. . . ."

Chapter 4

At the week's end Elizabeth was especially keen to get to Kendal, hope and possibility exciting her. She skipped almost all the way through the Serpentine Woods and didn't bother to stop at the Fleece Inn. In the last few days, Auntie had opened up to her as never before. They'd talked about wanting to live in a world where all people are treated as equals, about how each of them enjoyed the silence before meals, and about tithing — that it didn't seem like much of the collection went to help the poor. Auntie had agreed to meet Moe.

Elizabeth was hoping beyond measure that she'd see the disheveled child today, that Moe would find her. As luck would have it, just inside the town limits, she thought she caught sight of her by a stall selling gloves. She slowed her pace, anticipating that, as she had of late, the little girl would come and take her hand.

Moe peeked out from a corner and then came running to stand in front of Elizabeth. She tipped her chin up to catch the older girl's eyes and rapidly flexed her fingers in front of her chest.

"Want?" Elizabeth guessed. She copied the gesture and pointed to a carrot in her basket. "WANT? THIS?" She pretended to eat it. "EAT?"

Moe nodded vigorously, flexed her fingers again, and moved her hands from Elizabeth's basket to herself, her brown eyes wide with hope and desire. "WANT." She tapped at her mouth. "EAT. WANT EAT."

"You want to eat?" Elizabeth interpreted, charmed by the cleverness. She handed over a carrot. "Well, I just *happen* to have something," she mused, knowing Moe didn't understand her.

Moe bit at the root and chewed it hungrily. She reminded

Elizabeth of a mouse with her gnawing. As she watched her, Elizabeth decided she didn't have any purchases to make in the market that couldn't wait a week. When Moe finished the carrot, she offered her hand and started the two of them past the livestock pens. They skipped a bit through the Serpentine Woods, Moe giggling and seemingly unconcerned as to where she was going.

They were as far as the Holmes' cottage when Elizabeth saw that Lizzie and Hannah were outside hanging laundry. "Hello there," she called, the muscles in her throat tightening with anticipation.

"Hello back, dear," called Hannah, draping a piece of Kelsey's shirt front on a bush before giving over her full attention. "And who's this ragamuffin?" she asked as Moe angled back behind Elizabeth's skirts.

"Moe — her name's Moe," explained Elizabeth. "She's an orphan. I bring her food when I go to market." The story came out in starts and stops. "She doesn't hear, or at least not very well. Makes her own clever language with her fingers." She rested one of her own hands tenderly on Moe's shoulder and tried to move Moe into better view. "She'd probably be friendlier with something to eat."

Hannah chuckled. "Lizzie, would you go fetch something for this wee one?" She shooed away a curious hen who was trying to peck at Moe's torn stocking.

"I went to Minister Massey," Elizabeth went on. "But he doesn't seem able to help. . . ."

"Ah," sighed Hannah. She reached a chapped hand toward Moe.

Lizzie returned with a wedge of pie on a scrap of cloth and squatted down to Moe. She held it out to her. It was the poke of a stubby finger, a lick, and a shriek of delight that sent the women into hysterics.

"Your Auntie knows about Moe then?" asked Hannah, when she'd recovered. Moe continued to dance about, poking at the pie and licking her lips with great fanfare.

"We've talked about her, but she hasn't met her yet," admitted Elizabeth. She squinted over to the Fletcher cottage.

"I see," said Hannah. "Would you want me to go along over with you?"

Elizabeth shook her head. She wanted to face Auntie by herself. "Thank you, but no." She took hold of Moe's sticky fingers. "COME," she gestured. "Let's go see Auntie."

When they entered the Fletcher cottage, Auntie turned to the noise of the squeaky door.

"I've brought Moe to meet you, Auntie," Elizabeth said quickly. She pushed the child gently forward.

"Oh," peeped Auntie, startled. She held a chair to crouch down to Moe's level. "Hello little one," she whispered softly, reaching a hand out to Moe as if she was an injured dog. When Moe took it, Auntie shook the tiny fingers playfully. "Sweet little thing, isn't she?"

"She is," Elizabeth managed, her voice a prayer.

"Well, then." Auntie stood again, Moe's small hand still wrapped around three of her fingers, "might you find a way for her to sit high enough at the table? We should at least feed her, don't you think?" She gave Elizabeth a crooked grin and took a seat herself.

Elizabeth arranged Moe adjacent to Auntie and quickly buttered a hunk of bread for her. The child looked like a fragile little wren as she ate it.

"Might we help her?" Elizabeth asked softly. Moe began to purr like a kitten, smiling back and forth between Auntie and her savior.

Auntie pressed her fingers to her face. "Things are so

unsure these days," she said finally. She stared at a knot on the tabletop, her lips thin. "I just don't know."

Elizabeth's heart sank. Until that moment, she hadn't realized how much she'd hoped Moe would be able to stay.

"But then again," Auntie asserted suddenly, "We should help her, I suppose. She's so little. Can't eat much. . . ." Before she could say more, they were interrupted by a series of brisk knocks at the door. A surge of happiness engulfed Elizabeth as she rose to open it.

It was Lizzie, standing proudly, if not a little hesitantly, with a small wooden chair in one hand and two eggs in the other. "Extras," she announced, offering the eggs. She set the chair down just inside the doorway. "Ma found this in the barn."

Moe clambered down. "WANT, WANT," she insisted, coming as close as she dared to Lizzie. She brought her two hands in and out in front of herself, grabbing at the air. This was the one who'd given her that pie.

"You want something?" Lizzie guessed. She copied the gesture and gave Moe a puzzled stare.

Auntie got up, too. "'Twas nice of you, Lizzie." She came to take Moe's hand. "Why don't I go outside with the child. Leave you girls to your chatter."

"Really, Elizabeth — Moe doesn't hear?" Lizzie asked when Auntie and Moe had gone out. She took Auntie's place at the table and bit at a fingernail.

"Some maybe. Not much." Elizabeth shrugged. "A few too many knocks to the head is what I've been thinking."

Lizzie repeated Moe's sign for "want" to herself. "Clever little thing, isn't she?"

"She is that," Elizabeth agreed. "Can you stay for a while? Visit?" She started for the clay pitcher of beer in hopes of it. "What have you been up to lately?" She left her hopes for Moe in Auntie's hands for the time being.

"Oh . . ." began Lizzie tentatively. She drummed soundlessly on the table. "Chores. Talk with Thomas. . . ."

Elizabeth hid her face for the hurt of it. Not that long ago she and Lizzie had talked so easily.

"He's full of talk about Seekers and Quakers and Ranters," continued Lizzie. "Excited by all the change he says is coming." She watched Elizabeth pour two mugs of drink. "After all those boring hours at the looms, I think he envies them their freedom. Says that if you're in . . . the . . . ho-ly *Spir-it*," Lizzie paused between the syllables and gave the last one a twist, "then sin is impossible and there is no worry to any way of acting."

Elizabeth sat down. "Those Ranters . . . curious lot." She took a sip of her drink, avoiding eye contact.

"Surely," Lizzie agreed, trying to catch Elizabeth's gaze. "Sometimes I see them in the market making a nuisance of themselves. Like noisy ravens, screaming at the women in their fancy dresses." She waited for Elizabeth to comment, to add to her description. It was an old game they'd had between them.

Elizabeth gave into it. "Spinning and reaching for their polished buttons and bright ribbons. . . ." She gave Lizzie a little grin. "Attracted like magpies to shiny objects."

"Well, then, I guess the two of us have nothing to worry about," said Lizzie, ruffling her plain skirt. "But I do say, all the new ideas confuse me. Thomas tries to explain to me who is saying what. . . ." She licked her lips, trying to recall what'd been told to her. "I'm not sure he really understands it all either. Repeats a lot of what he gets from Edward Burrough."

Elizabeth turned. "Edward Burrough?" He was the one Thomas had mentioned when they'd talked in the market.

"His new friend," Lizzie allowed.

"And what does this Edward say?"

"Dissenters," quoted Lizzie. "The Ranters, Seekers, Quakers, all of them. But the Seekers and Quakers sit in holy worship without clergy, thinking God can speak directly to each of us."

"And this Edward fellow, which is he then?"

"I'm not sure. Quaker, I think. Thomas says he doesn't bow, doff his hat, or use titles. Told him that everyone should respect everyone else, no matter what the customs." Lizzie raised her eyebrows and then went on. "The lad is full of ideas like that — and Thomas is catching them up, a spark to tinder."

Elizabeth picked her mug up and set it down again. "I hope he isn't the one who's put those scribbles on the church doors . . . or has been teaching the children in Kendal the taunts I hear them toss at Minister Blake. 'Deceiver.' 'Hypocrite.' Them, hardly older than Moe, and not knowing what those big words mean or what might happen to them for yelling them out. . . ."

Lizzie broke in. "I know he's excitable, Elizabeth. Makes sudden decisions sometimes . . . but Thomas wouldn't paint those doors or purposely put children in harm's way." She straightened, her chest out and her chin pulled in. "But really, isn't there a part of you that admires some of it, that people aren't just talking . . . complaining . . . but finding ways to show their misery?" She didn't wait for an answer. "I've heard the gossip, too. Did you know that someone took Minister Blake's ledger book of tithes so he doesn't know who's paid? And they say that men are driving their herds into their neighbors' pastures so they can't be taken for fines. That's brave." She finished her drink and stood up. "I, I should be getting back," she mumbled. She came around the table to give Elizabeth a hug. "I'm sorry it's been so long."

For the rest of the afternoon and into the evening, Elizabeth felt a glow of happiness. Auntie hadn't said anything to suggest that Moe had to leave. She and Lizzie had finally talked. Moe had helped with supper, carrying each bowl of mutton pottage carefully to the table. She'd played quietly afterward with balls of yarn, letting the women talk, and had gone to sleep easily in Elizabeth's bed. Auntie and Elizabeth had just settled down to their knitting and spinning when Lizzie came banging on the door again.

"Thomas hasn't been here, has he? He isn't home from Kendal yet." Her worry tumbled out. "Jennifer is pacing and Charles thinks he's been assaulted. We can't figure where he is." She started to gnaw on a fingernail.

"Oh, Lizzie." Elizabeth put her work aside and came quickly to console her. "No, no . . . we haven't seen him."

Chapter 5

"Thomas is back!" panted Lizzie, interrupting their breakfast. "Him and Edward, Edward Burrough. They're over at the Holmes'."

Elizabeth turned sharply from the hearth. "Thomas back?" she repeated with relief. Worry of it had caused her to wake often in the night.

"Oh, thank goodness," sighed Auntie. "What happened?" She handed Moe a fork, encouraging her to use it for the egg mixture she was eating with her hands.

"He was in Underbarrow, not far. An easy walk. The two of them." Lizzie rattled. "Spent the night camped out with some men and quite charmed by a Quaker fellow, a preacher." She held her stomach, breathing hard with relief and excitement. "The fellow had preached, Thomas said, in Kendal — yesterday, yesterday afternoon. Thomas said the prophecy went deep into him."

Elizabeth didn't ask for permission. She grabbed Lizzie's hand and went quickly back across the lane to see for herself. "Thomas, thank goodness you're safe!" she cried out when she reached the two of them. She turned to the stranger. "Elizabeth, Elizabeth Fletcher," she introduced herself. Dressed nicely in dark clothing, void of buttons and ribbons, she saw no sword at his belt. *The Quaker*.

"Edward Burrough," the handsome lad replied, extending a hand just as he might to another man. Elizabeth took it loosely and smiled weakly into his intense eyes, partially obscured by dark curls that fell forward from his cap. A thin mustache was trying to grow above his lip.

"Tell us all about it," Lizzie urged Thomas as the four of them sat down in a tight little circle on the grass.

"Well," began Thomas, happy to have their attention. "There were rumors about a Quaker preacher — er, a *Friend* — all morning in the market and after a while I got so curious. I couldn't stand it any longer." His voice rose with the thrill of the recounting. "I packed up my goods, took down the stall, and stashed it all with a neighbor vendor."

"With no regard for what your Da would say about it?" Lizzie gently scoffed.

"No, no." Thomas shook his head. "Ran with a herd of others to find a spot in front of Moot Hall. Stood in the shadow of the clock turret, trying to figure out where the preacher was going to be and searching for Edward." He turned to the lad. "Tried several places so's to see over the huge mass of folks who were assembling but I didn't see you. Spied this constable fellow that I knew from selling. He worried me. Used to come to the stall to harass me for goods he thought should be taxed. I saw him at the edge of the crowd, rubbing his hands over his gut, nervous for the swell of folks. I could see that. Bothered, I suppose that things might get out of hand."

Elizabeth turned her hands in her lap, wishing he'd get on with it.

"Then I saw this man, 'bout my age, on the steps of Moot Hall." Thomas obliged as if he'd read her mind. "Wide-brimmed hat with a high crown, pinched over his long, twisted hair." Thomas ran his fingers through his own. "Certainly didn't seem like anyone special. Wore a soiled, leather top and stained breeches, same as men who walk the cart trails." Thomas turned to an imagined person beside him. "'Is that him? Is that George Fox?' I asked this woman pushed up against me.

"'Tis,' she told me. 'Not your usual minister, now is he?' she says to me. 'Gonna speak to us now.' The preacher raised up his hands and a hush went through the market. He called out. 'Praise, honor, and glory be to the Lord of heaven and earth. Of the Holy Spirit within! Come, come receive the good news. Of Christ, alive and present, and of how you can know him!'"

Thomas turned to Edward. "It's like I can remember every word. "'Mind the Light of God in your conscience,'" he quoted. "'For Christ has come to teach the people himself. A Light that enlightens all men and women. If you are quiet and wait on the Lord, listen within, you will find God . . . Spirit . . . Truth . . . a Spirit that goes by many names . . . for the Light is shining on each of you and can be found in all places, at all times.'" Thomas threw both hands to his forehead and stared out above their heads. "'Open to it. Let the Light guide you out of sin, temptation, and disbelief — out of your evil ways, your evil thoughts.'" He glanced back at Edward. "'Tis right, isn't it, Edward. That's what he said, yes?"

"'Tis," Edward said simply, a kind smile causing dimples. He got to his feet. "And, then . . . 'The Light doesn't lie and it doesn't deceive,'" he repeated, "but asks that we enter a new relationship with ourselves and others and come into a new life of freedom and power and joy.'" He swiveled his head to each of them and then held his gaze on Elizabeth. "'Come, join a community of those who worship in Spirit and in Truth, to those who — both inside and out — are sorting out the distractions and temptation of the world. Be liberated from what holds you back. . . .'"

Elizabeth felt her heart skip a beat.

"But then," Thomas interrupted, jumping to his feet as well. "Someone yelled out from a pub door, 'Heretic, God talks to you, does he?' and I searched wildly for the constable, thinking he'd be rushing in for the arrest. But . . . and here's truly a miracle . . . when I spotted the man, he was bent forward like a hunting dog, rapt as any of the others, listening."

Edward raised his hands out from his sides, bringing them back to the preaching. "'Resist. Resist those who might dissuade you,' George Fox was calling out. 'Don't be made afraid by customs and fashion but fear the Lord God. He is mighty in his power. Mighty.'" Edward breathed in loudly and arched back. "'Be bold in the power of Truth. Valiant for it on this good earth. For what you seek isn't in the sacraments but in the following of Christ's footsteps. To be today as it was then.'"

"'And it is yours,'" bellowed Thomas. "'Yours for free.'" He sat down close to Lizzie. "Yours for free," he said again, bumping her shoulder. "That's about when I saw Edward. He was standing in the shadows behind George. His eyes closed and his hands folded." He squinted at Edward for confirmation.

"We call it 'holding in the Light,'" offered Edward. He sat down again, too.

"Ah." Thomas bobbed his head like a turkey, taking in the learning. "Well, holding George Fox in the Light, then." He clapped his hands. "So, I started trying to get to the two of them." He caught Lizzie's wide eyes again. "Honestly, I felt like a horse on a lead. And oh, I wished you, and your parents, and . . ." he looked to Elizabeth, "You and Auntie, too . . . had been with me then."

He started up again. "'I call you to action,' George Fox was saying. It seemed like his eyes were right on me. The blue of them was piercing. I thought my heart would jump right out of my chest." He beamed at Edward. "I was so glad to be with him — with you — right then." He paused, swallowing as if something was caught in his throat. "People were queued up to talk with him and when it was my turn and I went to give my name; I couldn't get it out. Stuttered like a fool. He took my hand and his grip was so strong and . . ." Thomas looked out beyond them again. "I, I felt like the world, everything, was just falling away. Gone."

"I took Thomas to meet a small group of men who were standing around," interceded Edward. "Introduced him to a couple of chums, John Audland and a boy, Will Caton. They and some of the other men were talking of going with George to Underbarrow."

"And," Thomas jerked back. "I was in. Truly, I was, Lizzie. I wanted to go with them so badly. Couldn't think of nothing else. I stood around while Will Caton told George Fox about where he lived — a place called Swarthmoor Hall — and gave him directions to the place for later in the week. And then the boy paired up with me and we started out behind the others."

Thomas gave Edward a gentle poke with his elbow. "Highly entertained by this one. Him and George arguing most of the hour it took to get where we were going. Backing up their ideas with Bible verses and drawing on what had happened to them in their lives. Edward was a good match," he checked with the lad again. "Well-spoken, but never got the upper hand." He shook his head. "You know, I had no idea where we'd eat or sleep, and I didn't care." Thomas flapped his hands crossed to his chest. "We came to a cottage where we were well-received . . . and fed. The host very glad to see us as if it was meant to be . . . all of us together. When I'd finished eating and everyone was sitting about talking, I saw that George was readying for sleep and I got up my courage to go to him. Told him he was 'a faithful servant and messenger,' my words surprising me. Didn't know where they came from, but I felt honored, honored to have heard him in

Kendal and to have come along to Underbarrow to be with him that night."

"And what'd he say back?" whispered Lizzie.

Thomas faced her. "Nothing. Gave me a tight hug." He sighed. "I left him to fix myself a spot for the night. I felt like one of the *disciples*. Laid out beside Will Caton and thought back on the day. How George seemed to want nothing from any of us but that we understand God's truth. 'Let the Light shine on your evil ways,' he'd said. The crickets were chirping so loudly. It seemed they were yelling at me to consider my faults and see the different sides of things."

Thomas jerked his head over his shoulder toward the Holme cottage. "I thought first about my Da. How furious he was going to be with me that I'd left the stall and the merchandise and not come home. In my head, I tried to explain to him and Ma. Knew she was up pacing as I thought of her, awake with fret, and wondering if I'd been attacked by robbers or was in a ditch somewhere." Thomas wrapped his arms dramatically around his torso and began to sway. "I felt myself hugging her and begging her forgiveness. . . ." He took Elizabeth's hand and she met the sorry eyes. "And then, I thought of you, Elizabeth. I know you are so wanting to hear any news I bring from my travels. Earnest, clever you. You ask such thoughtful questions, baffling me at times." He gulped loudly. "I know you see Lizzie and me wandering the hills together, the two of us spending too much time away from your friendship. You must hurt from it."

Elizabeth looked away. The admission was too much. Sitting with the others, she was too self-conscious to say anything, but her heart was singing with Thomas' unexpected empathy.

Chapter 6

Later, chores finished, the three of them, Thomas, Lizzie, and Elizabeth, sat around Edward to listen to his tellings. He was describing how a huge group of Seekers came from around Sedbergh to hear George Fox preach.

"In Kendal? Before Thomas heard him?" asked a puzzled Lizzie.

"No, no, at a place called Firbank Fell. A year ago," Edward countered. "But, in part, it's why so many were there in Kendal to hear him. He'd attracted hundreds at the Sedbergh fair and thousands at Firbank Fell." He reached to Thomas and took hold of his shoulder. "Taken as this one here. . . . They told family and friends. And when there was news of him being in Kendal yesterday, a whole huge crowd came to hear him."

"And you were there? At the fair?" asked Elizabeth.

"Well, no," admitted Edward. "But my friend, John Audland, was. He heard George preach, and was so taken. He invited him to come to a little chapel at Firbank Fell where he sometimes gave ministry on First Day, Sunday." Edward stumbled, correcting himself so they'd understand. "'Tis how we call the pagan days." He went on. "Firbank Fell isn't far from here, between Kendal and Sedbergh."

Elizabeth had never heard of the place.

"John, John Audland, was inside the chapel," Edward continued. "And anxious as to whether George would come or not. He told me that his heart pounded with joy when he saw him strolling up over the rise in the path, coming towards the chapel. He came and sat in a back pew. Didn't preach. At the end of the service he invited the congregation to come out into the meadow to hear him. By that time, there were droves of people pouring into it." Edward spread his hands out wide for emphasis. "A thousand of them."

A thousand. Elizabeth thought with awe. More than in Kendal on market day, she guessed.

"By the time the ones in the chapel had joined the others, I was among them," explained Edward. "All of us standing together, every kind of folk, waiting in the heat of the day for what George Fox had to say. He stood up there, above us, on a natural crag that forms a pulpit, his eyes closed and his head cocked as if he were listening to the lark soaring over his head. My face, and all the others, were turned up to him, still and waiting like hungry baby birds. Out of the silence he began to speak."

"'Christ is here, with us, with you.'" Edward raised a hand and swept it wide, as if to acknowledge the beauty of the hillside and the grazing sheep. "'There is no need for the steeple house there. . . .'" Edward quoted, pointing to an imaginary chapel. "'Or the ministers who collect tithes to pray for you. This ground and these hills are as sanctified as that building and you all are a congregation wherever you gather.' He went on for three or four hours, preaching as Thomas told you of Kendal. No one shouting or criticizing. He said that those in the steeple houses — that's what he calls churches — with their ceremonies, tithes, memorized creeds, and all the rest, have not understood Christ's message. That if you are truly to come and know what is divine, holy Spirit can teach you . . . if you believe it is so, that He is there . . . as the moon and stars are in the sky on a cloudy night. He asked us to turn towards the Light, find it. By the end of the afternoon, most of those gathered below him were convinced."

"Convinced?" Elizabeth asked. The word seemed to hold a special meaning.

"'Tis what we say when we're altered, ready to do as we are

asked, despite the risk," Edward explained kindly. "John Audland told me later that as he listened to George on Firbank Fell, he felt as though a river was running through him, washing him clean and carrying him along. Friends don't go so far as to adopt new names, different from those we were given at birth, as some sects do but just the same, we are 'convinced.' And on that day at Firbank Fell, a thousand people decided to live in the cross, abiding in divine love and power of a new way of being, joining a new community of others trying to live that way too."

Edward opened the flask that hung from his shoulder and took a swig. "When George came down from the ridge, he talked to anyone who was interested, no matter their sex, age, or rank. A common man conversing freely with gentry, no bowing." Edward chuckled, remembering. "Stayed for as long as he was needed, a couple hours at least, without any sign of fatigue, each person as precious to him as a newborn lamb."

"And then what happened?" Thomas interrupted impatiently. The image Elizabeth had in her head dissolved.

Edward smiled over to Thomas. "John Audland and his wife, Anne, invited him to their cottage for sup . . . and he and his companion, Richard Farnsworth, went along with them. The Camms — neighbors to the Audlands — were invited, too, all caught up in it, talking together, far into the night."

'Tis what happened to Thomas in Underbarrow, Elizabeth realized.

"After Firbank Fell, John and Anne Audland — them not much older than me — and John and Mabel Camm, took up the preaching of Friends themselves. They're traveling together now. The men were already trained preachers, but of course, the women hadn't been to Oxford or Cambridge."

"How were they allowed then, the women?" Lizzie asked

eagerly. The question surprised Elizabeth. She fixed on Lizzie as Edward answered.

"I'm guessing they went first with George," supposed Edward, rubbing at his chin, "him taking note of their gifts as they talked with others — across tables by the hearth and in parlors, then in the local markets and fairs — until he saw they were capable. 'Twas how he's been with me."

"Ah," sighed Thomas. He leaned back, nodding his head in a succession of little shakes. "Trained by Christ, fueled by truth," he mumbled, quoting someone else, Elizabeth was sure.

"Held in the Light in our conscience," Edward agreed.

"This Light," asked Elizabeth. "It's a heavenly light then? Like God?" She imagined the holy trinity as she had always thought of them, sitting on their golden thrones, looking down at her from heaven.

"It is," said Edward. "Within us. Enabling each person to recognize their wrongful, harmful thoughts and deeds, and to cast them out and move forward. Like a secret in your heart."

Like a secret in your heart, repeated Elizabeth to herself. The idea of such intimate examination both thrilled and terrified her. "And we all have this Light?" she asked gravely.

"We do," replied Edward.

"E-lizzzz-abeth," Auntie called from across the lane. Edward offered his hands to support her as she got to her feet.

"I'll save the rest of the telling for later," Edward assured her. "I'm going to stay with the Leavens."

"Oh? Oh you, you are?" Elizabeth stammered. She was glad to hear it.

"Who's that?" Thomas pointed as Moe came carefully towards them.

"Little Moe," Lizzie said simply. "She lives with the Fletchers now."

Chapter 7

The next morning, Elizabeth carried the milk buckets out to the cow barn, walking pensively across a yard that held the tellings of those who'd come before her. It was often her way to pretend that the stories of her parents and grandparents lay there still, available to her if she kicked up the dirt in just the right way. Now in the pale sky of daybreak, she called them to her as she lifted the barn latch and ducked inside the low, simple shed. She hoped they knew of the stir that this George Fox fellow was causing, that they might bring him to her so she could hear him for herself.

Drawn to the dust motes dancing in the shaft of sunlight from the only window opening, Elizabeth set the milking pails down and went over to the light, extending her hands into the tangible, dancing beam. She spread her fingers in the warmth and slowly twisted them, mulling over the way Edward, and now Thomas, used the word Light — Light of Christ, Inward Light, Light in the conscience — when they were talking about the gift of a holy presence shining on them.

Shaking her head pensively with the longing, Elizabeth picked up the pails and went to Queenie. It'd been Auntie's little joke to name the sweet cow after royalty. She began to milk, wondering if a lasting change had really come over Thomas. He'd almost swooned when he'd told her of his adventures with Edward Burrough and George Fox. "Such drama," Elizabeth scoffed out loud. It was if he were drunk on Kendal beer, a brew much stronger than what they drank at the farmstead. Thomas going on and on, talking of the Light and the Holy Spirit and Truth, repeating phrases he'd heard from Edward and the others. Surely, he'd now say he'd been convinced." She rolled the unfamiliar word in her mouth. "Convinced" as Edward had explained the term.

Edward. A warm wave rolled through her as she thought of him. She was pleased to have him at the Leavens', although Thomas was quick to report that his parents were uncomfortable with the arrangement. Apparently, Charles and Jennifer thought it quite possible that the authorities and rabble rousers alike would hear of the Quaker and come complaining to the farmstead. Someone would get fined or jailed or beaten.

Elizabeth had lived under such threats most of her life. She wasn't concerned. Edward brightened her days. He'd been with them a week now, going willingly back and forth across the lane in his attempts to be useful. He'd brought Moe a doll from Kendal when he'd gone into town and tried to lend a hand with a wide assortment of chores. Most certainly a better preacher than a farmhand, he was unused to the hard labor of their work. By the end of his second day with them, his palms had been covered with blisters and he'd sought Elizabeth out to help him tend to them.

"What did Fox preach that swayed you?" she'd asked as she'd turned his soft palms in her hands to examine them. She was interested to know exactly what had happened at Firbank Fell and later in Underbarrow, that he'd leave the obvious comforts of his home to follow the preacher. He hadn't said anything about being apprenticed out and his clothes were a fine quality. "How did it happen?" she pushed. "Your, your convincement?"

"Well, I was searching. . . ." Edward flinched as Elizabeth touched a tender spot. "Had been since I was a boy. I'd tried different faiths as I grew older, but no one seemed to understand what I was needing, what was bothering me, and I didn't have the words to describe it."

Elizabeth smiled shyly at his honesty. Wasn't this exactly what she'd say of herself?

"I'd been told that George Fox was going to preach at Firbank Fell," Edward went on. "So, I snuck off to hear him, for, of course, my parents wouldn't have approved of my going." He shook his head, unmasked. "And his words hit straight into my heart — until later, later as we were walking to Underbarrow. I, I began to have my doubts then and I had the opportunity to question him. . . ." He flashed a crooked grin. "Oh, you know," he pulled his hands back, flapping them with embarrassment. "Thought myself the more apt with the Bible."

Elizabeth gave a little smirk of comradery. She was enchanted with Edward's decency, his forthrightness — how he didn't seem to hold back when he talked with her. She reached into a pocket for a salve she carried.

"He praised my boldness and we talked, a group of us, around the fire as we ate that night." Edward put his hands back out to her. "It drew me in how he accepted me, listened in that probing way he has." He bent his head towards Elizabeth, trying to catch her gaze as she applied the ointment. "For such a long time, you know, it'd been as if I was standing on one side of a wall, peering over at things, but not part of what was going on." He wrinkled his forehead, moving his mouth to one side. "I'd grown up like that. Having to do things the way my Da wanted. No questions asked, no discussion allowed. Even as I got older, we didn't see eye to eye. The man never cared to ask my opinion or know what concerned me."

"I'm grateful you found George Fox," Elizabeth interjected softly, his hurt apparent.

"Oh, yes. Oh yes. Me, too. Spirit moving, surely. I was so hungry for it all — the faith, the work, the appreciation. To be used." He brought the worst of his hands up to inspect the salve.

"You don't see your parents any longer then?" Elizabeth asked the obvious.

"Ah, no. I tried to see them when I was in Underbarrow — I'm from there — but my Da was very displeased with my ardor for Friends, embarrassed by it really. Thinks it's a religion of country folk, the poor and lost." Edward cleared his throat with the insult. "Tells anyone who'll listen that I'm caught up in 'youthful rebellion.'" He wiggled his head and gave a mocking scoff. "His exact words. Wants his family seen on the pew each Sabbath, dressed as is our class, and zealously participating."

"First row," mocked Elizabeth subtly. She could feel the flush of her face.

"Absolutely," agreed Edward, returning her grin. "He can't grasp my discomfort with it or be happy for me that I've found a faith that fills my heart, my needs. If he saw me about with George Fox and John Audland, he'd be the one to fetch the constable for the arrest. No doubt about it." Edward popped an eyebrow at Elizabeth. "Thinks us immoral — unlawful."

"I'm sorry for it," Elizabeth consoled.

"I begged them to understand, my parents," Edward admitted, not able to stop his talk. "But no, Da wouldn't change his position and my Ma wouldn't stand against him. He yelled loudly when I'd no longer address him any different from the servants."

Servants? Elizabeth repeated to herself. She was only mildly surprised.

"They disinherited me and our neighbors were glad for it. They despised me, too," Edward wagged his head at the shunning. "No, no. There was no concern when I left home."

Elizabeth heard Edward's breathing shift with resolve. "But I've a new family now. Friends who enjoy me, strengthen my faith. Profoundly loyal. A whole new family of brothers and sisters."

Elizabeth wanted to believe that Edward was trying to find opportunities to be with her. He seemed to come routinely to the Fletchers at the end of the workday to sit on the step with her. One day he bought a little pamphlet. "'THIS IS LIGHT'S APPEARANCE,'' he read, pointing to the letters blocked boldly on the front of it. He held it so they both could see the print even though he knew she couldn't read. "This . . ." he put a finger on the first letter, "is a 'T.'"

Elizabeth could feel his warm breath as he turned to tell her.

"T," she repeated as she looked into his dark eyes, noting the flutter of his thick eyelashes. He named the letters in the word "This," and she dutifully repeated them, torn between attending to the diminishing space between their faces and remembering the letter names.

"I can help you to learn to read if you're willing," Edward offered gently. "You have a good memory."

Elizabeth tilted her head. She hoped he was right. She thought about all those times she'd fixed on the words in the church and still had no idea what they said.

"The letters say different sounds," Edward continued, bringing her back. "When you know the sounds of each letter, you can figure out words." It was if he were reading her thoughts, considering her worry. "This," he read, pointing again to the first word in the pamphlet title. "Th . . . i . . . ssss." He stretched the sounds. "This."

Elizabeth repeated them. "These two letters have one sound?" she asked, her finger on the "Th" of "This."

"They do," admitted Edward. "It can be confusing, I know." He wrinkled his nose, trying to make light of the difficulty.

Elizabeth took the pamphlet from him and turned the pages. "There is a blank last page," she mused holding it up to him.

"'Tis where your future is written." Edward said, flirting.

Chapter 8

Lizzie found Elizabeth in the cow barn with Moe, finishing the evening chores. "George Fox! He's come! He's here!" she cried, swiping at the smoke released by the hissing oil lamp. She purposely went closer to the smelly thing so Moe could see her gesture. "COME," she signed, widely arching an arm and then pointing across the lane in the direction of her cottage. THERE. "Fetch Auntie and come over."

Moments later, Elizabeth, Auntie, and Moe arrived at the Leavens' front room, the space transformed. Gone were the muddy footprints and spinning wheel. The bundles of hanging herbs had all been moved to a back corner and the family chairs pushed together, a bench added. Beeswax candles were set about, giving off a magical cast the color of egg yolk and marking the evening as a special occasion. Moe dropped Elizabeth's hand and went, baby doll Edward had given her in tow, to the beautiful bouquet of forget-me-nots, larkspur, and daisies that sat on a small, low table in the center of the room.

Elizabeth surveyed those in attendance. Thomas and Edward were there, of course, but Thomas' parents as well. That was a surprise. Elizabeth fixed on Jennifer, thinking it was her love for her son, a full head taller than she was, that had brought the devout Presbyterian to hear what the Quaker had to say. She and Charles were dressed nicely, their expressions reserved.

Edward was talking to a stranger, a rotund, older gentleman, who stood out among the country people in his fancy waistcoat, the ribbons of his loose trousers tied evenly at the knees. *He couldn't be the preacher, could he?* Elizabeth wondered, her eyes fixed on his polished boots. Her eyes flinted to Kelsey and Hannah, serving beer and making small talk. She shifted her gaze again. Her breath caught. George Fox — she was sure of it. He'd come from the back room and was standing beside Edward. Not much older than Thomas but younger than Kelsey, he was clean-shaven, and his cheeks were bright from braving the wind. Whereas Charles and Thomas were dressed as men in the trades, the sleeveless leather jerkin and dark breeches of the preacher were plain and his shirt was soiled. There was a tear down the side of one of his stockings, and there were no buckles on his shoes.

Auntie tapped Elizabeth's shoulder. "Stop staring," she scolded gently. She pointed to a couple of chairs and they sat down just as Moe returned. She lifted her tiny nose to make a pretense of sniffing the air and pointed to the flowers. Then she splayed her fingers on her cheeks several times. Elizabeth saw blossoms in the gesture.

"YES," she nodded to show she understood. She copied the sign. "FLOWERS. YES." Then she moved her arms as if she were rocking a baby and pointed to the doll left by the little table.

"BABY DOLL," Moe copied enthusiastically. She punctuated the exchange with an exaggerated facial expression and amble head bobbing.

Elizabeth faced a giggling Lizzie, delighted by Moe's antics. "Did you gather those?" she asked kindly, pointing to the bouquet. "They're beautiful, Lizzie. The room's lovely."

Lizzie nodded. She seemed ready to burst. "He's soon to start, I think," she whispered, a hand squeezing Elizabeth's shoulder. She greeted Auntie and left them to sit near Thomas.

Moe was back. Doll dangling in her grasp, she raised both hands up like a toddler might to sit on Elizabeth's lap. Then, settling there, she squirmed side to side a couple of times and purposely crossed her arms against the front of her little shift as if she were hugging herself. When Elizabeth smiled at her, she repeated the movements.

"LOVE." Elizabeth guessed, dipping her chin to meet Moe's gaze. "LOVE, YES," she signed. The room seemed filled with it. She opened her heart to the possibilities of the evening, pulling Moe into her chest and rested her chin on top of her little head.

George Fox stepped forward and smiled at Elizabeth. His blue, penetrating eyes caught her ordinary brown ones, and heat crawled up her cheeks. "Thank you for joining us tonight," he said as he gazed in welcome around the room. There was a murmur of anticipation and those who weren't seated found a place.

The preacher remained standing, in command as he brushed aside the long, scraggly hair that hung loose from his hat and began. "I've been all over this region, conversing with folks such as you." He glanced to Hannah and Lizzie, who were now sitting together on a bench beside Thomas. "I'm indeed grateful for the hospitality. Thank you."

Lizzie sank behind her mother to be out of his sightline. She began to chew on a fingernail.

"It is wonderful to be in your midst, for as we travel, we depend on folks like you."

It was then that Elizabeth noticed that Kelsey wasn't in the room. Perhaps the risk of staying to listen to the "dissenter" was too great for him. She wasn't sure. Kelsey was a reticent man, willing to listen to others but not one to share his own thoughts casually. At least not with her. He'd be the one held accountable, she considered, if George Fox brought trouble to the farmstead.

"I'm alive with holy Spirit and happy to share it," George

was announcing. He removed his hat. "God and Christ are very real and present in this moment, are they not? Near at hand." He seemed very sure. "Present within and among us." He let the hat drop to the dirt floor. "Not an imitation from the imagination of ministers with their formal prayers and false preaching but moving here. Available to all of you, to all people, without charge. Free to every creature, to live in the life and power and spirit as Christ did, in the beauty of the world as servants to Truth. For this Light is love, the immortal word, shining into you."

The message seemed to galvanize those in the room. If Jennifer Holme was offended or thought George Fox blasphemous, she gave no indication of it. Elizabeth couldn't read Charles. His head was lowered, his eyes on the floor; his fingers pressed into his temples.

But how, how does one reach this Light? Elizabeth wondered. There'd been plenty enough talk of it of late, but she still didn't understand how a person found it.

As if he heard her query, George began to explain the way to the calm. "If you allow yourself, if you expect it, if you can brush aside your thinking and will accept what is available to you, you will feel goodness, shining into all your hard places, wrongful intentions, and jealous desires."

As she listened, Elizabeth pictured a lantern lighting the way into her soul. She tried to think of an offense, the worst one, and how it'd be to face it, change it. "You'll find peace among the darkness," George was adding. "Just as the roses and lilies grow in the thorns." Elizabeth smiled with the familiar verse. *George Fox saw images, too — holy ones.*

"For once you have seen the evil within yourself, your bad habits, you can turn from them, turn from the dark to a living understanding of all that is divine. And be led to Truth, to be of good faith, and valiant," George preached. "Grounded in the holy presence. . . ." He licked his lips. "For it's there that you find the power and strength to fiercely challenge yourself, to act to change."

Act to change. Elizabeth rubbed a finger over her lips.

"Let Christ shine on everything you are doing," George was saying. "It is the daily cross you bear, to stand naked and find what you are to discover. For it is the Light in your conscience, the Holy Spirit, who can speak to your condition, to remind you of the lessons Christ preached when he walked this earth. God, in the flesh, come and come again. *To counsel us in the living of our outward lives.*"

The preacher fumbled his hands and, in the pause, Elizabeth considered that if people were taught to speak to God in prayer then surely a divine message could be returned as well. *To counsel us in the living of our outward lives*, she echoed internally. She saw a swooping mass of sparrows, whirling in the afternoon sky, and she let all doubt fly with them from her heart. Never once had she felt like this in church — open, trusting, filled with hope.

It was the scrape of Charles Holme's boots on his chair leg that distracted her and brought her back to stare at George. If he'd heard the noise, he didn't let it divert him. He pushed at a lock of hair and started up again. "You know of the disobedience of Adam and Eve, created in the Divine image and restored to it?" He swiveled his eyes about the room. "You, too, good people, you, too, can be restored as they were, to the original pure nature of humankind. You can root yourself in love, compassion, and justice. Free yourself from a tradition that has lost its way."

Elizabeth raised her chin, her lips thin, and held his eyes.

"Like many of you," George said as if just to her, "I've fasted and sat in solitude since I was a child, saying daily prayers and pondering Bible verses that I felt might hold answers for me. But I tell you now, it isn't the written verses, but the Christ, the Holy Spirit, moving through them, that can inform your life. It matters not whether you can read. Let your experience be your truth." His voice rang out and he let go of her. "Christ will reach you if you're willing and patient. So, come," he suggested, lowering his voice. "Come into the family of love. Be still and be counseled." He sat down and leaned back into the high, elegant chair that Kelsey had artistically carved from the lower part of a thick tree stump. Charles Holme got abruptly to his feet and pulled at Jennifer's elbow so that she, too, stood up. He herded her out of the cottage, the door slamming behind them.

Elizabeth angled her head, trying to see if Moe was asleep, her limbs dangling limp from her lap. She adjusted the sleeping child and turned back to George. His eyes were closed, his face slackened, his shoulders slumped. His hands rested on his knees and his feet were solidly planted on the swept dirt floor. She supposed he was well-practiced in the worship of Friends and could easily find his comfort in it. She copied his posture, relaxed her eyelids, and allowed his form to blur as she drifted inward.

It was sometime later when Elizabeth heard George stand, that she realized she'd been in a calm, thoughtless space. It surprised her. She opened her eyes to see the preacher briefly offer his hand to Edward and then turn to the rest of them. "Friends," he announced. "I'm thankful you've made time in your evening to meet me and experience our worship." He went to stand behind the stranger. "Seems time for a bit of a break. Then I'd like you to hear what Arthur Parnell here has to say."

Chapter 9

Elizabeth left the buzz of conversations in the Leavens' front room to run to the Fletcher's privy. When she returned across the lane, she briefly introduced herself to the merchant, Arthur Parnell, trying not to fix on the way his hair was slicked back with some kind of oil from his wide forehead. Before they'd said much to each other, George asked everyone to circle up the chairs and give their attention to him.

Elizabeth found a spot with Moe between Auntie and Lizzie. George took a chair beside Arthur and gave an encouraging pat to his back.

"Hello, everyone. I'm, I'm Mister Parnell," Arthur stuttered uneasily, as he rose. "I, I was in Kendal on business from Retford, asking about Quakers . . . er, Friends . . . in the area. Was directed out this way." He clenched and unclenched his fingers in front of his clean, tailored shirt.

Elizabeth gave Hannah a worried look.

"I, I mean no harm. I was careful as I rode out," Arthur added quickly, catching Elizabeth's expression. "I had to take the chance of it. Wanted whoever was out here to know of my son, James, James Parnell. We worry for him. My wife and I. Don't know his whereabouts, you see. He's attracted to you sorts, and, and I thought maybe your paths would cross with his."

You sorts? Elizabeth repeated in her mind, disliking the expression. It occurred to her that if she saw Arthur Parnell in the market cross, he'd expect a curtsey from her.

Arthur scratched his head and started anew. "What I mean to say is that James is off preaching somewhere and we haven't heard from him for quite some time." Arthur ran his hands down his waistcoat. "He's already run away from home a couple of times, fell in with Seekers and now. . . ." Arthur rubbed at his neck. "He and I have had a rocky go of it."

"Has he met George?" asked a frowning Thomas. He scratched at his stubble of a beard.

"He has," said Arthur. "Sent to find him by Nottingham sympathizers. They told him he'd find Fox in prison in Carlisle." He checked with George who returned a thin smile of confirmation. "He walked ten days straight . . . alone and out in the wild . . . to reach the man he thought would understand his struggle."

Thomas gave a soft whistle.

"'Tis true," George interjected, taking their attention for a moment. "He was limping and ragged when he came to me. The jailers, who'd turned away countless of other visitors, thought him mad, that his endless prattle would be annoying. So they let him visit."

"Fox . . . er, George . . . tells me that he and James conversed all that whole day," added Arthur with more confidence in his telling. "James, of course, had never been among the lice and stench of a cell where men and women are thrown together with no chamber pots or privacy for it."

Murmurs fluttered around the room, none but George ever having seen a cell either.

"Still, I dare say, when James came home after that, he was happier than I'd seen him in a long while. Would sing in an odd manner around the place. Said he learned the way of it from George."

"He did, did he?" interrupted Thomas a second time. He bumped Edward's shoulder and smirked soundlessly. "How's it go?"

Arthur nodded to him, wanting to please, Elizabeth thought. "Find holy Spirit," he sang softly. "Find holy Spirit in your heart. Find holy Spirit . . ." He stopped the toneless attempt. "A simple thought, repeated over and over," he explained awkwardly and then went on. "James was worried for his champion. Told us he was held in a place crawling with maliciousness. He left us again to go to London. Requested audience with the Lord Protector to ask if he might be allowed to switch places with George. His pluck got him admitted but the Lord Protector didn't allow the switch." Arthur paused for a moment, collecting his thoughts.

"It was during that time, the last time James was home, that he told of being moved to preach in the way of Friends. There was no arguing with him about it. And, you know, 'tis so dangerous on the routes. Gangs of highway men, bandits, all about."

"You've heard nothing about him?" Auntie interrupted, commiserating with the worried father.

"We hear a rumor occasionally. My wife especially when she does her marketing. James was arrested at some point and lay in a stale, dank cell for two nights before a jury acquitted him. He got word to us. Said he was driven out of town and must now carry a pass that describes him as a rogue." Arthur stared down at his shiny boots for a long moment. "I feel the shame of it, but, but he's our son . . . and that's why I've come to you."

George stood up. "If it be us who find him or hear word, we'll convey your worry and encourage him to write. If it's you who sees him first, tell him you've found his friend, George Fox, and he'd be welcome to join my travel. He can reach me through Swarthmoor Hall in Ulverston. It's southwest of here in the Furness area of Lancaster. Home to Judge Fell."

Chapter 10

Moe felt the knock on the door through her feet and slid off her little chair to open the latch. It was Edward.

"George's going to tell a bit about himself if you'd like to come hear him," he said politely.

Elizabeth gave him a little grin. "We'll meet you there." She set about to clean Moe's face and hands from breakfast and ready the child. There was still mist on the ground when the three of them joined the others at the Leavens'.

Neither Thomas' parents nor Arthur Parnell were among those gathered but Kelsey was there. He came to the Fletchers. "I'll take Moe with me outside if you're wanting. She can help with my chores," he offered. He reached for a lump of sugar he carried for his plow horse and held it out to the child. A happy Moe took the sweet and followed him outside.

"Come, sit, join us," George called over to Elizabeth and Auntie. "I've a tract I've written if you'd like a copy." He held it up as Elizabeth and Auntie found chairs. *He must know we can't read*, thought Elizabeth, not reaching for the pamphlet. She was thankful when Hannah distracted them with mugs of the light beer Kelsey made.

"I'd like to tell you about a woman, Elizabeth . . ." George began, giving Elizabeth a soft chuckle. "Elizabeth Hooten." He glanced at Hannah and then Auntie. "When I was about the age of this one," he reached for Edward, "I walked to Skegby in Nottinghamshire, searching for answers to the things that bothered me. I'd found none who could speak to my condition and was greatly depressed. A kind minister directed me to a woman of note, describing her as a 'frustrated Baptist who was allowed to preach.' He told me I'd find her in Mansfield.

"And I did find her — Elizabeth Hooton, a remarkable older woman. She and I spent much of the next days together. She knew how to ask probing queries to get at the heart of things and didn't judge." George stretched back his chest and then let his shoulders drop. "Imagine this woman, the wife of an important businessman, busy with her family and home, who found time for me when no one else had." He chuckled softly. He peeked again at Hannah and Auntie.

"Weak and ill-formed as my ideas were at the time, Elizabeth Hooten saw merit in them. She listened deeply to what I was trying to tell her, allowed me to clarify my meanings. When I said my thoughts aloud to her, I realized that I knew for sure that it was only Christ who could speak to my condition, answers given to me when I listened within for guidance. My heart leaped with joy when I saw that I was to go out and preach the good news, that I was to follow my leading."

Leading, Elizabeth repeated to herself, tasting the word. George had trusted the still, small voice within. *Like with Moe . . .* she realized. She'd felt compelled to do something for the child, a sureness to act, *a leading*.

"Everyone can act as the Holy Spirit directs," George continued.

Everyone, repeated Elizabeth. She heard the songbirds calling outside. *Everyone. Everyone. Everyone can speak as the Holy Spirit gives them utterance. Everyone.* Her heart was beating wildly. *If George Fox can find answers in himself, then I can, too. That's what he's been trying to tell us.* She saw a key open a door in the blackness, a nameless force tearing into her. What he'd experienced was available to them all.

She came back to him. "Elizabeth Hooten introduced me to a group of worshippers who met in spirit and in truth," George was saying. "Without clergy." He took a sip from his mug. "It was wonderful, really. I'd only ever sat alone and I flourished in the worship in Mansfield." He licked the foam from his upper lip. "I remember that during one of those meetings, Elizabeth's prophecy was about the injustice of the poor, them expected to tithe and be punished unfairly if they didn't. My heart opened to the Truth of it and I let images of the struggling and suffering wander in me, sure the wrong shouldn't be forgot. I sank in the quiet around the message, glad that no one spoke after it was delivered. I was moved to speak myself, Elizabeth Hooten saying the silence deepened with my message."

"Was it the first meeting for worship then, in the way of Friends?" Thomas asked.

"The first settled meeting? Yes, I believe so," George allowed.

"And she was the first convinced?" asked Hannah.

"Perhaps," considered George.

There was a long silence and then people began to stretch and stand to mingle and attend to their needs. Hannah and Lizzie served a nice cake and refilled mugs. When they regrouped again, George wanted to tell about what had happened to him after he'd left Elizabeth Hooten and had started to preach publicly. "I went into Nottingham," he began. "And was arrested for it. I didn't fight it but went calmly with the constable and then before the judge. He sentenced me to jail — my first time." He looked to those to his right side and then to his left. "But good can, and did, come from it, for when I was alone with the jailer, he apologized for all the goings on and wanted to discuss how I'd come to our ways. We talked long into the night, he encouraged me with food and drink — me in the cell and he just outside it. We tried earnestly to understand the deepest parts of each other, each calling our ideas and experiences by words that resonated for us though they weren't the ones the other used: God . . . Lord . . . Christ Jesus . . . holy Spirit . . . Seed." George articulated each term carefully. "Each of these had bubbled up in me during worship or flashed in me at other times. I realized that the naming is not the center of it, that it didn't change my experience if the jailer used words that brought him comfort."

Light, Spirit. Yes. Elizabeth decided. They weren't the names she associated with church — God, Father, the man up in heaven. She took the ownership that George offered, shivering with the joy that fell over her.

"In the morning," said George, "I was told that the jailer had sought out the judge for my release — and it'd been granted. It seems both men were equally concerned that 'a man of God' had been imprisoned. My freedom was a surprise, to be sure, but it was an even greater jolt when the jailer invited me to his home, wanting his family to hear me out." George's face softened with the recollection. "I spent a dear night with them . . . and when I departed, the sheriff, his wife, and his children were convinced." He paused and, in the space, Thomas clapped softy. George stared over at him and he stopped.

"I mark that time as the end of my years as a troubled lad. Done with blood-letting and worthless ministers." He put a hand on his knee and stood. "I'd experienced an ocean of pain and trouble, but I saw an infinite ocean of Light and Love that flowed over it and would be with me always." He looked about the room. "That ocean of Light will flow over your troubles, too, lift you up and show you the way."

For her part, Elizabeth imagined a swath of clear sky stretching across the hillsides after the dark of a summer storm. She let the blue color run through her. "I see images of guidance, too," she whispered aloud, her hands sliding down her hips and her heart galloping. "I see the birth of a new lamb, the gift of it making us happy and hopeful." She snuck a peek at Auntie who raised her eyebrows, then gave a smile.

Elizabeth's simple proffering hung in the room for all to quietly consider. After a while George rose again. "Mind the Light working in your conscience, the Bible of your heart, for the answers to all you are asking are within. You need no person, creed, or hymn to find your way. The true preacher stands at the pulpit within you. Let your doubt of it be hushed and fly away."

Elizabeth's chest felt as if it were on fire. *I need no one to tell me that what George Fox says is true*, she thought. The anxious place in her heart shifted and a new understanding replaced it. *It's the Holy Spirit I hear in the wind, in the spaces between the leaves and in the whisper of the rain. . . . I am asked to stand naked, stripped and uncomfortable in it all. I am convinced.* She heard the sound of shoes lightly dancing towards her, Moe tapping on her skirts.

"EAT?" the girl signed, a hand tapping at her mouth, her eyebrows raised. When Elizabeth didn't respond, Moe turned to Auntie. "EAT," she mimed again. Others were rustling and rising, too. Auntie took Moe's hand down from her face, stood, and motioned toward the door. She didn't suggest Elizabeth come with them.

Lizzie came quickly to Elizabeth's side. "I'm convinced. I am," she whispered hoarsely. "It only took George Fox to share what he did for me to know it." Thomas and Edward were staring over at them from across the room, their eyes twinkling.

"I am as well, Lizzie. . . ." Elizabeth stuttered, bliss trapping her.

Part II

Convincement

1654

Chapter 11

George was wanting Thomas to go along to Durham with him. Edward and his friend, John Audland, would be with them, too. The women weren't invited.

"If there's 'that of God in everyone,'" Elizabeth complained to Lizzie, the two of them sitting on the bench in the Leavens' garden, "Why weren't we asked to go as Thomas was?" She didn't wait for an answer. "Because we're women?" she scoffed.

"Would you leave Moe, so soon?" asked Lizzie, dodging the claim. "Who knows how long they'll be gone."

Elizabeth considered the remark. Moe was just settling in, learning the routine of the days at the farmstead, building trust with Auntie, the Leavenses, and the Holmes. How would she have explained her leaving to the child? How would she explain it to herself? That she and Lizzie were going to stroll off for four or five days, with no plan for what they would eat or where they would sleep, to witness George — and maybe Edward and John — preach? A fledgling, unschooled, she doubted she and Lizzie would be much help; they'd probably only be in the way. No, Elizabeth finally decided. She let go of her ire. She was happy enough to wait at the farmstead to hear how it went, to sleep in her own bed and snuggle with Moe.

When Edward returned a week later, he came eagerly to find her. The crowds had welcomed them, he reported. George, Edward, and John had all taken a turn to preach to the hundreds they'd attracted. Thomas had listened, rocking in silence nearby. He'd been so taken with the messages that he could be seen visibly shaking and contorting himself. "He's enthusiastic and willing," espoused Edward. "A bit zealous, but it's good, it's good. He's learning the way of Friends."

When Elizabeth asked Thomas about it, tears streamed down his cheeks. He blubbered through telling her that he'd felt blessed, wholly blessed, as he'd stood with George and Edward and John. He was sure he was to do the holy work.

"What does your Da have to say about it?" Elizabeth carefully asked. Thomas was still supping and sleeping at his parents' cottage as far as she knew. "You're not weaving or selling at all anymore? You've ended it?" she asked. She hadn't seen Charles since the first night George had come to them, and although she didn't feel close to him, he'd always been kind to her. She hoped he wasn't going to disown Thomas as Edward's parents had done.

"He's angry, my Da," admitted Thomas, scowling. "Says he's lost his only son and business partner to a man who's preaching against the Church, a man who's spending his time wandering the countryside instead of helping his family." Thomas folded his arms and lifted his chin. "I'm to preach with Friends. I'm sure of it." In the next days, he spent large parts of the day pacing the Holmes' garden, arms whirling like a Ranter, calling out his "prophecy." All talk of marriage, as far as Elizabeth knew, was suspended.

"And will we be able to preach?" asked Lizzie innocently one afternoon.

Thomas gave her a cockeyed gaze. "You heard George tell of Elizabeth Hooten. She's a woman, isn't she?" He threw his hands in the air, irritated. "One of the first of our preachers. Anne Audland and Mabel Camm, too."

"But I've never heard of a woman preaching in Kendal," Elizabeth countered, coming to Lizzie's aid.

"Well, that's right," Thomas allowed. "The time has come when God is reigning supreme in our hearts, and who's to say what will happen next? Christ has come again among us to do remarkable good." He seemed to be quoting someone else. He clasped his hands dramatically at his heart, his eyes unfocused on an imagined audience.

Elizabeth and Lizzie stared at him. "He has?" Lizzie asked, head cocked and leaning forward.

"He has. Inwardly," Thomas clarified. "And if I am to be a spokesman for God, I must practice my ministry." He turned from them and began pacing again.

"We're going to ride to Swarthmoor Hall," Edward told Elizabeth a day or so later. He was freshly shaven and wearing a clean dark shirt atop his breeches. Margaret Fell, the matron there, had sent funds so that George and Edward could lease horses and ride to the Ulverston manor. "We're going to discuss a plan to blanket the country with the Truth," explained Edward. He stood tall and confident.

"And Thomas is going, too?" asked Elizabeth, trying not to sound assuming.

"I haven't heard that he is," Edward said.

"And will it be safe for you all to be there?"

"Oh yes," Edward assured her, his eyes twinkling. "Swarthmoor is the home of Judge Fell. He's climbed the ranks of judges and was a member of Parliament until only a few years back. He quit because he doesn't approve of Cromwell thinking he's God," the lad scowled. "And Margaret's a landowner in her own right; well respected in the area."

Things reverted back into the familiar farm routines after George and Edward left. As it turned out, Thomas wasn't invited along but he was seldom at the loom either. One day when Elizabeth didn't see him about, she went over to talk with Jennifer, out in her garden hanging newly dyed squares of cloth.

Jennifer seemed relieved to have George and Edward gone away and not influencing her son. Perhaps Charles Holme was also pleased to have his partner occasionally back by his side, although Elizabeth saw Thomas walking down the road toward Kendal and then returning, two or three times a day. He was anxious to hear about Swarthmoor, she supposed.

He didn't have to wait but a week. It happened that he was practicing out by the Holmes' workhouse when he saw the two men riding down the lane toward the farmstead. Elizabeth was out in the vegetable garden and ran to meet them. By the time they'd dismounted and Thomas had lashed the horses, Elizabeth and Lizzie were both bunched up with him to greet them. "New hat?" Elizabeth asked Edward. It was all she could do not to take his hand.

"Margaret Fell thought the wide-brim more practical than my cap," explained Edward. "She used money from the Kendal Fund, set up to support those who travel."

Elizabeth wondered if it'd stung his pride to receive the charity. After all, if his parents had been speaking to him, they could've readily provided whatever he needed.

"And so, you made a plan?" Hannah wanted to know. She'd come out of the Leavens' cottage at the sound of the arrival to greet the preachers.

"Yes, yes we have," George informed her. He flipped his hair back from his face. "Decided to send pairs or small groups of Friends out across the country. Like a mass of ants combing the hamlets, towns, and villages."

"Come inside and sit," suggested Hannah. "Tell us all about it."

"James Parnell was there, at Swarthmoor," George told them when Hannah had served everyone a refreshing drink. He was sitting back comfortably on his chair while Thomas, beside him, was on the edge of his. "The youngest one of us," he added. "I told him of his Da's visit here and he agreed to write home immediately."

"He hadn't meant to worry his parents," Edward added. "Gave us two pamphlets he'd written and had printed. We can give them out to those who seem to want to know more about Friends . . ."

"Children of the Light," George interjected. "From the Bible."

"Yes," agreed Edward, "We can give the tracts out to those wanting to read about the 'Children of the Light.'"

Elizabeth watched him smooth back his curls. She liked that he was including them all with his choice of words.

"James was taking them to Cambridge..." Edward continued.

"Oh! Cambridge!" George interrupted again. "Margaret Fell showed us a letter that'd come about Cambridge and Mary Fisher."

"Mary Fisher?" Elizabeth didn't think she'd heard the name before.

"A maidservant. Smart. Fearless. Convinced about three years ago in Selby."

"Six or seven days walk east from here," Edward whispered to Elizabeth as he got up to answer the knock at the door.

"Wondered where you all were," explained Auntie. She had Moe in tow, of course.

"Come join us, Jane," Hannah invited. She went to fetch a pitcher and two more mugs. "George and Edward are telling us about a Mary Fisher. Convinced three years ago in Selby." She turned to George. "One of the first then?"

"Yes, one of the first," agreed George. "Glad you came over, Jane. Come sit," He stood up and offered his chair, but Auntie slid into a different one. Moe went from chair to chair, collecting a hug from each person. Then she came back to sit on Auntie's lap.

"The whole Tomlinson household was convinced," George went on. "But Mary Fisher was bold in it. Wanted to be put to use as soon as arrangements could be made. Was given a fresh set of clothing, a good bonnet for the weather, and sturdier shoes. Left with a companion for York."

Elizabeth glanced at Auntie, wondering what she was thinking."

"Freed from her duties, then?" Lizzie asked, tossing her mane of blond hair, unbraided and hanging loose below her shoulders.

"Yes. Glad to be discharged of them and able to travel," said George. "She arrived at the church in York there on a First Day and tried to speak at the end of the service. Arrested as a vagrant. Sentenced to sixteen months in the cell."

"Sixteen months," groaned Hannah, incredulously.

"She was there with Elizabeth Hooten, arrested for the same violation but a month prior," added Edward. "The older woman taught her to read and write." He gave Elizabeth a smile.

"'Lay it to your heart and let the oppressed go free,'" George quoted. "That's what she wrote to a judge. Her first letter. When she was finally released, her faith was stronger than ever. We learned at Swarthmoor that she went from jail to Cambridge — 'tis where college lads are taught to rely on earthly knowledge rather than on inward revelation to become ministers."

"The training ground for the Presbyterians — there and Oxford," Edward interjected. He rubbed at his temple. "Uppity, spoiled young men. Engaged in their sports and horse-racing. Not serious about their service."

"All true," George concurred. "Hireling ministry," he scoffed. "Mary Fisher chose Sidney Sussex College to proclaim the good news." He took a loud breath. "Apparently she was mocked and ridiculed by the students and their professors. Asked disrespectful questions."

"But she refused to be intimidated," interrupted Edward a second time. "Answered with authority." He dipped his chin abruptly in his sureness of it.

"Wouldn't be bullied," George agreed, his lips set. "Called right back to them, singing and rejoicing and saying, 'The Lord be blessed, the Lord be praised.' The students were so shocked by her behavior that some ran to the mayor in complaint, saying 'the fat cow' was unmarried and illiterate and had no right to be challenging them."

"And what happened to her?" Hannah asked. She slid a protective arm around both Lizzie and Elizabeth and pulled them into her.

"She was brought before the judge. He made sport of her size and unbecoming appearance, her lack of status. He asked who her husband was . . ." George nodded to Edward.

"She answered that Christ was her husband, that she was married to holy Spirit." Edward obliged him.

"Angering the man," Auntie guessed, her face firm with worry. She peeked around Moe to catch Hannah's expression.

"Speaking her truth," George corrected her, but kindly. "He issued a warrant that she be whipped in the market cross 'til blood ran down her back.'"

"No," moaned Elizabeth. She didn't know what to think. She looked out the window, searching for comfort in the blue sky.

After a heartfelt pause, Edward continued with the telling. "Margaret Fell told us that the mayor ordered three of his sergeants to see that the sentence was 'cruelly and lawlessly executed.' It was important to her that the suffering was recorded in the letter."

"You should know all of it," George said, looking directly

at Elizabeth and Lizzie. "That Mary's cap was thrown from her hair, her bodice, pulled to her waist, sleeves and all. The flogging was more malicious and heartless than for any man."

Elizabeth stared down at her hands and tried to imagine the humiliation. She was agog to think the woman would have borne such punishment to spread the Truth of Friends.

"But Mary Fisher," George finished, "astonished the crowd with her behavior. Prayed loudly and repeatedly for the forgiveness of her persecutors. When they untied her, she pulled up what was left of her top and called out her rejoicing. She proclaimed to all who were still in the market that she was honored to have divinely suffered, to have endured it for Friends."

Honored to suffer, Elizabeth repeated. Her skin prickled.

Chapter 12

"We need Children of the Light to travel, to spread the good word," George announced. The group of them, Kelsey included, were sitting in the Leavens' garden. Auntie and Moe, too, with Hannah between Lizzie and Thomas. "Friends," he clarified. "Friends of Truth." He seemed fueled by the planning at Swarthmoor.

"Edward and I are going to start off soon for Cheshire — to the town of Chester. Take about a week. Thomas is deciding if he's going along. Elizabeth and Lizzie, perhaps you'd consider whether you're led to go, too."

Auntie stopped in her playing of finger games with Moe and met Elizabeth's gaze.

Elizabeth suspected she wasn't going to tell her what to do. If she was going to travel such a distance with three unmarried men, the decision was going to be hers. Still, she felt the weight of it. *I wanted this, didn't I?* she thought. *To be asked to go with them?* It was a chance for a different future.

"I'll be with them for part of the way," George assured Kelsey, Hannah and Auntie. "And Edward, too, until he splits off for London." He turned to the younger preacher. "For those with land or station will see our faith is not only for country folks. And," he faced Thomas. "We need men in the trades." His eyes alternated between Elizabeth and Lizzie. "And women in the work so that all manner of people see by our example that they are capable. You've heard of Mary Fisher. And Anne Audland, John's wife, and her neighbor, Mabel Camm, too. They're preaching now. Not half a dozen years older than you girls."

"Can you tell us the route?" asked Kelsey. He rolled in his bottom lip and held it there with his teeth.

George got down on the dusty ground and drew something of a map in the dirt with a stick. "Let's say this is England." He made an oblong shape that was part circle and part square. "Kendal is up here in the northwest, far from London and near a large lake. It's mountainous — wild and barren in places — but some good farmland, too. You know that. . . ." He squinted up at Kelsey and then looked down again to make a little circle with the tip of his stick. "Let's say Kendal is about here. The Pennines are here to the east." He drew some jagged marks to show the mountains. "And the Irish Sea, here to the west — between England and Ireland." He moved the stick to where the sea would be. "Scotland's up this way, yes? And here, south of Kendal, are the Midlands. I've walked all through here, zigzagging to Chester."

George looked to Elizabeth, then Lizzie. "Not far — we'll only be half a day of it the first day . . . maybe stop near Oxenholme. Then through Endmoor, Lancaster, Garstang, Preston, Euxton . . . Wugan." He wiggled the stick southward. "Finally, to Chester. Take us, oh, about a week."

A week of walking? Elizabeth sat back. She stared at the map in the dirt. The names meant nothing to her and it seemed a long way.

"Perhaps you'd sit quietly and consider it," George asked solemnly. "To live in the life and power as Christ did. For now, the challenge has come . . . to be used."

"I'm going," Thomas blurted. He flung an arm over Edward's shoulder.

"And me," piped Lizzie, wiggling away from Hannah. The decision didn't surprise Elizabeth. Lizzie would want to be with Thomas and here was her chance.

Elizabeth reached for one of Auntie's hands. She'd been convinced, too, the Truth coming into her that first night George had preached to the group of them. *She'll support me,*

Elizabeth knew. Still, how was she to rise above the meek part of herself, with her devotion to Friends so raw and unproven? She knew nothing of sleeping out of doors or cooking in the wild.

"We need Friends to travel," George repeated.

"Do worship on your part in it," Lizzie begged. She leaned closer and clenched Elizabeth's forearm. She pretended to gently twist it. "That you might be led to join us as well, to go faithfully to others as George came to us?"

Elizabeth felt her chest constrict. Wind blew wildly in her head. Was she, a farm girl to go? To stand in public places and prophesize? She ran her hands down her top skirt allowing possibility to fill her.

"I'll worship on it," she promised, an imagined hand pushing at the small of her back.

The next day when she found Auntie and Moe sitting on the step, the older woman mending and Moe playing with her doll, Elizabeth came to sit with them. Her gaze held for a moment on how the sunlight caught in the gray strands of Auntie's bowed head and she was uncertain as to what she should do — what she wanted to do — what she was led to do.

She watched Moe, opening and closing her mouth without sound, pretending to talk to her doll. *'Tis how I feel*, thought Elizabeth. She wasn't sure what she wanted to say, what she expected from Auntie. "I, I'm wondering if I'm called, Auntie," she said aloud. Her stomach felt like there was a rock in the pit of it. "If I'm called as the others are to go to Chester. Not just wanting to go with them for the adventure but *led*."

Auntie slowly released a breath and studied the earnest brown eyes. "You listen, Elizabeth. You listen as you do when you're out with the sheep and I call you. It's the time of day for you to be expecting it, yes? And you hear the yell and turn

— and come. . . ." She gave Elizabeth a moment. "You *know*, Elizabeth. You do. Trust yourself — as you do that the sun's still in the sky when it's gray and raining . . . that there's an ocean all around England though you've never seen it. Trust the holy spirit we've come to know."

The next time Elizabeth had a chance to sit alone, she couldn't stop the flood of relentless questions that bounded through her. Was it fair to leave Moe for two or three weeks? There'd be no way to explain to the child where she was going, why she wasn't home. She closed her eyes and tried to quiet the whirl of what plagued her. Was it fair to Auntie to have to figure out what Moe was wanting? For Auntie to have to do Elizabeth's chores?

No one had said anything to suggest that a leading was easy or without consequences. Elizabeth listened to the cheep, cheep of a sparrow, expecting an answer in it. When she opened her eyes, she felt as if a fleeting acceptance had come over her and she knew what she was to do. It was a subtle message, as a shape in a cloud. "I am of the Spirit, I am," Elizabeth announced to no one, the muscles in her face taut, serious, mature. "Capable as any of ministry." She'd go with them, trusting her needs would be satisfied. She'd listen to the ministry of George and Edward, learning to give her own.

"You've my blessing, Elizabeth Fletcher," was Auntie's reply when Elizabeth told her of her decision after sup that evening. "What a fine preacher you'll be." She reached across the table for Elizabeth's hands and gently massaged her knuckles. "To go forth, denying what is dear to you here, and be in the power of the Holy Spirit." She brought her hands back and patted her heart. "A week, a month, a year . . . you'll be with me always, Elizabeth. Right here."

Chapter 13

Elizabeth stood in the back room, tying her second sleeve to a clean, gray bodice. She fastened up the colorless ribbons down the front and tucked it into the waist of a dark top skirt. She wore a second skirt underneath and a pair of Thomas' old breeches for modesty under those. Auntie had made them smaller for her. She picked up the new bonnet Auntie had sewn for her. Lizzie had been the one to quilt the maroon lining to keep her warmer in the morning chill and summer drizzle. She'd made the ribbon ties thicker than usual to protect her cheeks from the sun and rain.

Moe insisted on carrying the bundle she'd fashioned. It contained a scarf and shawl, and another set of sleeves. She'd added a couple of rags to manage her monthlies — they'd become regular in the past year.

"COME," Elizabeth signaled to her. The child had no idea what was happening, but she followed obediently with the bundle to the front room. When they came to the table, Elizabeth stood at it for a moment and then trailed the palm of her free hand across the top ridge of her chair. She looked about the front room, trying to make a memory of the sparse interior, of the furniture her father had made, and of the smells of the home she'd known for fifteen years.

Out in the front garden, Elizabeth knelt down to Moe's level and cupped her tiny chin. "I'm going to go with George Fox, Moe. I'm going to learn to preach." She spoke into her bright little eyes as if Moe understood every word. She wished there was a way to tell the child she'd be gone for a couple of weeks but then would come back. "LOVE YOU," Elizabeth signed at last, leaving her pointer finger to linger on Moe's chest, a lump in her own. Moe furrowed her brow when she saw the leak of tears from her hero's sad eyes.

Auntie found them there, a bag of apples swinging on her arm. "We'll take you over," she offered as she found Moe's hand and the three of them crossed the lane to where George and Edward, Kelsey, Hannah, Lizzie, and Thomas were gathered.

It saddened Elizabeth that Charles and Jennifer hadn't joined the little group to muster goodbyes, though Thomas didn't seem concerned. With a heavy heart, she searched the Holmes' cottage window openings, hoping to at least see Jennifer's face peeking from one of them.

Lizzie came to pull her over to where Auntie and Hannah stood with Moe. "A nibble for you," Hannah said sweetly, handing her one of the lunches she'd packed for each of them. Auntie distributed apples and farewell hugs. There was a round of hand shaking from the men until Kelsey, glimpsing the high summer sun, called a halt to it all. "Be off with you now," he said forcefully, shooing them all on their way. His eyes glistening with tears.

Elizabeth couldn't remember ever seeing Kelsey so weepy. She went to him one final time and wrapped her arms around his slender waist. "We'll be fine, just fine," she said, her chin tilted up and resting on his chest. "Back in a couple of weeks," she assured him, trying to convince herself as much as him that she and Lizzie would return safe and sound.

George and Edward took the lead, heading south into Kendal and then past it. Thomas and Lizzie, clasped fingers swinging between them, were next in line. Elizabeth brought up the rear.

As she moved along, Elizabeth sifted through her memories, letting the images ease her leaving: Auntie when she first ventured outside in the morning, alert as any fox, to survey her vegetable garden. Moe, legs folded under her bottom, signing to herself as she played. Hannah, carefully hanging clothes out to dry on the bushes and fence. Kelsey, the only father she'd ever known, creating the stump chair where George Fox had first sat among them.

It's but three weeks, she chided herself for her insecurity. She squinted to where the others had gone ahead, to where the lane split. She could only see Lizzie's bonnet and upper back, Thomas no longer beside her as she turned left. A turn right would end at the coast, the Irish Sea. No doubt George, Edward, and Thomas had gone to the left, too. Now Lizzie.

Elizabeth wished they'd waited for her at the junction. She was hurt by everyone's impatience and hurried down the rough trail, with its bumps and rutted places, to make up for it. An oxen-pulled cart bounced past, the unsuspecting driver giving her a wave.

Elizabeth waved back — as if it was an ordinary day, as if she always traveled out of Kendal, as if she was not leaving home for the first time ever in her life.

"'Tis Oxenholme," George announced an hour or so later when Elizabeth caught up to the others. The group of them walked towards the hamlet, passing slanted-roofed, connected buildings that reminded Elizabeth of home. She noticed that the walls guarding the fields were piled with a stone pattern unlike those of Kendal and that there were more cows grazing than sheep. *Oxen Holme*. She turned back over her shoulder at the sound of a string of men galloping past and kicking up dust. They were really on their way.

Up ahead, Edward waited for her so that they could walk together. She felt a grateful flare of happiness, a balm to the burn in her calves. She took in his playful banter and serious explanations, the two of them never seeming to run out of things to say to each other.

It was late afternoon when Elizabeth looked up to see a shirtless man chipping at the earth with his hoe. His breeches were gathered with a rope belt that swung as he worked. For the second time that day, she gave a wave to a complete stranger. *Auntie would be scolding*, she thought when the farm hand stopped his work, wiped the sweat from under his large, floppy hat, and waved back.

Just a bit later, when the group of them stopped for a rest in the shade of some pines, the same farmer found them there. Perhaps for the kindness of it or as an excuse for a break in the heat of the day, the good man offered them fresh water and small portions of hard rye bread. "Name's Roy," he said by way of introduction. He passed around the bread and some pale cheese.

Hannah or Auntie would have done the same, Elizabeth considered. She introduced herself, keeping her gaze on Roy's rough beard rather than his eyes. *Cut by hacks with a knife*, she decided glancing over to Thomas. He'd shaved his poor beard and mustache after he'd been to Durham, saying Friends were careful so as not to be accused of trying to appear like Jesus.

"And this is my son, Gus," Roy explained as a young man came up to them and dropped his hand cart with a thud. His dog, panting madly, was quick to lie down beside Roy.

Elizabeth ate the meager offerings and then stretched back on the rough grass across from the rest of them. She worried that they'd only just begun, and she was already feeling weary. What if she didn't have the stamina to walk for a week?

Gus plopped his lanky body down beside her. "Hello, "he mumbled as he hunched his reedy body over the soiled knees of his breeches and took her in. He smelled thick from a long morning of labor, a hunk of damp hair sticking out from his hat and plastered to his forehead. "Seekers are you then?" he asked, eyes on the men for his answer. He began picking at the dirt under his fingernails.

"Friends," George corrected, and Elizabeth, new to being included in the growing sect, felt a stir in her heart.

"Have all the answers, do ya?" the lad smirked, his eyes sharp on George. He unfolded himself and leaned back to match Elizabeth.

"The important ones," the preacher replied calmly.

"Do you now?" poked Gus. "And what would you have us know then?" He threw his hat from his head and brushed his sweaty hair with both hands.

"That I was a lad like you not all that long ago — feeling trapped and dissatisfied." George took the final bites of his bread and cheese.

"Were you?" Gus mumbled. He reminded Elizabeth of a mosquito, with his spindly arms and legs and bothersome manner. "I feel those things," he allowed. "Sometimes."

"Where are you from, the group of you?" Roy asked abruptly. Elizabeth thought he was perhaps trying to offset his son's challenging behavior.

"These three are from Kendal," said George. He threw a hand to reference the Kendal Friends. "We've just come from farms near there. Edward Burrough here is from Underbarrow." He laid a hand on the lad's knee. "I spent my youth in Fenny Drayton . . . in Leicestershire. Though I left there some ten years ago."

"Were you apprenticed out then?" Roy probed.

"Twice. My fadder had me trained as a sheepherder and later as a shoemaker." George reached to finger one of his worn shoes. "Made these." He went on. "I saw that those who came for shoe repair were treated differently, the poor waved away but those with money given more consideration . . . and I decided I'd offer my abilities equally to each, at a fair price, no matter what a person's station or sex. That was the beginning of it."

"The beginning of what, what exactly?" puzzled Gus.

Elizabeth attended to how George steered the simple conversation, not saying too much at any one time and leaving space for the men's questions.

"The beginning of knowing that I didn't care to treat people the way the owner did, the way society dictated. The shoemaker ended my apprenticeship and when that happened, I began to take my mother's Bible and go into the countryside to read for long hours in the hollows of giant yew trees. By that time, I'd found little value in the church services and I decided to leave Fenny Drayton and seek my answers elsewhere."

"I bet your fadder was pleased about that," Gus scoffed sarcastically.

"I think he was relieved to have me go," George replied frankly. "Embarrassed by me." He nodded to confirm it. "I trudged down to London, but the place was too big and busy for a country lad. I felt lost there. And the influence of the Crown and Church was everywhere. I came back north where the Presbyterians don't have such a grip."

With that, both Roy and Gus gave a snort and Elizabeth suspected they were glad for the lack of authority in the north.

"Fight in the War? You're the age." Roy wondered. "I lost a boy to it. Gus's older brother."

"Sorry to hear it," Edward murmured. He picked up the bucket of water and dipper and passed it around to the others for a second drink.

"I didn't," George answered. "I was wrapped in my personal battle and wasn't made to go." He waited for the farmer to say more.

"The War took the lives of so many," lamented Roy, "Without any satisfying result — Cromwell and his cronies not bringing any solution to us poor and landless. . . ."

"How did you support yourself in it all?" Gus interrupted. He stared at George.

"I was never a vagabond," George clarified quickly. "My parents gave me some money at the start and I used it sparingly. I see now it was how they showed their love." The water came to him and he took his turn. "I spent that time going from village to village, talking to ministers. Some were helpful. Most weren't. They didn't accept me or my questions or see me as any kind of an equal." He tittered. "Or I them. Still, I was gaining on my understanding that Christ was my only teacher."

Gus stiffened at the mention. "The land is *my* Christ," he huffed. "Can't read the Bible and no one in these parts pays much attention if we work on the Sabbath." He held up his large, calloused hands.

George obliged him, avoiding confrontation. "Many ways to be holy, son," he said kindly. "Think of what you know about planting and caring for crops."

Elizabeth saw Roy dip his chin in agreement. A smile slowly spread across his face.

"A person doesn't need schooling or the church to know how things can grow and change," said George.

Elizabeth immediately found the double meaning in the phrasing, the lesson in it as true for her as for Gus and Roy.

"George and Edward here have a passion for the Bible," Thomas blurted out. "Me, not as much." He grinned infectiously, blinking his eyes.

"I do," agreed George, "love the Bible. My Da considered sending me to train as a minister. He decided in the end that I was too contrary for Oxford or Cambridge. . . ." He caught Gus's gaze. "But I love the land, too. Lots of lessons here. . . ." He patted the ground beside him.

Roy stood up and slapped at his hands, an indication that their break was over. Edward welcomed the hint. He got to his feet, glancing at the sun as he did so. "We best be on our way," he nudged. "Want to get through Endmoor and Preston Patrick yet today."

"May you be led by what is important to you," said Elizabeth to Gus as she slid her legs under herself, rose, and offered him a hand. She thought he surprised them both when he shook it.

Chapter 14

All through the long afternoon Elizabeth was flooded by feelings of doubt. As they passed through Endmoor, she fought with herself as to whether or not she could make it to Chester, work there for a few days, and tread home again. *I could turn around now*, she considered as she rubbed an ache in her hip. She was sure her feet were blistered. She began to do some figuring in her head. The day was much more than half gone but if she turned around now, she was pretty sure she could get to the farmstead before it was really pitch-black outside. *What would Auntie be doing?* she wondered, squinting at the sun. She wiped sweat from the edges of her bonnet. *Probably stirring the big cooking pot. Washing and chopping food for sup*, she speculated. She pictured Moe carrying things back and forth to Auntie. *If I missed them on the first day, how's it going to be tomorrow? In two weeks?* Her throat tightened. *I'm going to do this*, she decided. She watched herself take the next step, and then the next one on the dirt of the trail.

"Are you ok?" Edward asked, coming up alongside of her. There were beads of sweat on his forehead and his shirt clung to his chest.

"Mostly," Elizabeth answered, not wanting to complain or share her uncertainty. The two exchanged a few pleasantries and then Edward moved off to be with George. Elizabeth was disappointed. She wanted his comradery. When they stopped in an idyllic cemetery not long after and it was clear they weren't going to go any further, she realized it'd been Edward's suggestion to George.

It was a lovely spot. The group of them chose places to relax among a smattering of thin, rounded headstones, stuck at odd angles in the ground and covered with lichen. Elizabeth put her bundle aside, sank down in the tall, lush grass, and said a little prayer of gratitude in the familiar Presbyterian way. She checked the others, all a good distance from her, relaxing and talking softly to one another, and then discreetly took off her shoes. She pulled out each foot as if it were an over-ripe piece of fruit and boldly rolled down her stockings to inspect her blotched heels.

"Really, Elizabeth!" she heard Thomas whine. He flapped a hand in front of his face and rolled his eyes. Crunching her toes in relief, she returned an unembarrassed smirk and waved her feet in his direction for good measure. She had to stifle a laugh when Lizzie came over to her, found a soft spot, and released her feet as well. She took a pebble that had been rubbing inside her shoe and threw it a headstone with a ping and a gay giggle. They were on their own. They could make their own rules.

As Elizabeth and Lizzie massaged their toes, they talked about how they might arrange themselves for the night. They thought they'd spread out away from the men in the knee-high grass, the thick blades for their pallets, and use their shawls as coverings. Elizabeth laid back to test out their decision, grateful that Lizzie had come over to keep her company. Recent images rolled through her — Lizzie's unquestioning acceptance of Moe, her yielding posture when she worshipped.

"Oh, my," Lizzie said just then. "What have we got us into?" she asked plaintively. "Every part of me is sore from the walking, from the uncertainty of what we're doing." Elizabeth thought she heard Lizzie sniffle. "I don't mean to be complaining. . . . I, I *am* here for the right reasons. I am," she asserted. It was as if she were continuing a previous discussion with someone else. "To deepen my faith . . . to preach and serve as Christ did, to see how we might bring our ways to those who wait to know us." She sucked in a quivering breath and began to chew on a fingernail. Elizabeth kept quiet. "I'm truly thrilled, thrilled to have this opportunity." Lizzie clasped her hands together and rested her chin on them. "There are moments when I'm filled to overflowing with happiness — to be with all of you, to have the model of George Fox, to be my own person. And it's a relief not to be doing chores and pretending that market day is an adventure. . . ." She peeked at Thomas. "But, oh . . . I see how Thomas is shifting. Going to Underbarrow and not telling me of it, not including me in the decision. Then to Durham and not inviting me along." She wiped at the corner of her eyes. "Now he can hardly wait for his chance to preach, to show George and Edward that he's ready for it."

"Perhaps you could share your worries with him, let. . . ."

Lizzie jumped back in the exchange. "I should, I should," she interrupted. "See what his plans are after Chester — if he's going to stay with us or go with Edward — or off on his own, for that matter." Lizzie sprang up, wiped her eyes a second time, and smoothed her skirts. She went to where Thomas was laid out.

Edward came to Elizabeth as if he'd been waiting for the chance. "Would you like another reading lesson?" he asked in that charming way he had.

"I would," Elizabeth replied, the strain of the day eased by his kindness. She got to her feet with renewed vigor, a hand on the stone marker behind her. She began to trace the letters of the first word, rough under her fingers, naming as many as she could remember.

Edward leaned over her, ready to supply the names of the ones she missed. Elizabeth's pulse quickened. "Lu . . . see," she read, sounding out the name. "Lucy," she repeated. They read the last name together. "Garr . . . nnneettt."

When Edward reached around her to the verse at the base of the headstone, Elizabeth could feel his chest against her back. She held her breath as he slowly read it. She felt almost hypnotized, the words blurring. She sprang up and danced over to the next closest marker just to collect herself.

Edward came to her, a balmy, sweet breeze cooling them, and they knelt down together in front of the stone. With his help she read the full name, the dates of birth and death, and the verse. Edward pointed out the large and small forms. "Some of us capitalize more words than others and spell them every which way," he quipped, glancing at George. "Here," Edward referenced a nearby marker. "'Tis your own name." They moved to it and he showed her.

Elizabeth went gingerly off on her bare feet about the little cemetery to find her name again by herself. When she tired of that, she searched for other names she could read herself. "'Mary,'" she said loudly. "Mary Fisher learned to read in jail," she called back to Edward.

"That she did." It was George who responded. He waved the two of them over to where he sat. "Mary's my mother's name, too." He patted the grass beside himself. "Mary Lago Fox. She was of the stock of martyrs." Elizabeth settled on one side of him and Edward on the other. "You would have liked her," he said to Elizabeth. "Well-educated in school and quite able to read the Bible. She filled me with stories of those hounded for their faith — vivid tellings of church history. The sacrifices of those lives impressed me."

Edward got to his feet and went into the woods adjacent to the cemetery.

Elizabeth kept her face turned to George, letting Edward have his privacy. *Attending to his needs*, she figured.

"It is important work that we do, Elizabeth," George said, catching her eyes. "I expect your mind is on it."

Elizabeth hung her head like a child caught out. "It is, George. Truly." She met the piercing, blue eyes, a hot blush coming to her cheeks.

"We are walking in the glory of the Holy Spirit, are we not?" the preacher reminded her kindly.

"We are," Elizabeth agreed, suddenly committed to however many days it took to reach Chester.

When Edward returned, he sat down where he'd been before and he and George started up a conversation about the Christian martyrs. At first the exchange held Elizabeth's interest, but eventually she lay back, crumpling. Drowsy from the day, the last thing she remembered hearing was something about walking in the morning to "Preston Patrick," wherever that was. She didn't recall falling asleep but she woke later, crickets screaming in the night. The rest of the group was laid out next to her like corpses, Lizzie on her one side and, with an expanse between, Edward, Thomas, and George on the other. Her bonnet was off and she'd been covered with her cloak. Using her chin to hold it over her front, she sat up lethargically. The moon caught her eye and she considered it for a moment. Wisps of clouds were traveling rapidly passed the orb like ghosts. *Holy Spirit is moving about us.* It was her last thought as she lowered back, asleep in a blink.

Chapter 15

Elizabeth woke to gray skies and drizzle, surprised to find she'd slept without waking in the night. Flicking the wet from her eyelids, she sat up, found her bonnet, and wrapped her cloak tight around her neck and shoulders. She dragged off to squat in the woods, heading in the direction she'd seen Edward go the night before.

When she returned, Lizzie came right over to her. "Do you think we'll make it to this Chester place?" she asked.

Elizabeth tried not to look at her trembling mouth. "I think so," she murmured. She tucked a piece of her unruly hair under the side of her bonnet and tied it tight under her chin. "Depends, I suppose, on how often we stop and visit like yesterday."

The two of them fell in behind the men, the last in the string of hunched travelers. "Let's list all our complaints," Lizzie suggested. She tilted in close to Elizabeth so that the brims of their bonnets were touching. Alternating back and forth they had no trouble humoring each other. Their skirts were damp, the ground had been hard for sleeping, their bellies were growling, their calves ached. Before they knew it, the rain had let up and they were in a place Edward told them was called Burton, a large village with a church but no market. Elizabeth's shawl smelled like dirty sheep and the bottom edge of her top skirt was splashed with mud.

Edward used his last coins to buy each of them a mug of hot cider and a slice of breakfast cake from a woman who was selling out of her cottage window. As he paid, he gave the lady one of the pamphlets they carried. Then he called the men and Lizzie over to retrieve the breakfast and took Elizabeth her drink and one of the treats. As they ate, they talked about how they'd slept and where they were going. He left her shortly thereafter to go to George and the two headed off together into the bush.

As soon as they were gone, Thomas went back to the woman selling from her window and tried to begin a conversation with two hefty men who were purchasing cakes there. Elizabeth guessed the filthy men to be gravediggers, the larger one holding two shovels. His sleeves were rolled tight over his beefy arms. She thought both her legs could fit in a half of his mud-splattered breeches.

Thomas tapped at the pamphlet Edward had left on the counter ledge and tried to engage the two. Elizabeth could only hear bits of what he was saying, but it didn't seem to her that the gravediggers were much interested. Suddenly the bigger man let out a roar like a wild animal, demanding Thomas leave them be. "Been up all night, you dog," he bellowed. He reached for the pamphlet and tore it up, throwing the flutter of pieces in Thomas' face. Then he wiped a dirty sleeve across his nose and dropped the shovels.

"Come, good men," Elizabeth overheard. She saw Thomas lay a hand on the fellow's shoulder. "Hear the good news."

The man threw off Thomas' hand as if he were swatting a fly. Then he took a step back, hitched up his wide belt, and cocked his fists at the ready.

Thomas wagged a finger at him. "Some ignorant folks say our prophecy is false but. . . ."

"Oh, Thomas," Lizzie whispered, watching, too. "No. . . ."

"You calling us unschooled, dog?" the smaller man taunted. He stomped his thick work boots on the ground and began to circle Thomas like a vulture. "Pit scum," Elizabeth heard. She turned behind her to check for George and Edward, but she didn't see them. She had no idea what to do.

"You can be part of Christ's flock, be of the living Christ…." Thomas was trying. "If you but heed the Light. . . ."

"Moonlight? Rushlights?" The big man jeered. He punched a fist repeatedly into his large palm as he sidestepped closer to Thomas.

"No, no," Lizzie moaned again.

"Speak more kindly," Thomas suggested, seemingly oblivious to the threat of the men. "Our ideas deserve your fear and reverence."

It was the entirely wrong thing to say. The men started swinging, the big one going for Thomas' face and the other one kicking at his legs. Elizabeth wasn't sure if she should go to his aid or pull Lizzie farther down the trail — but when she saw Thomas duck away from the bullies and start running towards her, she put an arm around Lizzie and ran herself.

"Those evil dogs," Thomas muttered as he bunched behind the women, his cloak held wide like wings over their shoulders. Stones began to whiz past them and they picked up their pace.

"Heretics! Whores!" the gravediggers were yelling from where they'd stood. A rock hit the back of Elizabeth's bonnet and another her skirt.

"Blasphemers! And don't come back again," Elizabeth heard as the three of them reached where George and Edward had returned on the path. George shooed them all into the dense bush and they galloped, half buckling, down an incline and into a ditch.

Elizabeth was panting hard by the time they fell down together at its bottom. She fixed on Thomas' bleeding forehead. *Surely, he was led to talk to those men*, she thought. She wanted to say something comforting to him but she kept quiet. She swiveled instead to George for leadership and found him sitting back against a tree, his eyes closed. Edward was beside him, looking much the same. At their model, she shut her eyes tight and tried to calm her thumping heart. The rain and damp were the least of her worries, she realized. The gravediggers had purposely tried to hurt them. She heard George rustle to stand.

"We are in the hands of God. Obedient," he announced firmly. "The Light shining through us. Honored to be called to serve, to preach." He folded down again.

No one moved for a long while. When they did, Lizzie leaned, shoulder to shoulder to Elizabeth. "We're okay. We're all okay," she whispered.

"We are, we are," Elizabeth whispered back, squeezing her hand. They brushed themselves off and climbed back up the slope to the path, and then fell in behind Thomas, who was keeping a wide space between himself and Edward, who was trudging along behind George.

Elizabeth felt oddly stronger and more sure of herself. George's simple ministry had given her what she needed, fortified her. She left Lizzie and passed Thomas and then Edward, to sidle up to him. "How do you figure the way of it, George?" she asked. It wasn't exactly what she wanted to know, but it perplexed her how his perfect message had reminded her of the reason for their travel, of why she'd wanted to come. "How do you know what to say?"

"Well. . . ." George let there be a long pause. He didn't deny it. "I trust that when I'm led to give a message, the right words will come, that they are the ones I am to deliver."

Elizabeth tried to accept the honest response. *Trust that the right words will come,* she thought. "And is it the same when you're preparing to preach — like at the Sedbergh Fair and Firbank Fell — when hundreds are waiting for you? You don't prepare ahead or practice your preaching?" She hoped it didn't sound like she was doubting him.

"Worship is the root of it, whether I'm alone or with others, but no, the ministry isn't planned. If something comes to me, something I think I am to share, I let Spirit ride through me, my heart beating encouragement, until it seems I have the kernel of what I'm to say. Sometimes I add a line or two of Scripture if it occurs to me, if it feels that I am to do so. Sometimes I give examples." He rubbed at the scruff on his chin. "Then I repeat most of what I'd already said, maybe using slightly different words, so that the meaning is emphasized — and so those who are milling about have the chance to hear again what they might have missed."

"Hmm," Elizabeth hadn't expected that answer. She wanted a pattern, as there was with knitting. Something she could follow when she first tried to preach. It would be hard to trust that she'd say the right thing, that people would want to hear her message.

"Let's say I come up against opposition," George continued.

"You try to weave the opposing thoughts into our ways," Elizabeth interrupted. She'd seen this in his conversation with Gus and Roy. "You use their understandings to lead them to ours?"

"I do," George grinned at her, pleased. "And when I'm preaching in a market cross, I consider that some folks find themselves standing before me, unsure as to why they feel compelled to listen, not expecting to have been caught up by Spirit."

"Ah . . ." Elizabeth muttered, her head wobbling up and down. She'd felt that way.

Edward was behind them now and listening. He butted his head between theirs. "'Tis holy Spirit that brings them," he confirmed solemnly, "or keeps them. 'Tisn't in our control."

"Truly," George agreed, glancing fondly at the profile of the younger man. Edward came through them so he was in between George and Elizabeth. Before long, the two men moved ahead of her and she drifted back behind them. It didn't bother her. She was glad to have some time to herself to sort out the swirl of emotions of the last couple of days — her growing attraction to Edward, the decision to leave Auntie and Moe, the satisfaction of the way she'd interacted with Gus, the panic of the clash with the gravediggers. Elizabeth let the surrounding landscape soothe her. It didn't seem to change much. Granite hills and grazing sheep, hamlets with an occasional kitchen garden.

They passed through Carnforth and Bolton-le-Sands. Elizabeth spelled the names of the places over and over, wondering how long they'd existed. Were the hamlets named for the first landowners? There only seemed to be the one trail through them. Could she find her way back on it after Chester? *What if Lizzie goes on with Thomas? What if I go to London with Edward?*

Elizabeth let thoughts of Edward go round about in her head. She listed all his becoming features, found words for the aspects of his personality that charmed her, reviewed some of her favorite exchanges. Eventually, she walked off the path and into the wildflowers beneath a limestone outcropping to relieve herself. Leaning against it, she hiked her skirts and squatted down so there wasn't a splash. When she finished, she checked her skirts, then went in the direction the others had gone, listening for their voices.

"There. Yonder," Edward shouted just as Elizabeth caught up to the bunch of them. He slapped George playfully on the back and pointed up the trail.

"Richard?" George gaped at the approaching figure. "Richard Farnsworth?"

All heads turned to the rider, loudly clicking his tongue to guide his horse carefully towards them. He was a jovial looking lad, Elizabeth thought, stout, with a wild little beard.

"Hello, Friends," he called out. "My good fortune to be headed this way from Lancaster."

"Now you'll hear the story of Pendle Hill!" Edward told Elizabeth, his eyebrows raised with intrigue as the rider came stiffly down from the horse. He met George in an energetic handshake that collapsed into an embrace.

"Ah, the religious fanatic," Richard sang in jest, a muscled arm close around his friend. "Let me see that *face*," he laughed, grabbing George's chin. "Doesn't seem 'overzealous' to *me*." There was delight in his voice as he released George and smacked a kiss on his cheek. "Has it been two years, old man?"

George introduced them. "Elizabeth Fletcher, Elizabeth Leavens, Thomas Holme — this is Richard Farnsworth, my young but weighty Friend."

"Had a run in, have you?" Richard asked, staring at the dried wound on Thomas' temple. He took a moment to go back to his horse, dig in the saddle packs, and return with some wrappings to the group. "Have you told them of your own, George?" he asked, squatting down. He laid out his cloak and Elizabeth saw a fat flask, too. "Manhandled by ministers and magistrates, thrown down steps by infuriated villagers, pelleted with clods of dirt and stones . . ." Richard shook his head. He glazed solemnly at George. "Or do they only know of the thousands who have been convinced by your brilliant ministry?"

Richard didn't ask if they were hungry. When he gestured for everyone to sit down, Elizabeth purposely positioned herself beside Edward, everyone complying. "Be not anxious for your life," he quoted from the Bible. "What ye shall eat, or what ye shall drink." His eyes sparkled into Elizabeth's. "Is not the life more than the food. . . ? Behold the birds of the heaven, that they sow not, neither do they reap, nor gather into barns, but they are divinely fed — as you, too, shall be," he finished. He opened the wrappings and began to lay out mutton, sage cheese, and strips of cold bacon.

I am here and it is right, Elizabeth thought. She was sure. She watched Thomas grab up a portion of the bread and gobbled it down, and wasn't bothered.

Richard handed Elizabeth a hunk from the bread loaf, his expression kind. "Restocked just this morning. Elizabeth . . . Elizabeth Fletcher is it?"

She nodded into the ruddy face. "And we call Elizabeth Leavens — Lizzie — to keep us apart," she explained. "You travel and preach alone then, Richard, Richard Farns-Farnsworth?" she asked formally.

"I do, but my part has oft been to work in the shadows, to assist those convinced by the preaching and to host the first meetings."

"Important work, to organize and settle the meetings," George assured them.

Elizabeth stared over at the huddle of George, Richard and Edward. Surely, they possessed a greater measure of Spirit than the rest of them. She was abashed to be in their presence, nourished by the strength of their faith. "How do you explain it then, that there's no clergy?" she asked Richard, wanting to continue the topic, to glean more from his experience.

Richard tipped his head slightly one way and then the other. "Well, I start by asking them to sit — all mixed — the men and the women, the young and the old, the poor . . . and those who dress like this one," he poked at Edward.

"Ah," Edward pushed him gently and returned a good-natured grin. His nice waistcoat and breeches were now wrinkled and slightly soiled with the travel.

"I usually say a bit of an introduction, but not always," Richard continued. He seemed pleased by Elizabeth's earnestness. "People figure out the way of it. How the glory of the Lord fills the spaces given if they trust in it. Expect it. . . ."

In her mind's eye, Elizabeth saw the bowed heads. It was what she'd first wanted, hints as to how to find the sacred. Still, she'd only ever worshipped at the farmstead and now with her four fellow travelers. *To be in a group of fifty . . . or a hundred . . . a thousand,* she considered, wanting it.

"And if I'm led to speak, I do, not forcing it." Richard sat back. "There's good as well in a completely silent meeting and, of course, it's rare that those so new to it find a message to share . . . but if they do . . ." He held Elizabeth's waiting eyes. "I explain that we are *all* clergy, all responsible to give a message that comes to us if it rises up and persists." He stretched his hands out behind himself to brace his bulky frame, his shirt tight across his chest. He seemed to listen to the birds for a moment.

"In due course I end it and thank them for trying our way," Richard started up again. "Often people come in private to tell me how they were moved in the Presence. I usually hold at least one more meeting with those who request it before I move on and we talk about how it might go after I'm gone. How to meet safely. What to do if the constables come clubbing and arresting." He gave Thomas, snuggled up against Lizzie, a fleeting look.

Thomas straightened a bit with the attention. "And do you broker decisions and mediate quarrels?" he tried to joke.

Richard didn't return the lopsided smile. "I model what it's like to give each person's notions equal weight, despite what society has taught them," he replied sternly. "Ah, but they *are* earnest," he softened, peeking at George. "It's been a joy to see how people work to agree, to find a solution to a concern — how they consider the best of what is suggested and credit each other."

"It's good work that you do, Richard Farnsworth," complimented Edward. "Stirring up what's pure." He took in the fading daylight and encouraged everyone to lay out their bedrolls so they could drop out of the conversation when they tired and go to sleep.

Elizabeth was glad for the decision. They'd reach Lancaster soon enough.

"Any news of others?" George asked Richard.

"Just left George Whitehead. Imprisoned under the Vagrancy Law — the judges stretching its purpose to use it against us."

"We abide by the highest laws and not the government's regulations," George reminded them, popping up again. "We speak honestly, have no need of their oaths in court, find equality in all people, and preach against tithes." He sucked in a deep bracing breath and Elizabeth wondered what'd set him off. They were all quite aware of these things.

"'Tis just that conduct that's landed George Whitehead in a cell," said Richard, his face drawn. "Wrote that it was an awful place, stinkin' rye straw for bedding. Was given but tainted water because he wouldn't buy beer from the jailer." He shifted his tone. "George and his group have found a peace in their capture, grateful to be tested. They're using the time to write a book — a book about us."

Us, repeated Elizabeth. *Us*.

Chapter 16

Richard shared more of what he carried for breakfast, and after breakfast, Elizabeth was ever so pleased to have her hunger satisfied for a change. It was one thing to live on a farm and eat whenever you wanted. It was another to never know when your next meal would be. *Moe*, she thought suddenly, missing the child and happy she was with Auntie now.

As they ate, George told of his desire to make a long day of it to preach in Lancaster. Maybe Scotforth and Galgate, too. Perhaps even Garstang if it worked out. Richard was going to come with them.

"People in these hamlets and towns are cut off, going their own way for several years," Richard counseled. "Many will welcome what we offer." He encouraged everyone to let his horse carry their bundles.

Elizabeth stood last in the little queue of them by Richard and his horse, rubbing a hip that was already aching. She'd slept fitfully, dreaming that the gravediggers had come after her and Lizzie, giving them a hard time. She'd known it wasn't going to be all walking in comradery, learning to read, and sharing stories, but she hadn't counted on nightmares. Morning hadn't come too soon.

"Rough night?" Richard guessed when she handed him her things.

Elizabeth put a hand self-consciously to her face. She was sure she looked a mess. She didn't want to complain. "No regrets in your work?" she finally managed. It was an awkward thing to say.

"Oh, can't think how better to use my life," Richard replied exuberantly. He turned from her to secure the last of their belongings. "Come with me?" he asked, taking a broad step to start them off behind the others. He guided the horse, snorting and tossing its head, behind them. "The Day of the Lord is at hand and we saints will soon triumph. No regrets," he confirmed. "Are you missing the loved ones you left behind?"

"Yes, some," Elizabeth admitted. "My aunt and a little sister, Moe. She's deaf. And Lizzie's and Thomas' parents. They live just across the lane from my aunt and me. On a farmstead just north of Kendal. They'd give you hospitality if you're ever out that way. . . ."

"My parents died when I was a child," lamented Richard. "Don't have anyone missing me. I was raised by relatives who didn't welcome another mouth to feed. They hired me out as soon as I was old enough for it."

Elizabeth glanced at Richard's sad face. Auntie had been so good to her. She'd encouraged her to travel with George and Edward. She was doing her chores now so that Elizabeth could have this opportunity. "How did you meet George?" she asked, taking several hurried strides to keep up with Richard.

"In Balby. Couple three years back. There's a story to it," Richard hedged enticingly. He checked his horse. "I'd had severe pangs of conscience since I was a boy. I wanted to be worthy of a place in heaven and didn't see any way I'd get there."

"I used to complain about that, too," interrupted Elizabeth. "A challenge when you're of our class."

"Or so the Presbyterians would want us to believe," Richard smirked. "Back then I thought that if I prayed long and often, memorized lots of scripture, and piously listened to the sermons, the ministers would take notice and find me worthy of their prayers. All that happened though was that the neighbour lads mocked me for my strict ways. They badgered me to play cards, bet on the cocks, try a woman — though I wasn't but twelve or thirteen. . . ." He caught himself, stopping with the litany of temptations. "I think I went into some kind of crisis, God's curses ringing in my ears. I prayed even more fervently and for long hours. But then, sitting alone one evening when I was about fifteen, I heard a voice saying, '*I will teach you. I will teach you.*' I was stunned. I wondered if I'd really heard it. Not long after, I heard that a powerful Quaker was going to preach in Balby. . . ."

Elizabeth gave a little giggle. She knew what was coming.

"Hmm, yes," Richard smiled, shaking his head. "Found George Fox preaching from a roof ledge in the Balby market cross. He was incredible. Authentic. Honest."

"Simple. Brilliant," Elizabeth added.

"Yes, all those things." Richard tapped his hands to his heart. "I was so giddy with his message, the whole of it resonating in my being." Richard jumped over a large hole in the path and waited to see that both Elizabeth and his horse made it safely around it. "I was reborn in Christ that day, my life given depth and direction." He shook his head again, the emotion of it fresh. "I went to him like a wee dog afterwards, excited and energetic for the work."

Elizabeth thought back for a moment on her own more subtle convincement. "And Pendle Hill?" she finally hinted.

"You've truly not heard the telling?"

"Some of it . . . from Edward. It mystifies me as to why, with paths around hills as they are, you two were compelled to climb it. . . ."

"Ah," sighed Richard, preparing to explain.

"But wait, wait." Elizabeth grabbed his sleeve. "Let me call Lizzie and Thomas to hear it. After all, you were *there*, and it's already a favorite telling among Friends. Surely we'll be asked for it ourselves. . . ." She waved an arm back to where Thomas and Lizzie were strolling along. "COME," she signed, her arm arced wide with the gesture.

"Ah, well, then," Richard started when they'd joined him and Elizabeth. "George Fox and I came to Pendle Hill . . ."

"Last year?" Thomas interrupted.

"Two years ago. 1652," corrected Richard. "The winter snow had melted and the place was the lime-green color of early summer. Have you seen it?" he asked abruptly.

They wagged their heads like three lazy dogs. No, they had not.

"Well, it rises distinctly above the hills that surround it, a bald, moreland ridge. We'd been fasting and as we came nearer George said he was called to climb to the top. I've a bad knee and didn't think I could make the hike. It's pretty steep. I waited for him at the boulders below, and, oh my, he came down afire! Full of joy and purpose. Confident that he'd been called to preach his message. He'd looked out at the expanse of hills and valleys, could even see the sea from up there. He'd had a vision, a vision of 'a people gathered.'"

Lizzie moved over beside Elizabeth and took her hand. "It's us, Elizabeth," she whispered, her blue eyes sparkling. "He saw us."

Elizabeth liked the idea. They were the people George had seen, their numbers now rapidly multiplying. She nodded solemnly.

"I believe that, too," agreed Richard. "George saw us all, 'a people gathered,'" he repeated. He positioned himself between the two women, with Thomas on Lizzie's other side.

"We went on afterwards, refreshed, and George convinced many with his fierce preaching. That evening, we lay out in a field with underbrush for blankets, me feeling so good to be with him." Richard swallowed, basking in the memory. "Next morning, George was sure we were to split up. Like seeds, he said, to be strewn in the wind. It's from the Bible. He'd had a dream and felt sure he was to go north. People in white had come towards him, walking by a river. The River Kent, he supposed."

"The River Kent?" Lizzie stopped in the track. "'Tis when he came to us."

They arrived in Lancaster, Richard's horse clopping noticeably when the dirt path turned to uneven cobbles. The six of them spread out in the market.

"Come, come and hear George Fox, a Friend," Elizabeth called to a woman riding by on a donkey with a plentiful basket of produce tied down behind her. Elizabeth waved the pamphlets she was selling and pointed to where Edward, Thomas, and Lizzie were standing around George. "See the ones there," she encouraged. The woman turned her braying beast and a nearby carpenter took note and went towards the Friends.

Not long after, Elizabeth joined them, too. She stood like a peaceful sentinel to the side of Richard who was closest to George.

"Friends," George called out as he stepped up on a barrel. "Come. Learn how to turn inside yourself to hear the wisdom there. Learn to wait upon the living Christ. Listen inwardly for hope and peace. . . ."

Before he could say more, two constables were on him, yelling loudly of the Vagrancy Law and ignoring the rest of them.

The muscling stunned Elizabeth. It was the first time for the Kendal Friends to see one of their own arrested and she watched dumbfounded as one of the men slapped George hard across the mouth and buckled his hands roughly behind his back. He didn't resist or call out as they pushed him away and down the street from the little crowd that had gathered for his preaching.

Richard advised them to wait a few moments and then they went in a little huddle to what Elizabeth assumed was the courthouse. Thomas came between her and Lizzie, his arms around each of them. He pulled them close.

Elizabeth's thoughts were flooded with the tellings of Friends and the possibilities of what might happen to George. *Trust in holy Spirit*, she told herself. She found it challenging.

Once inside the building, Elizabeth watched some of the townspeople who were there for the proceedings. They pointed and murmured at the Friends as she took her seat beside Lizzie. "Unchaperoned women, dirty and unkempt, sitting among 'Quaker lads,'" she heard. She kept her eyes forward, her hands folded piously in her lap, and didn't acknowledge the comments.

George was led in and positioned before the robed judge for sentencing. When he didn't willingly remove his wide-brimmed hat, it was ordered off his head and the arresting constable swiped it rudely to the floor. Cheers erupted in the gallery.

Elizabeth kept her attention on George, taking note of his conduct, proud of him. He stood rigid, his legs stiff, his hands folded in front of him. He was elegant, she decided. Yes, elegant as he waited patiently for the judge to begin his questioning and then answered politely. He quoted from Isaiah, Jeremiah, and Ezekiel to justify his preaching, slowly rotating his head to include not only the judge but the constables and the commoners, too. She was pretty sure he saw the row of them sitting on the bench behind him and that his voice strengthened because of it. The judge leaned forward, the courtroom heckles ceasing, as George's message hit its mark. In the end, he was but fined and ordered out of town.

Elizabeth peered over at Richard, who remained expressionless. She wondered how they'd come up with the money.

When the court dismissed and the group of them were outside, Richard told them his plan. He was going to go quickly to sell his horse. They were to wait at the courthouse, not talk to anyone, and keep an eye out to see where George was taken if he came through the doors.

"We should get to walking," George advised when they were together again, gathered on the outskirts of Lancaster. "Away from this place and its constables. Let's get to Garstang if we can, yes?" He bounced on the balls of his feet, anxious to leave. Richard threw an arm around him, both of them seeming relieved it hadn't been worse. Elizabeth was glad for it too; thankful they were obeying the court order. If George wanted them to walk for the rest of the day, she would do so without complaint.

It pleased her when Edward paired up with her. She saw that Thomas was talking with George and Richard and that Lizzie had drifted to the end of line of them. She had told her earlier in the day that she had her monthly. *Probably has cramps*, Elizabeth supposed. She began to spell words with Edward. She could spell "Ma," "Da," and little words easily, but "Moe" was her favorite. "Who do you think I'll meet as I travel?" she asked after a time, tiring of the spelling game. "Which of the religious groups?"

"Ah, Elizabeth," Edward wheeled his head with delight. "Travel? After Chester? Are you one of us then? An itinerant Friend? A Publisher of Truth?"

Elizabeth blushed. "Yes," she granted cautiously. "If I continue to be led." She bit her lip. "And if I can defend myself against all those who'll surely be against me." She stole a look at Thomas, thinking of his interaction with the gravediggers again. "There're so many different kinds of people, so many groups rising up. I hardly know anything beyond the names. . . ."

Edward put his hand up in front of them and splayed his fingers. "Well, could be Presbyterian, Independent, Baptists — dissenters," he listed as he wiggled his thumb, pointer, and middle finger in turn. "Those seem to be the most common in these parts." He bent his ringless ring finger forward. "Even the Catholics have regained some footing in the North." He made his little finger dance. "Ranters, of course. . . ."

Out of fingers on the one hand, he put up his other one and flicked his fingers to name more groups. "Puritans — who want all traces of the Catholic faith gone. There might still be some Diggers around . . . but they're not really a separate group. Fifth Monarchists, who are waiting for the second coming of Christ, them saying 'till be but in a couple of years."

"But Friends . . ."

"Ah, Friends . . ." barked Edward. He dropped his fingers and grabbed up hers.

An odd sensation rippled through Elizabeth at his warm, sincere touch. "Friends, Friends believe Christ has come and is here with us now, do they not?" she choked. She turned her face away from him so he wouldn't see her blush.

"Yes, yes, we do. Surely," agreed Edward. He bent to catch her bright eyes, shielded by the bonnet. "But we are more than talk . . . not like the others who blabber on professing. We are about action." He took a long sure stride. "You'll find your way in it, Elizabeth, you will. Use your own experiences to explain things. Speak your own truth."

"I will, I can," stuttered Elizabeth. "But I want them . . . men, men especially . . . of any status . . . to heed my preaching. . . ."

"They may be more open to you than you think," asserted Edward, his voice softening. "More to you women than to us men. Some consider women the handmaids of God. . . ."

"And some consider us geese," Elizabeth huffed.

"Elizabeth." Edward stopped to face her. "You're going to be wonderful at whatever you're to do with your life," he assured her. "There will always be those who don't listen to our ministry, but we aren't the ones who do the convincing, now are we?" He held her gaze. "If you're to preach, you won't be able to resist the call. You'll be forced to speak out, and you will."

"You're so sure of it, Edward, are you?" Elizabeth flirted, turning them to continue walking. "Though ministers have warned us all our lives that we'll be denied heaven if we don't take their sermons to heart?"

"'*All our lives*,' little maiden?" Edward stopped in front of her again. He threw back his head, his voice rising with such enthusiasm that a covey of quail, feeding in the grass, startled skyward in mass. "Our lives have just begun!" He bent and kissed her cheek. "We are heaven! We're creating it now by our zeal and faithfulness. Right *here*, right here on earth!"

A spark flew through Elizabeth and she giggled into the gay eyes, the lovely mouth. She could spend the rest of her days looking at the fresh face, the whole of it forged by a blend of commitment and cheerfulness. "Edward, truly, I believe you could convince a stone!"

They walked together past Garstang, stopping only briefly for a drink of water, some food and a rest, and headed south to Catterall. Suddenly, Edward threw a stiff arm out across her waist, stopping her next step. He stared at something in the distance that unnerved him. Then Elizabeth heard it too — something coming, fast-paced through the crackle of leaves and twigs. Before she could distinguish what it was, George and Richard were bunched up with her, strangers just in front of them all.

"No harm, no harm," the taller of two men called from where he'd stopped. He bent an arm up at his side in a stiff wave. "Friends, friends," he smiled. "We come in peace." The men wore rugged shirts and soiled breeches. Farm hands, Elizabeth guessed.

"We've been watching for you," explained the other one, his hands relaxed at his sides. Elizabeth saw no sword. "Sympathizers sent word to us, saw you along the path. Our farm is just up the way a piece, he added, his expression kind. "We came to offer lodging for the night. Got a nice barn with fresh hay. . . ."

"Ah, well then, that's good of you," Edward replied. He came forward, his arm extended.

Introductions were made and when it was Elizabeth's turn she clasped each of the rough hands with gratitude. She envisioned a barn loft of soft, sweet hay, as she followed the men, able to hear the deep voices as they drifted back to her.

They were talking about James Parnell, the young preacher who'd been with George and Edward at Swarthmoor Hall, Arthur Parnell's son. It seemed he'd been preaching among soldiers and had been welcomed. Then he'd returned home for a time, saving the money he earned working in the family business and eventually left again. Elizabeth bet Arthur was pleased to have him at home, if even for a little while.

The men were agreeing on James' ability and success — too much of it, perhaps. Apparently his prophecies of hope and possibility had caused villagers to riot. Elizabeth didn't catch where. He'd been arrested as "an idle and disorderly vagrant." "Fined five pounds and sentenced to five months in prison," she heard. "Treated harshly in the cell, prey for the hardened criminals."

Elizabeth moved a little faster to stay close to the conversation. She thought the men were saying James was in Colchester Castle, a dungeon with a terrifying reputation, and Lizzie feared for him. He'd asked Friends to find George Fox.

George stopped on the trail and waited for everyone to come to him. "James Parnell is sentenced to Colchester Castle and is wanting me. There must be good reason for it," he explained, recapping what he'd been told. "Friends have been ill-treated in that place. He isn't one to ask for us unless we're needed."

The next morning, when George came to Elizabeth and Lizzie, they were picking straw out of their hair, contented after a pleasant night's sleep. His plan was to preach in Preston and Euxton, he told them. They'd mingle in the crowd and distribute tracts, hold him in the Light. Then he and Richard were going to James. "Edward will preach in Chester and then split off for London," he reminded them. Elizabeth listened to the plans without comment. He was their leader and they accepted his decisions.

As they paired up, Elizabeth walked on the sides of her shoes, her stride tight. "What do you know of London, really Edward?" She knew nothing of the place, the home of the kings and queens of the past, and now of Cromwell. There was a part of her that wished he wouldn't go, that she'd have the chance to see where their friendship took them.

"Only what George has told me," Edward confessed. He was in his usual good mood this morning. "He was there once. Remember what he told those farmers back near Oxenholme? The place wasn't at all to his liking. Too loud and corrupt for him — but I'm excited for it. For the good work I can do there. All those people! Why, there are more folks in London than in all the places we've passed through *combined*."

Elizabeth watched her shadow shift in the sunshine. Edward was destined to be a great preacher, a great Friend. She felt it in her heart and gave over to his enthusiasm. "And you'll be there alone then?"

"No, with Francis Howgill. He's written me all about it and is waiting for me. There's certainly work enough for the two of us, the place spreading out to grab the villages at its edges." He put his hand out in front of them, imagining what lay ahead. "Francis says that it's to the east where the hovels are. . . ." He moved his hand opposite to where it'd been. "And to the west where the rich are building. Across that expanse are thousands of people, people from all the groups we've named and then some. All waiting to be caught in the net. All waiting to hear of our good news." Edward held his eyes wide. "This is Preston," he said as they came to the outskirts of the village.

This time there was no trouble. A small crowd gathered before the preacher, listened without insult, and when he was finished, they all talked with those who came to them. Then they went on to Euxton. It was Richard who started there, George preaching after him, the ideas of their ministry familiar to Elizabeth now. She listened for the frequent phrases and Bible verses, repeating them to herself. Afterwards, she strolled along contentedly, their little band coming to a nice spot beside the River Yarrow. George decided the younger men could take a try at fishing so they might have a last hearty meal together.

Elizabeth and Lizzie untied their shoes and crawled out on a thick limb of a great sycamore tree that had twisted out over the water. They sat like Kingfishers dangling their blistered feet in the cool breeze to watch the young men, their jerkins and shirts off. Richard, Thomas, and Edward waded into the rippling water.

"You're staring," Lizzie giggled.

Elizabeth couldn't find words. Edward splashed into the water, his muscular torso bending and swooping upright with his repeated attempts to catch a trout.

"Oh, my . . . Richard's got one!" Lizzie yelped, blinking against the sun.

The women clambered off the branch, grabbed up their shoes, and ran carefully down to where a good-size fish, sparkling pink and silver in the last sunlight, flopped on the ground. While Edward and Thomas kept up their efforts, playfully competing and soaking themselves, Elizabeth and Lizzie went off, at Richard's direction, to gather kindling. When they returned, six grand fish lay near Richard, flies buzzing about them. No one could talk of anything but of how they'd feast.

Richard and George built a fire and lit it with a flint. The others gathered round them, shifting from foot to foot, waiting. When the flames had died down to red and orange embers, Richard and Edward poked each fresh fish onto green sticks and handed them about. Richard showed the women how to squat close to the fire but avoid the little sparks of flame that jumped up from the dripping spit.

Soon a wonderful aroma filled the air, the meal a sweet farewell as George and Richard prepared to leave them. George started with Edward, whispering privately to him. Then Thomas, who hugged the preacher for a good, long while. Elizabeth thought she heard him sniffling.

When George faced her and Lizzie, it was as if he was offering a blessing. "Elizabeth Leavens," he said, using Lizzie's proper name. "You are firm in your leading and a helpful companion. Have no doubt but that holy Spirit will surround you when you begin to preach." He hugged her briefly and stepped back to gravely shake her hand.

"And you, Elizabeth Fletcher," George embraced her as an older brother might, tight to his chest. "You are filled with faith and wisdom beyond your fifteen years. Your unique perspective will bring women and their families flocking."

Color rose in Elizabeth's cheeks and tears came to the backs of her eyes. "May Spirit guide you, too, George Fox, my dear friend," she whispered. As he and Richard vanished down the lane, she kept her eyes on his floppy hat, wishing only for their safe travel.

Edward took the lead in finding a spot to spend the night, each of them suffering privately in their thoughts until they fell asleep. Next morning, they begged breakfast in Wigan and headed for Warrington. George had given them the name of a family there, the Betnels, and Edward had told them it'd be near evening before they arrived.

For Elizabeth, the sadness of losing George and the rawness of her feet after four days of walking manifested in a nagging irritation with Thomas. With each step she reviewed his annoying behaviors — every silly little remark he made, his lanky, exaggerated gestures as he monopolized Lizzie. She spun with retorts to the questions and comments she imagined him throwing at her. Edward was only a step or two in front of her and she pinched her lips raw, withholding the grumbles and moans that almost escaped her mouth. She certainly didn't want to spoil whatever opinion Edward held by saying something rude about Thomas. Luckily, the hospitality of the Betnels changed her foul mood completely.

The four of them were met at the door by the woman of the house, Sara Betnel, and welcomed like royalty. They were escorted to the most comfortable chairs, served beer and cakes, and asked provocative questions by various family members as they rested in the dim interior of the modest home. Lizzie pulled out her embroidery for the first time on the trip and engaged with Maryhelen, one of Sara's sisters, in a discussion about the various stitches while Elizabeth sank quietly into the hospitality and Edward and Thomas talked with Mark Betnel, Sara's husband.

Maryhelen found a private moment to ask discretely if Elizabeth and Lizzie needed clean rags for their monthlies. Elizabeth was glad for the offer. Hers had just started and it was difficult on the trail to hide the smell, change the rags, and find peppermint or yarrow to smooth the cramping. "Might you want a drink with ginger?" Maryhelen asked, hurrying off to fix it.

After sup, neighbors joined the family and the others. They sat about the largest room of the Betnel cottage to hear Edward, "the seasoned Friend," talk about each person's right to freely develop their beliefs. The tender scene caught Elizabeth up as she watched the attention the twenty year old commanded. With neither George nor Richard to overshadow him, Edward's charismatic manner seemed magnified. He confidently led the conversation, expressing his own thoughts on the matter but leaned forward regularly to ask others their opinions. As the pleasant evening ended, Mark Betnel asked Edward if he planned to preach in Chester. "'Tis a big place. Your prophecy will be much welcomed there."

Chapter 17

It was another full day of walking to reach Chester, but worth the wait. As Mark Betnel had forewarned, it was the biggest town Elizabeth and Lizzie had ever seen. People scurried about like worker ants even in the late of the afternoon. When they reached the market cross, Edward found a large sturdy crate, turned it over, and stepped up on it. Thomas moved quickly to stand beside him.

Elizabeth didn't let it annoy her. She was fresh from a night in a soft bed with linen that smelled of lavender, and it was easy enough to accept that Thomas was only copying the duty he'd seen Richard model. She worked, instead, to imagine Light surrounding both men.

With a variety of townsfolk all about and children circling with excitement, Edward began. "Friends, friends. We are here to tell you that Christ has come again, the Holy Spirit available to everyone. Rich and poor alike. To live within us, guide us, be with us as we battle the cruelty of our government and authorities. Join with us. Stand up for peace." He punched a hand into the air.

Elizabeth saw how confidently he spoke. He was compelling, charismatic. "The Lord will bring a candle to your dark thoughts, without need of a minister," Edward called out to the growing group, turning from their errands to listen. "You can decide for yourselves if the guidance rings true, if the Holy Spirit within is sufficient to reprove each of you of every evil deed, word and thought. For I can tell you, *it is.*"

As she listened, Elizabeth filled with a soaring hope — for herself, for the people of Chester, and for the whole of society. In her mind's eye she saw a sweet flock of sparrows leaving their homes and soaring uncharacteristically to every English village and town in England. She saw herself among them, too, delivering missives in places she'd never seen. It was Thomas stepping up beside Edward, wiggling like an untethered garden pole that brought her back to the preaching. He was distracting everyone, she thought, especially Edward, with his closeness on the crate.

"There is a witness . . . of God . . . in every man and woman." Edward faltered as he swiveled to quickly check Thomas. "Against all unjust laws and rulers . . . and governments . . . which can be turned to work against wickedness and oppression . . . We stand with the Light. With God," Edward called out suddenly. He reached an arm to emphasize his phrasing and almost knocked Thomas off the crate. "We'll bear witness against the wrongs of the world, you and I together. We'll speak out to correct things as they are, living as Christ, here on earth, heaven on earth. . . ."

Thomas shuffled forward. *Come on, Thomas, come on*, Elizabeth mouthed, impatient that he find his nerve and take his turn. She clenched and unclenched her hands, praying silently.

And then he did it. Bothersome Thomas — with all his irritations. Dear Thomas, who had told her stories of witches when they were children and brought her the news she longed to hear as she matured, who'd first talked with her of Seekers and Friends and brought Edward to the farmstead. Thomas reached his long arms broadly skyward and waved them, a fledgling taking flight. "You," he screeched. "You here with us today," he called out as if he'd just spied his best friend. "Do you, do you now, not find hope, hope it is, in the preaching of Edward Burrough?" He rocked back and forth on the crate, loud and repetitive. "You can, can, oh yes, Lord, believe this preacher. . . ." He threw an arm toward Edward. "Praise God

. . . for he . . . we . . . we bring you Truth. Truth. A holy message in these difficult, difficult times. Praise God."

Edward respectfully stepped off the crate and let Thomas have his time. Thomas held his hands out wide and shook them mightily. "You need not kneel, no not kneel, before the ministers, the authorities, or their crosses in fear of their threats . . ." bloomed Thomas Holme, the Friend, the preacher, "or pay them in the steeple house for what is freely, freely, I say, freely yours. Praise the Lord."

Elizabeth thought Thomas seemed more like a crazed lunatic than a man with a message, but she couldn't deny the shift in the crowd, like an abrupt change in wind direction, from Edward to Thomas. When she surveyed the throng, she saw that he held them, the whole swarm of those gathered around him in the market. Edward seemed to realize it, too. She saw him slip from where he stood near the back of the crate to merge into the assemblage and then she was drawn back into the rhythm of Thomas' preaching.

As he shifted back and forth, back and forth on his heels, she listened with rapt attention to Thomas tell of his spiritual journey as if she hadn't been part of it. She saw how people drew in closer to him, no one heckling him as he shared how it had only been recently that he'd stood in the Kendal market cross and listened to a Friend preach, same as they were doing now. How he'd been touched so deeply that he'd left his sure place in his family business to travel the routes and bring the message of his unfolding faith to anyone who was waiting, seeking.

"We are Publishers of Truth. We gain nothing by our work. We have no income from it," Thomas declared. "But only bring the message of Friends, Quakers as some call us, to you with neither exaggeration nor boast. We offer but the simple, pure Truth. Praise the Lord." Then he listed the towns they'd just visited, the large numbers George Fox, Richard Farnsworth, and Edward Burrough had convinced — and it was enough and all. His impact was undeniable.

When Elizabeth glanced over to Lizzie, she saw that her shoulders were back, her chin forward, and her front puffed out like a stiff soldier at allegiance. Clearly she was soaked in love and admiration for her man.

Thomas went on for a while, Elizabeth relaxing in his ministry. By the time she realized he was ensnarled in a tangle of unrelated ideas, and repeating them over and over, she didn't see Edward anywhere. Thomas, pausing at awkward times and still in his rocking, seemed to be searching for him, too. His arms hung deflated at his sides and he began to stutter.

Clearly, Elizabeth realized, Edward wasn't going to rescue him or he'd already have stepped back up to take another turn. She jabbed Lizzie. "What should we do?" she whispered hoarsely. Lizzie didn't react. She seemed glued, defeated, where she stood.

Elizabeth picked up her skirts and rustled quickly through the crowd. She deftly stepped up onto the crate beside Thomas, the relief on his face palpable as he yielded his position and shuffled back behind her. When she caught on all the faces staring at her, her heart started thumping like it would fly right out of her bodice. She was grateful she could feel Thomas just behind her shoulder, that he hadn't left her to stand there alone.

"Our, our faith is full of stories," she called out, trying to think of a way to bridge from Thomas' ministry to her own.

"Tell us," encouraged an older woman standing at the front. "What is it, this Quaker Way?"

Elizabeth met the woman's kind eyes and matched her soft smile. Just for a moment, the two connected and Elizabeth imagined herself the woman's young daughter, a girl really, so short and unworldly, who wanted only to give back what she'd been given. She ran her hands down her skirts.

"I'll tell you of the Quaker Way," she replied, lifting her head to project out into the crowd. "For not very long ago, that was my question, too. 'Twas when George Fox, the great Friend, came to preach in Kendal. Have you heard him? What a preacher! His message is honest and straightforward, wanting only for those like you and me to know what is available, how *Truth* and *Spirit*," she emphasized the words, "can shine into you and you can be *changed*. For that is the peace of it, the harmony of it, within you and without. That is the *way* of Friends."

She went on, trusting the words that came from her as George had advised. She told of how the group of them from a farmstead north of Kendal had all come gladly into the Light, repeating some of the first preaching she'd ever witnessed. "God, Christ, holy Spirit . . . very real and present in this moment. Near at hand. Within and among us. Available to *all* people," George had told her. She heard her voice, as if a different person had emerged, strong and sure. "Oh, tender plants," she swept her gaze bravely, easily, out though those gathered, looking directly at various people, "suckle the milk, free to everyone to live in the life and Power, in the beauty of the world, as servants to Truth and Right."

Just as Elizabeth had imagined, people moved forward, captivated. They raised their hands to her and waved them, wanting more. She went out from herself and saw the scene as if she were flying above it — a young woman standing strong and confident, alive with the power. She came back to the crate, fixing on a maiden about her same age who stood just below her. She was dressed nicely for market day. "And you have a story, too, do you not?" she asked the girl. She felt completely sure of what she was doing. She moved her gaze from the young woman to two older women who stood beside her. They could have been Auntie and Hannah for how they were dressed. "About how you want something more from this life than what is already decided, decided by men in power and control — and ministers who profit off your tithing but can assure you of nothing. For it is all hollow, isn't it? And you've been searching, searching for something deeper, something to fulfill you and give you purpose. Am I right?"

Elizabeth ran her hands down her top skirt again and then lifted them up wide. "Edward Burrough, Thomas Holme, myself — all Friends — we were searching once too. Just as you are. Take courage from our tellings. Discern your part in them as you worship in Truth." Her eyes came to rest on a babe, tucked in a farmer's arm and she thought of Edward telling her to use what she knew. "Come to the Light within. Come like little chicks and follow. Follow in the footsteps of Spirit to be gathered in. COME, COME," she signed with an outstretched, slow-moving, circling gesture. "Come find the searing, unmistakable . . ."

"You're mad," a man blustered. "'Tis sacrilege!"

Elizabeth saw a determined fellow cutting quickly through the front of the group, pushing people aside, and coming at the crate. *Give me grace*, Elizabeth thought as Thomas stepped in front of her and swept her back behind his frame.

He meant to aid me, she thought later, *as I had him*. She didn't think Thomas had realized until the plain-clothed constable was upon him, yelling, yelling loudly and swinging his club, that he was being arrested. Elizabeth wished she'd stood more boldly, come forward as an ally — but she hadn't. She didn't know why or if it would have mattered. Perhaps because she was a woman, perhaps because of her short stature, the constable hadn't seemed to consider her but had only tightened his grip on the one he thought the leader.

The Ranter had emerged in Thomas then. He'd stared down into the constable's miserable face and publicly challenged his authority . . . and the poor man had fainted, gone down in front of hundreds of people who had begun to mock him.

Elizabeth had immediately knelt down to pull the feeble man's head off the hard cobbles and onto her lap. Lizzie, too, suddenly beside her, had bent to pat at his cheeks. When he'd come to, he'd popped open his eyes and pushed both women away as if he'd been only further humiliated by their kindness. He'd stumbled to his feet and gone after Thomas, not seeming to realize at all that if resistance had been Thomas' intention, he could've escaped well away while the man laid unconscious on the ground.

"Why did he confront that officer?" Lizzie moaned, twisting back and forth, her arms wrapped tightly across her bosom.

"I don't know, I don't know," mumbled Elizabeth. She tried to put an arm around the tense, rigid shoulders. "The man could've simply demanded we leave," she commiserated. "Not beat at Thomas with that club as if he were some common criminal."

"But no," Lizzie muttered. "Thomas had to get in the last word. . . ." She bent over and put her face in her hands.

"Caught up in the power of it, in the greater good," interjected Edward. He'd reappeared only moments after the confrontation with a spindly woman at his side. She was dressed unconvincingly in boys' clothing and wasn't much older than they were. She stood with the group of them now as they watched the agitated constable move Thomas down the street. When he was out of sight, the "boy" stepped forward. She was about Lizzie's height, but alarmingly gaunt, with sunken eyes and a bony nose. The drawstrings of her cinched breeches swung long from her waist when she offered her hand. "Jane Waugh. Friend."

Chapter 18

Elizabeth held a sagging Lizzie as the group of them started slowly in the direction Thomas had been taken. She expected things would go as they had for George, but when they arrived at the courthouse door, the constable guarding it denied them entrance. He threatened to arrest them for loitering if they didn't leave.

"You're welcome to come with me," whispered Jane as they moved off. "I'm camped out on the grounds of Chester Castle."

Elizabeth wasn't ready for arrest, possibly jail. Spent, Lizzie was willing to leave, too. Edward let the decision be theirs. With little conversation between them, the three soberly followed Jane up a hill to the expansive castle grounds.

"'Tis his part," said Lizzie finally, the conviction in her tone a relief to Elizabeth. They'd reached an overgrown place in the shadows of one of the high towers and its adjacent massive walls. Jane went to dig about the bush and came back to them with stale bread and discolored cheese.

"You did well today," Edward offered to Elizabeth as Jane passed portions around.

"Yes, yes, you did, Elizabeth," agreed Lizzie.

Elizabeth wished they'd say more. She could hardly remember how it'd gone. The image of the old women who'd encouraged her to start came to her, then that of the farmer with the infant who reminded her of chicks. She felt the vindicating power of her preaching, shivering with the recollections even now. Edward gave her a reassuring smile, thanked Jane for his share of the meager sup, and pointed to where he'd be laid out nearby. He took a long swig from his flask and handed it to Elizabeth and left them.

Jane spread out her cloak and bid Elizabeth and Lizzie to come sit beside her on theirs.

"We've been told of you, you and your sister," Elizabeth started. "You lived near Firbank Fell, was it?"

"Yes, with the Camms," replied Jane. She was sitting with her tattered breeches hanging loose over her thin, crossed legs. She'd already kicked off her shoes. Her disguise wasn't very persuasive but neither Elizabeth nor Lizzie commented on it. "You've met the Audlands and the Camms along the way then?" Jane asked, nibbling at her cheese.

Elizabeth eyed Jane's holey stockings. "No, it's only that Edward told us," she clarified, untying her shoes and stretching her legs out beside Jane's. "We're recently convinced. Just started out a few days back from Kendal to travel with George Fox and Edward. Richard Farnsworth was with us for a bit, too, but now he and George have gone to Colchester Castle." Jane nodded with each mention as if she knew the men, so Elizabeth went on. "James Parnell is there and asked for George."

"Oh, James Parnell," repeated Jane. "I celebrated his sixteenth birthday with him last year after a marvelous day of preaching. He's brilliant." She covered her knees with what was available of the cloak. "Kendal, you say? Never been there but Anne Audland came from those parts — then were sent elsewhere in her childhood and raised by relatives."

"Were Anne Audland and Mabel Camm good to you?" asked Lizzie, wanting in on the conversation.

"Good to us, yes, and like sisters to each other. We worked for Mabel for about two years before George came into our lives. We adored Thomas, her young son." She scratched at her mess of hair. "And you? Were you maid-servants too?"

"No, farm laborers," Lizzie corrected, taking a gulp from the flask to wash down what she'd eaten. "Though Elizabeth and her aunt own their cottage and the land around it. . . ." She wiped her knuckles across her mouth and peeked over to Elizabeth.

"Well, it's the same work, isn't it?" Elizabeth shrugged. "Curing bacon, salting meat, preserving pickles . . ."

"Making jellies and jams," Jane added, warming to them.

Elizabeth caught Lizzie's eyes. "And rushlight candles and soaps," sniggered Lizzie.

"Ah," a little titter escaped Jane as well although she knew nothing of their little game. "Your days filled much as ours then. I worked mostly in the kitchen — scouring pots, cleaning vegetables, plucking poultry, and tending the fire in the parlor." She let out a long sigh. "My sister Dorothy had the out-of-doors responsibilities. Fetching the water to the house, harvesting from the vegetable garden, sweeping in and out. A marvel with livestock."

"Can't say that I miss any of it," groaned Lizzie falsely. "Especially that early morning milking." She stretched back.

"Don't know anyone around Camm's Dell who doesn't have a cow," Jane reminisced. "And chickens and a cock or two. Bees . . ." Her voice trailed off. "There are days when I long for a goose pie," she sighed. "Mabel Camm made the best you've ever tasted." She licked her lips and settled back beside Lizzie. "And hers was a *safe* home, it was. No worry that the men would bother us. We'd a featherbed with a nice quilt in a room to ourselves, Dorothy and me. It had a picture of dells on the wall." She took a long, slow inhale. "'Twas a new day for us when George Fox stayed with the Audlands after Firbank Fell. So powerful, yet kind. Those blue eyes, that deep voice. He lay it all out for us. A miracle, really. We were all so taken. Everyone captured."

Elizabeth laid back beside the other two, content to listen to Jane's prattle.

"We women prepared for a year. Mabel and Anne abandoned the felts they'd worn over their petticoats and exchanged their white neck handkerchiefs for woolen shawls." Jane reached her hands up behind her head as a pillow and Elizabeth copied her. "They had skirts sewn up for all four of us. Dark brown and sage green. First new clothes I ever had. Before we set off to travel, they gave us new white linen caps and black capes. Sturdy shoes, too."

Elizabeth imagined the fresh outfits, unexpected in the lifetime of a servant or a farm girl. She wondered what had happened to Jane's outfit but decided not to ask.

"Do you know of Anne Askew?" Jane asked, suddenly. She wiggled on the hard ground to get comfortable.

Elizabeth and Lizzie said they didn't.

"'Twas Mabel's favorite telling. Might help you in the days ahead to know of it." She scratched at her dirty head again. "Well, Anne Askew was a Protestant. Lived a hundred years ago. Mabel liked to quote the Bible when she told of her, where Peter is advising the first Christians to be loyal — loyal when others have power over them . . . over us." She clarified, clearing her throat. "To be faithful and devoted even when harassed, beaten, tortured. . . ." She sat up and turned from one of them to the other. "Back in the days of Anne Askew, when Henry VIII was king, he kept the Catholic ways. Protestants, like Anne, were bullied for their beliefs, and when her Da forced her to marry a Catholic husband, it wasn't long before he threw her out, her only about fifteen years old at the time. . . ."

"*We're* fifteen!" Lizzie interrupted.

"Shhh. Edward," reminded Jane, turning her way. "Well, then. When Anne was your age, she found her way to London and to the kinship of women, women of her dear faith. Together they held meetings to study the Bible and she began to preach."

"And she wasn't arrested for it?" asked Elizabeth.

Jane turned to her. "Oh, but she was. Several times. The frustrated authorities finally took her to the Tower of London." In the impending dark, Jane took in one of the foreboding towers of Chester Castle. "The only woman ever tortured there."

"What did they do to her?" whispered Lizzie.

"Declared her a heretic and put her on the *rack*. Thought the stretch of it would convert her, pulling the limbs as it does, until they are far from where they belong."

"Oh, my." Elizabeth sat up.

"But Anne Askew didn't cry out. Mabel always was quick to remind us that that's the lesson."

"What is?" peeped Lizzie.

"Shhh," scolded Jane. "Edward, remember?" She put a finger to her lips and then resumed the telling. "That Anne Askew rose above the torture, it so unbearable that the tower constable couldn't watch and had to leave the room." Jane drew in a jagged breath. "But Anne wouldn't renounce her faith or give the names of her women friends, so they condemned her to burn."

"To burn . . . alive?" asked Elizabeth incredulously.

"At the stake," Jane confirmed, her tone grave. "They had to carry her to the place of it, the rack having done its damage — and . . ." Jane's voice caught for the dead martyr. "Anne *sang* as she was chained to the post. Sang so that all those watching could hear that she was not defeated, that she'd kept her faith. She was put between three fellow martyrs and she called out to them with her final words: 'God is with us. We go to him now. Re-jo-ice!'" Jane elongated the whispered word in hushed triumph. "And so, she died, loyal for her faith to the end," she finished, her voice cracking.

"'Tis why the telling is a favorite," confirmed Elizabeth. "For we too, are a great threat in our defiance to the church and the authorities, and those who think we should curtsey to them for their rank. . . ."

"And do we not remain strong in the face of the ridicule and, and punishment?" queried Jane, her voice steady again.

"We do, we do," confirmed Lizzie.

"'Tis like Mary Fisher," Elizabeth whispered.

Jane jerked up and faced her. "Did something happen to her?"

"She was led to preach in Cambridge — among the students there," Elizabeth answered, the idea that she and Lizzie could go to Oxford occurring to her.

"I hadn't heard," whispered Jane.

"The ministers and college lads think only men can be trained — ordained — for ministry," explained Lizzie as if Jane didn't know as much. She sat up. "And poor Mary Fisher came to them boldly. . . . She was arrested for it, of course. Stripped to the waist and whipped in the market cross. Publicly humiliated. They thought it'd stop her."

"Have you seen it? Seen it done?" Jane asked. "I have," she answered herself. "A man. Whipped furiously with heavily braided strands. The snake of it brought down full-force, time and again on his back — the cuts deep, the blood spurting. By the end of it, his skin was but long ribbons." She stopped talking, checking the darkness that surrounded them now. "Mary Fisher will have raised scars on her back for the rest of her life," she muttered and then went quiet.

In the space of it, Elizabeth wondered if she could endure what might await them if they went on to Oxford. She looked over to Lizzie, searching Lizzie's face in the dimness.

Jane started up again. "My sister, Dorothy . . ." she looked at Lizzie and then to Elizabeth. "Went to preach at the crossroads in Carlisle. This was just last year — when she was but twenty years old. She was so fresh in our faith and filled with purpose, declaring happily to any who'd listen in the market cross that there was that of holy Spirit within. She was led to enter a church — walked straight up to the front where she could be best seen, took a deep breath, she told me, and began her prophecy."

Elizabeth had heard others tell of doing this. Men. George Fox in Mansfield. James Parnell in Colchester. George Whitehead somewhere else. She pictured herself at the Kendal church, opening the grand doors and taking bold strides to address a startled congregation.

"'Tis remarkable," acknowledged Lizzie. "A servant girl. . . ."

"Anne Audland oft recited a quote from the book of Peter, that we are *all* priests. Dorothy believed we are all the messiah. She *welcomed* the chance to challenge those men." Jane turned from Lizzie to Elizabeth's profile. "You might not think that you know how, but something inside you does." She laid a hand on Elizabeth's arm. "For it's our advantage to be women, isn't it? We've no position, no obligation to act a certain way, to model our preaching after the men. We're free to find our own manner."

Edward had said as much. Elizabeth turned to where he was sleeping. "Edward told me that our way in it could be the very thing that attracts. It might not be like that of George Fox, who knows the Bible so well, or of the way of the poetic Edward, but we country women can use our chores and what we know of plantings and animals in our ministry."

"Ah, as the songbirds, delighting us with their distinctive calls?" Jane sniggered softly.

"What happened to her?" Lizzie urged. "To your sister? To Dorothy?"

"Well, of course she was punished for her courage — that a woman, a *woman*,'" Jane emphasized the word, "would be so daring." She took her sister's part again, whispering roughly.

"'You, each and every one, can hear, can feel the divine within your own heart.' And 'you need not pay this man.'" She pointed in the dark to the imagined clergy. "'Not this false minister, who can do nothing to save you from hell. A hell you create with your own inaction. Face the Light in your conscience. Stand still in it.'" Jane paused, swallowing loudly. "That's about when the constable came at her, screaming about the Blasphemy Act."

"Which one is that again?" Lizzie interrupted earnestly.

"That it's a punishable offense for a person to declare himself to be God or equal to God," Jane explained dryly. "Dorothy told me that when she stood before the mayor, she locked her knees, threw her breasts out, and glared at him. He called her a 'whore' and 'unwomanly,' and reminded her that 'wandering Quakers' were already in jail for what he called our 'immoral beliefs and exploits.' He ordered her bridled."

"Bridled?" peeped Lizzie. "Like a horse?"

"Have you seen one?" Jane asked. Neither Elizabeth nor Lizzie had. "It's a medieval contraption, fashioned after a horse bridle but made of metal. The wicked jailer dangled the thing in front of Dorothy, she told me, playing with her like a cat with a mouse. When he finally clamped it over her face, forcing her mouth open and the rusty pins, three facing up and three facing down through her tongue, he took no caution."

Elizabeth put her hands over her eyes, not wanting to acknowledge the images that flooded her. It did no good. She saw Dorothy gagging, blood spilling over her jaw and trickling down her neck.

Jane swallowed hard again. "The horrid man pulled her up like a prized fish and paraded her about. Charged anyone available two pence to watch her staggering about like a drunk from the weight trapping her head. Then he led her down dark passageways to the pit of the castle dungeon and when he got her to the cell, the lecher claimed he had to check her for witchcraft. He stripped her to the waist with a single pulling down of her front and Dorothy said that when she felt his cold fingers, she thought of Anne Askew. 'Tis why I told you about her. When he was done with his fondling, he yanked off her stockings, saying he needed to see her bare legs 'for bumps.' That was when Dorothy took herself to a higher place. She said it felt like the deepest worship, how she turned herself completely over to Spirit, despite what was happening to her, trusting it was part of a divine plan even if she didn't understand it."

"We are innocent lambs, we women," murmured Lizzie. She fell back on the ground and pulled her cloak up around her.

"We don't fight," said Jane, lying back so her head was touching Lizzie's. "We accept what's happening is what is supposed to be, that God is over us," she repeated. She sounded to Elizabeth like a mother reprimanding a child. "And so," her voice softened, "when she was finally left alone, Dorothy said she felt victorious, like she'd run a race and won. She gave thanks — to have been chosen for the honor of the work we do — to be confirmed that Spirit is truly within us, to have been her best self." Jane turned to Elizabeth. "No one is going to know these things save us. It's the men mostly who can keep a journal and none is going to write of what was done to Dorothy or to any of us, how we've suffered in the Lamb's war. . . ."

The Lamb's war, Elizabeth repeated. She snuggled down beside Jane, the three women nestled in the night chill like tender rabbits.

"And loved for it by God and Friends," finished Jane.

"It's a witness, yes . . ." Elizabeth whispered to her in the dark. *Oxford*, she thought again, filled with conviction. "That we do what is asked of us."

Chapter 19

Elizabeth inhaled the sweet, fresh smell of the dew again and again as they worshipped the next morning and let the Silence sink into her bones. She envisioned each of them, surrounded by sunlight, brave in whatever lay ahead. At the rise, Edward told Jane the names of those who'd assisted them and Jane did likewise. Then, feeling strong from the week they'd been traveling in their faith, and the day sunny and new ahead, Elizabeth joined the others as they huddled in farewell, each with an arm around the waist of the other.

Jane wasn't sure of her plans, but she didn't want to go with them to check on Thomas. "Holy Spirit is with you . . . always," she called back over her shoulder as they split from each other. "Be valiant in your preaching. You never know who might be influenced by it."

"Heroic pioneers all," Edward confirmed, giving her a final wave.

At the courthouse, the guard informed Edward, Lizzie, and Elizabeth that Thomas wasn't getting out any time soon. The judge was angry with him. Thomas hadn't removed his hat, taken the oath, or pledged allegiance to the Lord Protector. "You're not allowed in," he said firmly. "No visitors." He stepped in front of the heavy door to make his point.

The night jailer overheard who they were and came over to give them an earful. In the cell, it'd been one thing after another all night long. "The ferret said he was 'led,'" the man told them sarcastically, clearly not understanding the meaning of the term. "'Commanded by the Lord' to deny the mattress provided and to not buy food or drink. He jumped and skipped around, humming a dull tune over and over again until all the sods were complaining of it." The jailer let out a hiss of outrage. "About midnight he began bellowing like a drunk, singing and carrying on . . . us all having to live through it."

Edward and the women left the courthouse and went to find a place off the trail out of town to worship. As she closed her eyes, Elizabeth mulled over Thomas' antics. *Who was she to say he hadn't been divinely called to act as he had?* she considered. Edward's tellings of Ranters and Friends danced through her head — those who'd earnestly walked in sack cloth made from coarse, black goat hair as an outward sign of inward shame and remorse for regretted behavior. Others who'd smeared ash on their foreheads or gone "naked for the Truth," to show their humility and total allegiance to God. Still more who spoke in tongues or cast demons out with a thumb print of holy oil on an afflicted forehead. All felt genuinely guided by the Holy Spirit. Surely Thomas had felt led in his refusing and singing, she decided.

Without quite knowing why, Elizabeth opened her eyes and reached a hand into the sunshine. As she'd once done in the cow barn, she twisted it slowly, watching the light fall on her fingers. Her eyes fell on Lizzie and she watched her in prayer, her belly swelling in and out, in and out, with her breathing. Her shoulders slumped and she quivered slightly. Her eyes flicked open.

"I'm grateful for you," Elizabeth whispered with heartfelt sincerity. "The newness of all this has been eased for me by your ways — your excitement when convinced, your happiness in the travel, your commitment to the faith. . . ." A lump rose in her throat as she met the innocent blue eyes. "Who would trudge so far, have so little to eat, and sleep on ground so rough, but you, so deeply pledged?"

Lizzie stared back at her. "I, I feel blessed to be along, to be with you, too, Elizabeth," she said quietly.

Elizabeth took a long breath and let it out slowly. "I am led, Lizzie, led to go to Oxford. I wonder if you'd accompany me in it."

Lizzie relaxed her posture. "Thomas is solid in his faith," she replied. "I've been thinking of our unity, no matter if we are apart. . . ."

"Sink down in that which is pure," offered Edward, his eyes still closed. It was a few more minutes before he opened them and rose. As they stretched and readied themselves for the day, he shared a name Jane had given him — a Matthew Alton, a Whitchurch merchant. Edward had directions to his home. "Not but half a day's walk," he smiled.

They were to the timber home with its wattle and daub walls and the cheerful family who occupied it by late afternoon, welcomed in and served a huge scramble of potato and sausage. Then the wife, Bridget, suggested that Elizabeth and Lizzie might enjoy the privacy of a shallow river that ran behind the place. Edward could stay with Matt while they went to clean up. Smiling their gratitude and hands entwined, the two took their bundles and followed a narrow path out to the bank.

They were both in pensive moods. Elizabeth stripped off her stockings and shoes and dipped her feet into the cold current. Eventually, she let the water run over her bruised feet, and focused on a shiny bit of something half buried in the river's sandy bottom. The way it was partially covered made her think about leadings, how they seemed only partially revealed.

Was it right to go onto Oxford and not return to Kendal? *What will Moe think?* she wondered. *And Auntie, when we're not back as expected?* She watched the rush of the river for a time, splashing its way downstream. *I'm to go*, she thought, remember all the times she'd sat on the back step at the farmstead and watched the River Kent. She turned to Lizzie who was perched on the bank, leaning over the water, her feet submerged as well. "Have you decided about Oxford?" she asked solemnly, a surprise of tears welled up in the backs of her eyes. "To be the first to preach there, you and I."

Lizzie rolled her bottom lip under and released it. "I will," she answered solemnly. Then, without warning, she threw a foot deeper into the water and splashed at Elizabeth.

"No, no, no," Elizabeth feigned in protest, laughing with the relief of the decision. Not much later, skirts darkened by their splashing, Elizabeth and Lizzie washed their faces and under their arms and changed their sleeves and skirts for the fresher ones they carried. They tugged their shoes back over their cleanest stockings and helped each other up. Then they started back down the path.

"Spirits lifted, girls?" inquired Bridget, coming towards them.

"Yes, thank you," replied Lizzie politely. "The break of it will surely get us through this day. . . . Here," she said suddenly, rummaging through her bag. "I'd like to share something with you." She pulled out a pretty square of cloth with the cross and feather stitches embroidered on it.

"You stitch?" the older woman asked, a curiosity to her tone. She examined the piece.

"Some," Lizzie replied. "We only use a flat stitch in Kendal but recently I've learned these sews," she said modestly. "'Tis but a knack of fancy work for your kindness."

Bridget put out her sleeve. "I'm most proud of one they call the French knot," she beamed, rotating her cuff. The white threads of little raised dots accented a larger beige flat-stitched area so that she had to twist her arm in the light for them to see the little dots. Lizzie leaned in for a closer look. "I use the same color thread as the cloth so it's not so easily seen," explained Bridget. She gestured towards a handsome bench near the back door. "Might we take a moment to show each other our stitches? The men are minding the children."

"They are?" Lizzie and Elizabeth chimed in unison. Then they sat and waited for Bridget to return with a scrap of fabric, a little hoop of bent wood, and threaded needles poked into a tuft of wool. She sat down between Elizabeth and Lizzie, moving the piece on the hoop tighter before starting the special knot. With the hand that wasn't holding the needle, she held the thread taut a few inches from where it exited up through the bottom of the fabric. Then she put the needle in front of the stretch, wound the thread twice around, and kept tension with her other hand to prevent it from uncoiling.

Lizzie was mesmerized. "Are you watching this, Elizabeth?" she pleaded.

"I'm trying," Elizabeth laughed, dutifully focusing on the tight coil on the needle as Bridget re-inserted the tip of it into the fabric. A little miracle ball was forming.

"Don't enter the same hole exactly," Bridget cautioned. She gave the thread a quick downward tug, the special knot finished. She handed the scrap to Lizzie who bent to the hoop to make the cross and feather stitches.

"We are grateful to you who hold up the meetings," Lizzie said gravely to Bridget when she was finished. "For we all are of the same purpose, wanting guidance and growth."

Elizabeth stared over at her. It was the wisest thing she'd ever heard Lizzie say.

Chapter 20

A night with the Altons and it was on to Birmingham. Edward guessed it'd take about three days. The first night of it was warm and, hardened to sleeping outside, they decided to save the coins the Altons had given them and not go to an inn. Lizzie was disappointed, but Elizabeth convinced her it'd best to save the money for when the two of them were on their own.

The following day they strolled on to a place called Wolverhampton, arriving by early afternoon. At Edward's suggestion, they treated themselves to a decent meal and then roamed the market cross, Edward preaching, and Lizzie, fortified by the events of the last days, taking a turn afterwards.

Lizzie did well. Elizabeth beamed with pride as Lizzie told those who gathered around her that she was living as Christ first had, coming to bring good news — that the Holy Spirit of righteousness was within each of them and available should they listen with intention. It was the message of Friends, the "Quaker way."

"Quiet and find peace in the Light," Lizzie finished, her voice strong and sure.

A woman came out of the little crowd circled around them and took her hand. "Very bold of you, girl." She'd never heard a woman preach and thanked Lizzie. She gave no indication as to whether she accepted the ministry or not, but even so, when Edward, Elizabeth and Lizzie were on their way again, Lizzie gushed with delight in how she'd been received. "I am resurrected as Christ was," she told Elizabeth solemnly. "Him come again and again in my thoughts and actions."

Elizabeth praised her as she'd wished Lizzie had complimented her after her first attempt. Edward did, too, though only briefly, wanting them to find a place on the outskirts of town for the night. They slept soundly in a hidden spot behind some bush, worshipped the next morning, and bought a little meal from a vendor who passed them going in the opposite direction. Then it was an easy stroll to Birmingham.

Elizabeth didn't have to be told that they were approaching the city. The trail widened, more horsemen rode by, and carriages began to lurch past them. She held her breathe as she walked alongside heavily laden, foul-smelling pack animals and stepped around their droppings.

Edward began to whistle a little tune, seemingly quite at home in the rush. *This is how London will be for him*, Elizabeth supposed. "See there, the pillory and stocks," he pointed. A man was held in the contraption, his head immobilized in an upright board, his arms forced toward the ends of a cross piece. Elizabeth willed herself to be distracted by the shops they passed — glove making, tailoring, and printing — on the lower level of the two-and three-story buildings that trimmed the cobbled streets. There was even a watchmaker.

"Look at the height of this steeple house," marveled Lizzie, tiling her head back to follow up the massive walls. When Elizabeth gazed up to the multiple spires towering in the summer sky, people bumped on either side of her, shoppers coming in all directions.

Lizzie caught her hand so the two might better stay together. She leaned in close to ask where they might set up to sell the pamphlets they carried. "Oh my, Elizabeth! Look over there," she whispered suddenly. A nobleman, dressed in a satin waistcoat with a wide, white collar, was stepping from a finely trimmed coach pulled by two magnificent horses. His breeches were thickly stitched, and he wore fancy, high-heeled shoes.

"Not from these parts," Edward surmised as the man moved forward to allow the doorman to attend to his lady. She was adorned in a costume of white silk covered by a blue jacket. Her jewels glistened in the sunlight. To Elizabeth, the couple was a striking image of undeserved wealth and false power, people bowing and curtseying to them as they strutted their way on the cobbles.

"A duke and duchess?" supposed Lizzie, her eyes on the huge broach that lay low on the woman's cleavage.

"How do they ever stoop to pick something up?" Elizabeth wondered, eyeing what seemed to be hoops under the skirts and the tight and rigid stays of the woman's satin bodice.

"They have *no need*," Edward reminded her. "Servants for that."

"May . . . be," mumbled Lizzie, each syllable soaked in awe. She watched as the lady flounced toward a group of men and women who were dressed nicely but in much simpler, dark attire. The men wore black hats and the women narrow bonnets that sat straight on their heads to frame their faces. They neither bowed nor curtseyed as the noble couple passed by them.

"They're Friends!" Elizabeth guessed. She started over to them, Edward and Lizzie trailing behind.

An animated young man extended a hand and held it out to her as she reached him. "Robert Byrd," he offered.

"Elizabeth Fletcher, Edward Burrough, and Elizabeth Leavens. Friends from Kendal," Elizabeth offered, shaking his hand. "We're traveling in ministry. Just came from Chester."

"Well, very good then." Robert's eyes flitting from one to the other. "You've come a long way."

An older man came alongside them. "David Lewis. Hello."

Then, two women and another older gent bunched around as well, exchanging names. "Yes, yes," agreed David. "Sleeping out, are you?"

Elizabeth put a hand to her bonnet and tucked in a loose strand of her auburn hair.

"You must be tired to the bone." David's voice was deep, his tone kind. His gaze caught on their worn shoes.

"We'd welcome you as guests," a woman named Susanne offered. "If you'd like to come with us to Small Heath. Won't take but an hour."

Edward nodded, accepting for the three of them. He moved up to be with the men, the women following.

"How fortunate that you saw us and came over," said the one named Janet. She was walking beside Lizzie. "For, once we're home, we can feed you well and all worship together. It's rare for us to have the Silence with anyone but ourselves."

In no time at all the group of them stood before a large, handsome house of white stucco. Decorative brown boards trimmed it vertically and framed the second story windows. Elizabeth began to imagine the meal they'd be served. She wasn't disappointed. Almost immediately, a servant girl showed them to comfortable places in the attractive front sitting room and brought beer and cakes.

Janet handed a pamphlet to Lizzie for discussion while they ate. From where she sat beside her, Elizabeth could see, too, that it depicted a block print of a devil who was whispering into the ear of a woman dressed as a witch. She could read the word under it. "Quaker."

Lizzie handed the tract to Susanne. "They think us scandalous for our speech and 'sexual looseness,'" the woman scoffed as she ran her finger over the horned figure with wings and claws who seemed to be reaching towards the woman preacher. Elizabeth guessed she could read the tract.

"She's not a witch," Lizzie declared, "but a daring girl."

Susanne passed the pamphlet over to Edward who was sitting beside her. "Perhaps the maker of it fears you women," he offered. He glanced to their bonnets, all carefully set over wooden forms on a side table near the entryway. "Depicting your bonnets as witches' hats, pointed when they are not."

Janet rose, gesturing to Robert and David, to come and help with the various aspects of the evening meal. Delicious smells began to fill the room. Elizabeth became distracted watching the men set the serving dishes on the dining table.

The invitation to come pick a place came soon after. Heads bowed in a weighty silence; Elizabeth imagined the touch of Auntie's hands. *She'd be proud of me*, she thought. *Approving of Oxford.*

The meal was a feast — a meat stew with an added array of garden vegetables and mint.

Lizzie began with the compliments, and Edward and Elizabeth added to them with such enthusiasm that the Altons began to tease them in their delight. At the end of it, Elizabeth made it her job to help the servant girl collect up the dishes. Then she and Edward helped Janet serve large slices of berry dessert while Lizzie told of the first time Moe had tasted pie. There were chuckles all around, a tired Elizabeth appreciative of Lizzie's ease among their new friends.

"Where are you headed?" David asked as some of the men lit pipes and Robert served a last round of beer. Eyes shifted to Edward, but it was Lizzie who answered. "Edward is led to London. Elizabeth and I to Oxford. . . ."

"Where young men are trained up in the church ministry," Susanne asked. "Will you be safe there?" Her eyes narrowed.

"We trust Spirit," said Lizzie matter of factly. She sat back.

"Might you want men's clothing?" suggested Janet, echoing Susanne's concern. "Women dressed that way during the War, you know. Come see what we have." She rose. "Were my son's."

Elizabeth and Lizzie followed the older woman to her sleeping chamber, a curtained bed in a corner, a beautifully carved chest and table beside it. Elizabeth didn't feel it right to ask what had happened to Susanne's boy. She surveyed the homey room, the floor planked where the back rooms at the farmstead were dirt, and fixed on a lovely painting of flowers. Susanne found a small dark shirt and folded breeches for each of them.

Elizabeth went to a corner to turn her back to see if hers fit. She felt exposed with only the shirt covering her breasts, but the freedom of the breeches was astonishing. She took a few tentative steps, then a few more, enjoying the comfort. Lizzie, changed now, too, giggled at her.

When they returned to the outer room to add the clothing to their bundles, Elizabeth saw that the men were preparing for evening worship. Friends had come to join in it, thrilling Elizabeth to find that at such a distance from Kendal, others were well-practiced in their manner. She sat down beside Edward, easing back into the soft cushioned chair, and found her way down into her well of solitude. When a neighbor, Jaime Clausen, expressed gratitude for the traveling Friends, referring to the preachers as 'radical stock,' a great force came over Elizabeth. Trust and desire rose up in her like a huge hawk, its wings spread wide. No matter what lay ahead, she and Lizzie were ready.

As others excused themselves to their various evening routines, David asked Edward, Elizabeth, and Lizzie to bring their bundles and come to his study. They passed a room that he offered them for sleep and talked about a recipe he'd made for ink. It was from berries, rusty nails and soot, heated over the fire and strained. He showed them a bottle of it at his desk.

"Has Edward told you of my learning to read and write?" Elizabeth asked the gentle man.

David pointed to a quill pen and paper on his desk in response. "You might practice here," he offered and then moved about the room to light the candles. Lizzie retired to an elegantly upholstered chair opposite the desk and readied herself to embroider. David excused himself for the evening and left them.

Edward picked up the pen, inked it, and handed it to Elizabeth. "You hold it as a schoolboy might," he teased.

"Ah, I should have been so lucky," she scoffed playfully, bending over the coarse paper. "Look here." She sounded out simple words as she spelled them. "Mmoo. Moe is hoomm." She put the pen down and rested both hands on her hips. "What do you suppose Moe's doing?"

"Getting ready for bed, I suspect," Edward mused.

"As we should all be doing soon, as well," Lizzie muttered at them from where she'd sequestered herself.

"And kissing Auntie 'goodnight,'" Edward flirted.

Elizabeth let herself forget about her rough feet, her aching hip. For a few happy moments, she leaned into Edward's firm shoulder, engulfed by the special feelings she held for him.

"Oh, for heaven's sake," huffed Lizzie. She noisily packed away her things and left for the offered chamber.

"She stomps a touch like Moe might." Edward chuckled, so softly that only Elizabeth could hear. After a while, he went about the room, puffing out the candles and meeting Elizabeth in front of the fire. She was patiently holding a poker to the flames. Then, with a little giggle, she spelled out "LOVE" with the orange tip.

The image dissolved quickly and Elizabeth put the poker down. She went to curl up on the rug, Edward coming to fold in against her back. He found her hand and lightly moved his thumb back and forth across her knuckles as he bent closer. Elizabeth twisted to him. She closed her eyes and found his mouth.

Edward left them the next afternoon in Coventry, the logical place for him to divert for London. "We submit to the divine master," he reminded them both. "The power of the Lord is over us." He hugged Lizzie. "Thomas will be fine. You'll be fine," he assured her. When he moved to stand in front of Elizabeth, he took her hand and held it longer than necessary. "We all walk the pack horse trails. Our paths will cross again." He drew her in. Elizabeth kept her jaw clamped and blinked rapidly. "We're ordinary people," Edward said as he released her and then leaned in to give her a quick, fumbling kiss. "But in our hearts we know extraordinary things."

Part III

Oxford and Chester

1655

Chapter 21

Alone, just the two of them, Elizabeth and Lizzie ate a meager sup in Coventry, too depleted and anxious to converse much with anyone seated around them at the alehouse they'd chosen. "Oxford?" the bar maid asked them, taken aback when they told her where they were headed. "You two maidens? Alone?" she glanced at their worn shoes. "Will take you three or four days, ya know?" she squinted at them, her head drawn back. "Through Banbury and then just after a little place called Kidlington." She went off to get their food.

Elizabeth suggested they use the money David Lewis had given them for a night in the Butterworth Inn adjacent to the place. She thought they'd be more comfortable inside and they could get an early start in the morning.

As it turned out, she had trouble falling asleep. The place was swollen with arguments over the merits of silk rather than wool for industry, a brawl breaking out and the shouts drifting up through the floorboards in the chamber they'd been assigned. Elizabeth lay with Lizzie, spooning like the sisters they'd always been, and longed for the forest. She finally fell asleep imagining Spirit surrounded them, rocking her with long glowing arms of Light.

Next day, Elizabeth let the ribbon of trail consume her. There were no signposts where she expected at intersections and in some places the way dwindled out and disappeared altogether. Few people passed them and neither Elizabeth nor Lizzie felt it safe to inquire if they were, indeed, headed the right way, lest they call attention to themselves, young women traveling alone. They simply had to make their best guesses; the walking seemingly more arduous without the men. It wasn't long before they decided to find a secluded spot to change into the boy's clothing Susanne had given them in Birmingham.

The second day went better. They got up with the sunrise, thinking that time of day would be safer for them. When they arrived at Banbury in the afternoon, they used the last of their money to buy fruit and bread, ready to preach afterwards. The work was like a tonic.

"Join us," Elizabeth beckoned enthusiastically when it was her turn. "I'll tell you how an unschooled farmgirl once ruminated on sheep before learning to sit in the grand Silence. How a living faith grew as the corn, waving full and strong in the wind. How purpose was discovered, and with it, a deep and satisfying joy. For it isn't a college education that's required to bring good news to people as yourselves, but inward attention, trust, and obedience."

"This is what will save each of us," Lizzie claimed, trembling with her Truth in the little village of Kidlington-on-the-Green. "That we'll break up the hard earth within ourselves, so that the seed can be planted. And once planted, a new self will rise — strong and determined." Her ministry included the basic ideas of Friends that she'd heard from George and Edward, but she found inspiration, too, as Elizabeth did, in the birds and animals, the encompassing sky, and the changing weather.

Elizabeth stood nearby Lizzie, holding her in the Light, not always following her ideas, but accepting what unfolded. She was glad they were together — thankful for Lizzie's ever cheerful demeanor and increasingly fine phrasing when she preached. Elizabeth thought it was because of Lizzie that folks warmed to them, seeking her over Elizabeth to answer their questions. In the whole of their work, Elizabeth felt free and right, much transformed in the brave space they created and bursting with the joy of it. That night, she kept an arm over Lizzie, the two of them sleeping like innocent babes on the warm summer ground.

It was First Day when Elizabeth and Lizzie arrived at the Oxford city gates. They found a discreet spot under the full leaves of an aged sycamore tree and prepared internally for whatever they might encounter in the city. At the rise of their worship, Elizabeth suggested they change back into their skirts and bonnets.

"On this day especially," Lizzie agreed, her blue eyes fixed on Lizzie's brown ones. "We should appear as our honest selves." She led the way with their bundles to dense shrubs, modestly turning her back to change. As if still in worship, Elizabeth humbly untied one part of her outfit and exchanged it for another, averting her eyes from her own unblemished skin. While she did so, she thought about the female Friends who'd preached and suffered and of Mary Askew who had died for her faith. *Would she be welcomed or arrested?* she wondered. Whatever was to happen, she was led to this day and she welcomed it.

"Look how your skirt hangs," whispered Lizzie when they faced each other again. It was the result of days of meager meals and long hours of travel. They repacked their bundles and hid them. Then they meticulously tied each other's bonnet ribbons.

"Holy Spirit between us," Lizzie announced as they threaded their arms to walk abreast through the North Gate.

"Wherever two are gathered. . . ." Elizabeth agreed, her bright eyes focused straight ahead to the highest church steeple. She felt strong and capable, her shoulders back and her chin up. "Wrap us, wrap us in your love," she said aloud, feeling the presence of Auntie and Hannah, Elizabeth Hooten and Mary Fisher; Jane and Dorothy Waugh.

As the two grave women went down Cornmarket Street, Elizabeth repeated the words she'd heard from Edward. "Be guided to do good in the world, to see what love can do." They reached St. Martin's at the crossroads and Elizabeth untied her bonnet, pulled it from her head, and began to preach to those milling there. She'd thought about how she'd start, deciding on the words she first heard George Fox preach.

"I'm alive with holy Spirit and happy to share it. God and Christ are very real, very real, and present in this moment, are they not? Real and near at hand. Near at hand, yes. In my heart and yours. For there's that of God in each of you. Available to everyone, young and old, poor and wealthy, trained and untrained.

There were murmurings among those gathered, hopeful gazes on her as a growing number of villagers clustered closer. Elizabeth fixed on a well-dressed businessman. "Choose your clothing as you do your words — for what rings in you and not for another — the more simple and plain, the better, and not for pride or class." When she felt finished, she sucked in a long languid breath and closed her eyes for a moment. It was going well. She went slowly to where Lizzie stood in front of St. Martin's massive doors and the two of them slipped inside.

The service was just ending as the women went assertively down the center aisle, Elizabeth in the lead, to the front of the stone sanctuary. The minister startled to see them, his mouth agape as Elizabeth came confidently to where he stood. She turned in front of him to address the congregation. "There is that of Spirit in each and every one of you," she began, chin up, eyes on the many who were standing. "And we Friends have come to tell you of it," she called out triumphantly over the rising clamor. "For you have no need of this minister . . ." She pointed to the robed clergy, her arm straight and steady. "or any other." The rumble of outrage grew louder.

"Blasphemer!" she heard. "What right do you have to speak for God?"

"To testify that it's robbery that takes place in this steeple house," Elizabeth answered, turning to the source of the challenge. "Keeping you, you my good man, and everyone here from what is already yours. . . ."

A sergeant was on her then, muscling her from where she stood. "Vagrants. You ain't allowed here," he screamed.

Elizabeth felt no hurt from his grip. She met the menacing eyes, the cheekbones prominent with anger, took in the foul breath. Another man was on Lizzie. His dark hair, once parted and flattened for church, fell into his face.

Arms pinned, the two of them were pushed down the aisle, back out the sanctuary doors. "We're not vagrants," Elizabeth said softly as she tripped into the sunlight.

"Witches, whores," retorted the one with Lizzie, his spittle splattered her cheek.

The women were hustled off in the direction of the courthouse. "Light within, holy Spirit. Freely available. To all. Light within, holy Spirit. Freely available. To all," Elizabeth chanted as they went through the streets. Lizzie joined her, their volume together loud enough to bring a handful of jeering students from the entrance to St. John's College out onto the cobbled street alongside them.

"What gives Quakers — girls at that — the right to be preaching on our streets?" boomed a lad, his puny face twitching as he waited to see what the constables would allow. Other students, guffawing and jabbing, closed in around Elizabeth and Lizzie, the constables permitting it. "You can neither read the Bible nor understand it, and yet you oppose our study!" the student snorted.

"Those whom Christ has inspired are surely justified to speak," Lizzie replied with temerity. She was pulled into a dark corner of the wide, stone entrance to St. John's.

Elizabeth felt a hard jab at her back and she, too, was dragged into the shadows, out of view from those on the street. After she was forced down, one of the students threw a leg over her, pinning her face up on the ground. "If we women don't speak, the serpent speaks," she said into the young face, her eyes on the stubble that sprouted between pock marks there. She squirmed away from the attempted kisses, rough on her mouth, and swiveled her head to those who'd squatted around the scene. Clenched hands dug into her shoulders and held her flat.

"Ah, but no! You are the evil serpents!" hooted the one on top of her. He ground his hips down below her stomach as he jabbed a hand up under her bodice. "Like that, do you, whore?" he sneered.

Elizabeth stared unflinchingly into his face and willed herself not to show the fear that was rising up inside her.

"Let's give the filthy wench a wash," a lad roared, completely ripping off one of her sleeves. Cheers rose up at the sight of her pale flesh. Elizabeth felt invading fingers traveling over her like giant spiders. She was pulled to her feet; she and Lizzie shuffled a short distance to a horse trough and ducked under in the slimy water.

"Better yet, to the fountain," an excited youth shrilly screamed. Pushed to it, Elizabeth caught the sparkle of the gushing water in the sunlight. She was made to squat, her soaked skirts draping over her scraped calves like pieces hung on wash day. Lizzie's back was pushed up against her own and the two of them tied tightly together, Elizabeth wincing as a leather belt was cinched into the soft flesh of her wrists. A bucket of fountain water came crashing over her head.

Coughing, she bent to her chest, trying desperately for breath. Hands pried her jaw open, splashing a pour sloppily down it. She couldn't breathe. She couldn't breathe.

Holy Spirit guide me. Holy Spirit be with me, Elizabeth tried to pray internally. She was drowning.

"St. Giles," Elizabeth heard as Lizzie fell against her and they were dragged again. No constable or college professor stopped the violence. At the St. Giles graveyard, a woman came out of nowhere and pushed her hard over a headstone. She felt the jolt of a sharp pain from somewhere beneath her ragged skirts and a sound like a gunshot in her head as it clanked against the marker.

As she sprawled the open grave, lads were back on her in seconds. Two of them roughly grabbed at her caved body. She shrieked in agony as they hoisted her out of the pit.

"Stop this ruckus at once," a man demanded then. Elizabeth couldn't see him through her damaged eyes, only hear the authoritative voice spitting orders that quelled the attack. "Get these Quakers to the Bocardo." It was a fortress that towered over the street that was attached to the tower of St. Michael's Church. The worst felons and murderers were housed there.

The lads complied. Two each trudged the women down the street towards the tower entrance and into the hands of the jailer on duty. He pulled the crumpled women up the steps to the cells and threw them through a set of iron-barred doors. Elizabeth immediately passed out on the straw.

It was a different guard who roughly woke the preachers in the morning. He gave a disgusted frown when he saw Elizabeth's blotched face, the blood crusted on her lips. He threw a muscled arm around the waist of what remained of her darkly stained skirts and carried her down the steps as if she were a feed sack to a chamber adjacent to the jail. Lizzie hobbled behind them, entering the room to stand before an assembly of red-robed men with white wigs, all seated behind a long, polished table.

One of the men came over to them and dismissed the guard. He wasn't dressed in the court regalia of the others but a fancy black jacket and breeches, black stockings, and black square shoes. He introduced himself as Martin Layton, the mayor of Oxford. That was all that was allowed before the Vice-Chancellor took over the proceedings. With his dark goatee and the collar of his red robe high on his neck, he seemed to Elizabeth to be the devil himself. "Why were you in Oxford?" he boomed. He stood up from the table to loom over them.

"We were commanded by the Lord to come," Lizzie replied hoarsely, meeting the coal-black eyes.

"And what were you to do here?" the Vice Chancellor asked sarcastically. He pinched his lips and raised his eyebrows high, a finger re-curling one end of his waxed moustache.

"To preach against *pride*. . . ." Lizzie emphasized the word, her voice forceful. "Lust and failed worship. . . . Sins that are alive *here* contrary to the commandments of God."

The Vice Chancellor frowned. You," he addressed Elizabeth. "How do you know you were called by God and not the Devil to preach as you say?"

Elizabeth took a slow breath in and released it calmly. "We prepare, we wait." she managed, her phrasing measured. "Love presses on our hearts, and we feel the word of life in our whole body and soul." She rolled her shoulders down her back, feeling as if there were wings attached there. "We trust," she continued, her chin high. "We see with new eyes. We obey."

"Blasphemy," The Vice Chancellor bellowed. "Do you not read the Scriptures?"

"We are farm girls from the North. Not taught to read," said Lizzie, her eyes directly on the man. "Friends believe scripture is important," she added, a force in her tone despite her appearance. "But it's the Holy Spirit moving *through* the verses that informs."

"Ah," smirked the Vice-Chancellor. He checked with his cronies on his right, pounding his gavel as they began to mutter to each other. "But are you not advised to be obedient to your superiors?"

"We are obedient to the divine power of holy Spirit," answered Lizzie. Her blue eyes twinkled as she moved them up and down the table to fix on each of the men.

"Girls? Instructed by the Holy Spirit? Ha!" the Vice-Chancellor mocked. There was a smattering of nervous sniggering from the others.

Elizabeth slid her hands down her skirts and lifted her chest. She stared confidently at the Vice Chancellor. "If the power of God speaks in man or woman, is it not Christ?" she asked, purposely quoting the Bible.

"My comely, young maids," the Vice Chancellor chided, fidgeting with the gavel. "Your voices remain unstilled? You profane the word of God, whom you do not know, yet you speak so much of him?" He stood abruptly, his robes swishing. "Get them from my sight!"

Elizabeth and Lizzie were taken into a small anterior room and left alone there. They slumped together on the cold stone bench searching each other's faces but not daring to touch each other's wounds. Through the thin door they could hear the mayor pleading on their behalf.

"I won't sign it," Martin Layton was saying about whatever punishment was being devised. "Let me offer them food and drink, a little money if they need it, and have them escorted to the city limits."

"They'll just return to contaminate our city," decreed the Vice Chancellor. "We mean to make an example of these Quakers. Whip them out."

A constable came to fetch them, a huge man following their escort outside. He was dressed all in black. *The one to do the whipping*, Elizabeth realized when she saw him uncoil the thick cord he carried and slap it repeatedly against his hand. She thought he was only wanting to terrorize them in front of the onlookers who had turned from their errands. "Good, good man," she started, her tiny, bent frame eye-level with his thick black belt. "We're a peaceful people. There's no need for the whip."

Her plea seemed to ignite the man's fury. "You're to be whipped out, you bitch," he disparaged, raising the whip handle high above his head. He wore a headband to keep his hair out of his eyes and the ample construction of his shirt allowed a full range of motion. Not four feet back, he hurdled the barbed rope into Elizabeth's back with a monstrous force. If she'd been trying to control her reactions to any part of the punishment, she let go now, giving herself completely over to Spirit. She turned to him with the shock of the blow, a second one cutting deep into her cheek.

Nauseated by the pain, she glimpsed Lizzie go down beside her. Hot tears burned her eyes but she clearly heard Lizzie sing out. "There's that of God," she started but stopped suddenly. Elizabeth couldn't see why.

"I love you. You are loved," Elizabeth began repeating at the sound of Lizzie's voice. She couldn't tell if she was saying the words aloud or only to herself. The flogging stopped. She was pushed through the North Gate, no one following them. She saw only Lizzie, collapsed beside her, moaning on the cobbles.

Chapter 22

Elizabeth woke with searing pain corkscrewing through her body. Her belly hurt something awful. An elderly, brown-skinned woman came into fuzzy view with her moaning. "Friend?" she tried to ask through her puffed lips. Her speech was unintelligible even to her.

"You're safe, child," the woman cooed into the swollen, purple face. "You were brought to the Bettris' house after. . . ."

Elizabeth passed out again.

The next time she awoke, the ordeal of Oxford flashed in fragments. She'd done as she was commanded. She'd preached and been abused for it, nearly drowned at a huge stone fountain. A woman had pushed her hard at a grave marker and she'd fallen into the fresh hole behind it. They'd spent a night in a cell that smelled like cat piss. She was whipped. She snaked a hand tenderly to her cheek and felt the bump of the wound.

It was someone blotting her check that next roused her. *The brown-skinned face?* Her vision was blurry, as if she were peeking through a crack in a wall on a foggy day. No maggots or leeches, Elizabeth hoped, wincing from the pressure of the cloth on the wound. It pulsed like a beacon, setting off all the aches and pains that stormed in her. She saw hands, the color of autumn leaves, moving about her and then felt them on her thighs. She began to remember things — the grinding on her hips, the groping hand on her breast, the invading fingers. She moved as far as she could into her refuge of black and stayed there.

Elizabeth had no idea how many days passed before she woke next. She came up out of her hiding as if she were surfacing from a pond of water. Her body ached but the pain was bearable, not as continual or as throbbing as it had been at first. She could see better. She learned it was the mistress of the home, Ellen Bettris, who spooned broth through her raw lips, and the dark-skinned Sara Timms, whose age-spotted hands cleaned her wounds and put the bed pan under her. She worked for Doctor Bettris and his family and was the friend of an older man, Christopher Ricks. He was a neighbor and a sympathizer. The three of them, Ellen, Sara, and Christopher, had been the ones to rescue her and Lizzie at the North Gate.

"I've sent word to Swarthmoor Hall," Christopher told them one morning. "To let them know you're here with us."

"I expect the folks there will get word to others to come for us," Lizzie said, her voice wobbly.

"I gave directions," Christopher assured her.

Elizabeth laid back weakly. "Means . . . authorities know . . . we're here," she worried, the wound on her face pulling as she spoke.

"We're not afraid," Ellen said boldly, coming to her as if she were a wounded bird. "My husband is a physician and in *very* good standing in Oxford. We're all glad to have been convinced by your preaching at St. Martin's." She held a vial of an amber liquid for Elizabeth to inhale.

"You're Friends, then?" asked Elizabeth.

"We've worshipped in silence for years," explained Ellen. "Waiting. Sara Timms wouldn't tell you, but she's suffered herself for preaching in Bristol. Arrested and reprimanded by the mayor to go home, sweep her house, and do her laundry." Ellen shook her head with the insult, the lines of her forehead furrowed. "We were lucky to be in the market cross the other day to hear you preach." Bits of confusing memories fluttered in Elizabeth as Ellen dipped closer to her and better inspected the bruises on her face. The black was softening to a deep yellow color.

CHAPTER 22

In the next days, Elizabeth allowed Dr. Bettris to check her for internal wounds. He gave Sara an ointment to apply to the cut on her cheek. "Try to get up and move some. Go out into the sunlight," he recommended.

That afternoon forward, Christopher and Sara helped the "Kendal Friends" to sit on the porch of the stone house. Lizzie was well enough to practice her sews and Elizabeth was given little tasks that helped her to think about something other than the pain in her stomach. She liked best to talk with Christopher. He was the one to tell her about Doctor Bettris, a man with a daring reputation for helping sorry men. A decade earlier, he'd cared for Parliamentary prisoners in the Oxford Castle and had been incarcerated himself by King Charles for doing so.

Once she could tolerate it, Christopher read some to Elizabeth from saved letters. He encouraged her to read along, although she had to pause often to swallow the saliva that collected in her mouth. Still, she was interested in how people expressed themselves and her confidence grew in sounding out difficult, unfamiliar words. Overhearing her read one afternoon, Sara complimented her intelligence, and Lizzie put down her needle to clap when Elizabeth read an especially long sentence with unexpected ease.

In the next days, something of a routine was established about the Bettrises'. Lizzie and Elizabeth were able to do more of their own care and assisted as they could about the home. They held daily worship with Richard and Ellen Bettris and Christopher and Sara, Elizabeth unable to go deep into it for the memories that would rise up when she closed her eyes. A woman named Mary Lee Loe began to visit and bring meals.

One afternoon, a wiry lad called Iggy came to the house. He turned immediately shy when he saw that Elizabeth and

Lizzy were among the others. "I, I have a letter," he stuttered. He took a long-legged step to hand it to Ellen, his hair bobbing at his delicate chin.

"Iggy and Christopher have a post system," explained Sara. "Christopher writes the letters, one contact often leading to another, and Iggy rides to deliver or fetch them. That's how we're kept informed of Friends' activities."

The young man gave a crinkled smile and sat down in a vacant chair. As Ellen broke the seal and unfolded the paper, he crammed his hands between his knees and stared at Lizzie.

"Lizzie Leavens," Lizzie introduced herself to him. Elizabeth tried to reach out to the boy, too, but sharp pain in her gut stopped her. Unwelcome tears filled her eyes.

"Beautiful handwriting," mumbled Ellen as she scanned the letter. "It's from young Margaret Fell at Swarthmoor Hall," she announced. "Not the mistress, but the daughter. She sends her love for the living God, and to us, and writes first of a Thomas Holme of Chester."

"Thomas Holme!" Lizzie exclaimed. Everyone turned toward her. "It's, it's that we — Thomas, Elizabeth and I — we grew up together . . . in Kendal . . . and started out together in ministry a month or so ago." Emotion caught up with her and she couldn't say more.

"Says he was trembling and crying as he preached in Chester," Ellen read. "So much so that a constable fainted and the mayor had him arrested for disturbing the peace."

"Oh, that's only about half true," defended Lizzie. "We were there, too, for that part. It's that they feared the Light within, the message he was moved to deliver. It was his first time to preach . . . and Elizabeth's, too." She glanced over at Elizabeth.

"Yes, yes," Elizabeth agreed, choked, too, for news of Thomas.

"I see." Ellen returned to the letter. "Says here he claimed to be divinely commanded to lie on the cell floor and sing at midnight."

"We heard those rumors too," Lizzie said, her tone defiant. "Led, surely." She popped her eyes at Elizabeth again. "It got him mentioned in the letter," she grinned.

It was but a day or so later that from where they sat inside, they heard the fast approach of galloping horses. Lizzie was the first to the door to see what the ruckus was. "Thomas!" she screamed in sheer happiness when she saw the rider. She hurried down the front step, Elizabeth limping gingerly behind her.

Ah, Thomas. Elizabeth sighed with relief. Tears slipped from her eyes. Richard Farnsworth was with him, too.

"I came as soon as I heard," called Thomas as he dismounted. Lizzie flew into his arms, her face lit up. Over her head he beckoned Elizabeth to him as well.

Safe, she thought as he pulled her into the heat of his chest. They'd ridden hard. Tangled in his arms, Elizabeth closed her eyes for the undeniable bliss of knowing Thomas had come for them.

"And who are these good people?" Richard asked as Ellen, Sara, and close behind them, Christopher and Dr. Bettris came out of the cottage and towards the hitching post where he'd lashed the horses.

"Richard Bettris. Friend," Dr. Bettris volunteered, stepping forward. "Newly convinced." The others introduced themselves as well.

Elizabeth went to him then. "Thank you, thank you for coming," she burbled, more animated than she'd been in days. She folded carefully into his embrace.

"We only just *read* about you in a letter from Swarthmoor," Lizzie sang into Thomas' face. She was too thrilled to be with him to be courteous to Richard.

"You did, did you?" laughed Thomas, his face full of relief for having found them.

"Come, come in," Ellen fussed. "Let's have a proper welcome!"

They settled into the chairs around the front room. Sara and Christopher served brandy and sweets.

"'Twas the Friends in Chester who got me released," Thomas started up, ready to dominate the conversation. "I've stayed there since." He stopped to wolf down a biscuit while the others waited politely. "The Chester Meeting is well, though the constables come constantly to break it up." He sputtered to clear the gobbled food. "We stand up to them, we do. Refuse any kind of compliance: the walk from the courthouse to the cell, the swearing on the Bible. We hold our names when a judge asks them." He swiped crumbs from his beard. "Some from the meeting go discreetly about, gaining support for the ones jailed, bringing flowers and herbs for the smell of the hay, for . . . oh Lizzie, it's awful in those chambers." He wiped his mouth with the back of his hand and reached for a second biscuit.

Same Thomas, thought Elizabeth as Sara pushed the plate of sweets closer to him. He didn't stop for a moment to consider that she and Lizzie might have been jailed themselves since they'd last seen him. Didn't occur to him to ask where they'd gone after Chester. Or how they'd been led to Oxford. The brandy burned down her throat. Or what had happened to them there. She felt her face flush.

Thomas caught her eyeing him. "Did you know," he asked, looking straight at her, "that there's a herd of Friends holding you in the Light, wishing you good recovery?"

Elizabeth shook her head as if she was a little girl sitting at his knee again.

"'Tis true."

"We give thanks for it," whispered a solemn Elizabeth, tears welling up in her eyes. She welcomed his news.

"Might we worship in gratitude," suggested Sara, noticing.

Mugs and plates were set aside and they all settled back. They unfolded their legs, splaying their hands on their knees or curling them in their laps. Before Elizabeth closed her eyes, she took a moment to consider the solemn faces, the planted feet. Then she began her worship as she often did, starting down the familiar well of darkness, working to expand into the vastness out before her. Thomas' breathing seemed magnified, loud in her ears. She felt groping fingers come at her out of the shadows of the strained silence and she tensed her lower half. She flashed her eyes open, puffing out air, tears pushing at the back of her eyes again.

She adjusted her posture, hesitant to try again. She saw lads teasing her, pulling at her clothes, dancing about. She made herself stop them and took power from their vanishing. What might she do to show her obedience to the faith she loved? *Go naked*, she thought. She'd heard of it being done. *I need that now*, she decided. *To show my own self as much as anyone else that Oxford won't stop me.*

Elizabeth was tipped to her injured side, considering whether she could discard her clothing as she might the shards of fear and anger that poked at her, when she heard skirts rustle. She recognized Lizzie's voice.

"I'm led . . . led . . . to be stripped of my clothes," Lizzie sniffled, her words halting. To walk . . . as in olden times . . . as a sign that Cromwell and Parliament . . . and all who think they have power . . . do not have it. . . . Gone as clothes, the authority of the Church of England . . . and those training for it. . . . Shamed . . . shamed as I will be, a modest maiden. . . . Shamed for their cruelty." Elizabeth heard her swallow. "It's like death to me, this leading . . . but Spirit is asking, sweet as honey, and I must be faithful," Lizzie's voice wobbled. She sank back down in the palpable Silence.

In the mind, Elizabeth repeated some of Lizzie's phrasing. She slowly turned the words over and over as she sometimes twisted her hand in the sunlight. Was Spirit moving around the room, the kernel of action in the shudder of the prophecy as well as in her own deliberations? Was she being asked, too, to shed her outer clothing in divine obedience, contrary to her own will? She rubbed slowly down her skirt. *I'm to go. Go with Lizzie. Yes.* At the rise of worship, she stepped to her.

"Might I go with you?" she asked unassumingly.

Next morning, Elizabeth and Lizzie soberly prepared themselves for the day. Sara wrapped Elizabeth's injured torso for support and protection, then helped the preachers to dress. They went into the front garden where Ellen and the men were waiting.

Sara handed a jerkin each to Thomas and Richard. "They might want these," she suggested.

Elizabeth and Lizzie took the lead, Thomas and Richard walking a few paces behind them. The others stayed back.

Near the North Gate where they'd first called on Spirit to surround and guide them, the women went off behind a shed to disrobe. They reappeared, wearing nothing but their shifts and no bonnets. When they gave the men their clothes, they asked for the jerkins.

Elizabeth took Lizzie's hand and started toward Cornmarket Street, Thomas and Richard at a distance behind them. "Wherever two are gathered," Lizzie reminded Elizabeth.

"I'm remembering what Jane Waugh said," Elizabeth replied bravely. "'Discomfort completes the deed.'" She rounded her shoulders back and down. *Trust in Spirit, Trust in Spirit*, she murmured, struggling to keep herself prayerful.

Townspeople stopped to watch them as they retraced the course they'd taken initially, but no one hollered or interfered. "I'm led," Lizzie called out to those staring at them, "to be stripped of my outer garments. To walk in obedience. As a sign of truth." She didn't mention the Oxford students, even when they passed St. John's College. Ironically, no student or professor was out near the thick arched entrance where they'd first been attacked. Wherever they were, Elizabeth hoped that all who had been involved in their molestation were reflecting on their role in the violence, considering how they'd conducted themselves. She didn't see an older woman who came suddenly at her with two others.

"Thank you, thank you for preaching that day," the lady whispered earnestly, her eyes sparkling into Elizabeth's own. "It meant so much to us. To have you here. To hear your message at St. Martin's."

"Elizabeth Fletcher," Elizabeth replied. She extended her hand.

The woman, and then each of the younger women with her, took it warmly. Then Lizzie's.

"Your courage and blessings," a younger one beside her mumbled self-conscientiously. "Then and now. I'm, I'm much transformed by your model." Her lively gaze darted from Elizabeth to Lizzie. "We've burnt all our ribbons as a testimony against worldly ways," she added. The other one beside her nodded vigorously.

"We hold meeting at the Bettrises' house." Lizzie pointed in a general direction back behind them. "Not far from here. Come experience the Light within, the depth of our worship."

The three women faded in tandem back with the men. Not long after, at the St. Giles graveyard, Elizabeth turned to Lizzie. "I am no longer led to go as this." Without further explanation, she reached back to Richard for the bundle of her clothes and her bonnet. Lizzie did likewise and they went off together to a side of the grand church, the Oxford women encircling them, to change.

Attired again, Elizabeth went to the stone where she'd been injured. She stood reverently over the newly turned earth of the grave it marked.

"What happened here?" Richard asked solemnly, tapping her shoulder when she didn't turn to the noise of his approach.

"The grave was empty on the day we preached," Elizabeth replied. "Dug for this recent burial. After we were caught up by the students and brought this way, a woman . . . a woman came out of nowhere and pushed me hard against this headstone." She laid a hand respectfully on the granite. "Something happened inside my belly. I still hurt from it." She stared at the ground for a moment. "My heart is tortured, too," she muttered.

"I'm sorry for it," Richard consoled. "For it was important that you and Lizzie came here." He bent to fully see her face. "You realize that, don't you?"

"In part, yes," Elizabeth agreed softly, not able to say more about what the St. John's boys had done, of all she'd had to bear, of how her worship was hindered. "Realized it afresh when these women approached today," she said modestly, twisting away from his closeness.

"We rarely know how our actions affect others," Richard offered as they went to rejoin Thomas and Lizzie. The Friends said their goodbyes to the Oxford women and started back to the Bettrises', Richard and Elizabeth behind Thomas and Lizzie.

Elizabeth watched the couple, their hands clasped and swinging. *I've lost Lizzie*, she thought. *Unaccompanied now.*

Chapter 23

They had barely started lunch when Thomas noisily pushed back his chair saying he needed to tend to the horses. Not a second later, Lizzie followed him out the front door. Those who remained at the table exchanged questioning stares. Before anyone took a guess at what was going on, Lizzie burst back into the room.

"Thomas and I are getting married!" she gushed. "We're going to travel and preach together."

Thomas came in behind her. He stared over to Elizabeth in silence. She looked away for a moment and then back at him. His eyes were still on her. *Two branches of the same tree*, she thought. Thomas' proposal was interrupted when George Fox had come to the farmstead. Now that he was reunited with Lizzie, he wasn't going to risk losing her again. Elizabeth could see that. She rose and went to the couple.

"When? Where? Who will marry you?" she asked, joining in the excitement. She knew no Presbyterian church would have them — nor they the Church.

"As soon as possible. In Chester," said Thomas. Elizabeth saw relief in his expression. "Out of the Spirit and in Truth. Among Friends — the Morgans." He stepped outside again, as if the announcement and the attention that came with it were too much for him.

Lizzie grabbed Elizabeth's hands and squeezed them, then went out, too.

Elizabeth drifted back to the table.

"Might you want to ride with me to the wedding?" Richard asked. "I'm headed to Northumberland while the lanes are dry, but I could leave my work there 'til after."

"Oh, that's so kind of you," Elizabeth hedged. "I'm, I'm

not sure I'm . . ." she wrapped her arms protectively over her belly, "well, enough."

"It's a way. . . . Well, you know, you've walked it," said Richard. "Even by horse it'll take at least a week." His gaze flitted about the table. "But we could stay in inns so you'd be better fed and wouldn't have to sleep out."

"We should be by their side," decided Elizabeth, a nervous hitch in her voice. She picked up her spoon and raised it up as if it were a wedding toast.

"Don't look all gloomy," Lizzie chided, all smiles and delight, as she helped wrap Elizabeth's breasts and stomach a few mornings later. They'd been visited by the newly convinced Oxford women who'd given each of them handsome black bonnets, freshly sewn top skirts, and sturdy new boots. "I'll see you in but a week . . . at my wedding!" she sang.

Outside, Richard and Ellen Bettris, Sara and Christopher, and Elizabeth and Lizzie waited while Thomas rode his gelding from the barn. Then, without any dithering, Lizzie stepped up on the mounting block, threw a leg over, and wrapped her arms around her groom. When they trotted off, she didn't look back. Elizabeth could hear Thomas, though, singing loudly into the wind.

Her mind's filled with wedding plans, thought Elizabeth, hurt nonetheless. When the group of them went back inside, she was thankful they talked of other things.

They ate lunch and then Richard went for his horse, too. He'd agreed not to follow the lovers too closely, to give them time to get ahead, but now that they'd eaten, he wanted to get started.

Elizabeth, hands shoved in the pockets of her skirt, twisted back and forth as she waited for him. Ellen, Sara and Christopher stood nearby. "I truly thank you for your bravery in taking us in." She ran her fingers under her eyes. "And your tenderness in our care," she said to them, her voice quivering.

"Ah, child. . . ." It was all that Sara could manage as she pulled Elizabeth carefully into her. Ellen and Christopher came into the hug, too.

"We love you, Elizabeth Fletcher," Christopher said above her head. "We wish you but good health and peace of mind, that you heal inside and out."

Elizabeth backed out of the embrace so she could see his face. "I'm worried for the jogging," she admitted. Then she warily stepped up on the mounting block.

She'd never ridden a horse before. When Richard rode up alongside her, she swung a leg over the huge animal as she'd seen Lizzie do. Pain shot through her like fire. Dizzy, she threw an arm tight around his waist and buried her head in his back. As they trotted off, she clung to him as if he were a tree, grateful he couldn't see her wincing.

It never got much better. Every clop of the horse was like a knife in her belly. For most of the riding, Richard had no idea of her suffering and left her to own thoughts. *How can he help anyway?* Elizabeth decided. She tried to add comment to his occasional story, grateful that he was trying to help her pass the time, and that he didn't ask probing questions. She would have found it difficult to talk.

They stopped in Stratford-on-Avon around sup time. Richard rode them down Sheep Street through a sprawling market and vendors of skins and barley, and shops of glove-making, tanning, malting, and such. Elizabeth was surprised to find most of them still open for sales at that time of day.

Richard secured rooms at a place called the Rex Manor Inn and Alehouse, a rebuilt farmhouse with a pub on the first floor and rooms above. They took their meal among traders and craftsmen of all sorts, most of whom were associated with the market in some regard.

Aside from the girl who took their orders and brought their beer and plates, no one bothered them. Elizabeth caught tidbits about the town's aristocracy and the garrisons of the Civil War from the conversations around her. None of it seemed to be a warning or a threat — only small talk. Near the end of their eating, men at a nearby table engaged Richard, telling of a recent, raging fire. It'd wiped out the home and sheds of a man named Stuart Masters, a haberdasher, but had been contained before it spread.

Elizabeth listened, politely left out of most of the exchange. Two women sitting close by must have noticed, she figured, because they came over to her. Boldly, they slid into chairs, letting the men have their talk, and engaged her in theirs. One was employed as a collar maker and the other as a more general seamstress. They had their own money to spend and boasted of it. *It's a new time*, thought Elizabeth, *women able to sit and talk in a pub like this*. She told them how she used to eavesdrop at the window of the Fleece Inn in Kendal where no women were allowed.

People around them began games of cards and checkers, and a man started up on a lively fiddle and another to singing. Elizabeth didn't last long. Fatigued, she bid the women and Richard goodnight and retired upstairs. She shared a room with several others of her sex, sleeping better than she expected among them. The next morning, she woke and dressed, and came downstairs to find Richard already eating. He was talking with a pair who were passing through, much as they themselves were, sharing his plan to ride to Birmingham, the half-way point to Chester. He figured it'd take two days.

The exchange gave Elizabeth a goal, a hope that she'd

make it to the wedding. *Trust Spirit. Trust Spirit.* It came to her like a whisper.

In was in the afternoon that Elizabeth told Richard of the abandonment she felt. "I, I am unable to sink into the quiet of late," was how she started.

"Of worship?" Richard clarified.

"Oxford has stopped me," Elizabeth confessed. "I flit from one memory to another." She fought to mention the college lads who'd pinned her down, the 'fledgling priests,' as George Fox called them. She saw herself naked with indecency as they pushed her to the cobbles. "I have lost the safety of it," she managed. "Images attack me there."

"Return to it, Elizabeth," Richard counseled after a long silence, not able to turn to her. "Love and comfort await you there."

She squinted her eyes, swallowing and swallowing. "I, I struggle to believe my attackers possess the Light," she admitted. It was the core belief of her faith and the loss of it worried her the most. If she couldn't believe that the college students held a divine measure of good, how could she go on?

Perhaps it was the talk of Oxford or the stabbing pain in her belly but after only but an hour, in a place called Solihull, Elizabeth asked Richard if they could stop. She feared she'd lose consciousness and fall off the horse.

Richard helped her to dismount and they began to walk through the market, thinking it might invigorate her. Despite it being mid-morning, most of the stalls were vacant. "Trades people, like meself are struggling," a woman told them when they asked her about it. "People gone from here or buying elsewhere," she mumbled. She gave the name of the proprietor of the McClure Arms as a recommendation of a place to stay.

"Damaris Page?" Richard asked when the entered the shoddy place.

"It is," the woman replied loudly, as if there were a large group of them. She tipped the narrow brim of an extravagant, oversized hat, a few of the decorative feathers on it wavering as she did so. Elizabeth diverted her eyes from the woman's low cut, loose blouse. It did a poor job of covering her immense, flopping breasts and forearms. "Well, go ahead and sit," Damaris commanded, flinging an arm towards a table. "Welcome to the McClure Arms." Then she flounced back to a wooden bar along one wall. Her sashaying petticoats fanned a pair of button-up shoes and Elizabeth caught sight of her ankles.

Not useful in walking any distance, thought Elizabeth as Damaris began to fill mugs, slopping much of the drink on the long counter. When she delivered the beer, Elizabeth extended a hand. "Elizabeth Fletcher," she offered.

Damaris gave her an odd look for the novelty of the gesture between women, set the mugs down, and unexpectedly joined them at the table. Her fancy underskirts rose and fell like bellows as she did so. "And you?" she asked Richard, batting her eyelashes.

"Richard Farnsworth. We're Friends," he explained. "Some call us Children of the Light. Given your name by a woman down the road."

"This is your place then?"

"Surely, surely," sniffed Damaris. She took a long swig of beer, smearing her red lips, and embarked on a one-sided dialogue. "Worked hard for it, too. For what ways are open to a poor girl? Not many." She patted Richard's arm a couple of times. "Suppose you've heard that those Parliament men just voted away our hunting rights. . . . We do poach, though." She smirked like a naughty child. "Quaker, are you then? Not inclined to poach, I expect." She swiveled to Elizabeth. "No lace or buttons at all?" She fingered one of Elizabeth's plain cuffs and then touched her stiff black bonnet.

"'Tis that our inward life is more important than our outward one," Elizabeth countered softly.

"I see that," Damaris chuckled sarcastically. She swung her mug up and took another swig. "I've had a few of yous come through," she burped. "Most want to exchange a night in the barn for workin'. Polite enough, but don't drink more than a mug or two. Hardly buy nothing for grub." She leaned in as if she thought they knew a secret. "Seems to be more and more of you though. What's the advantages of it?"

"The *advantages*?" Elizabeth repeated, an eyebrow raised to Richard. "Of being Friends?" He left her to it. "Well, there's a responsibility to go within and trust you'll find guidance there. To find the good in each person no matter how hard it is or what stands in your way." The words struck her as ironic, given her own condition. "When you're convinced, that is," she added weakly.

Damaris drummed her fingers on the table. "None of you around when I was a child. Beat us with a twig if we didn't stand still in church for hours and hours. I spent the time admiring the fancy clothes of them that sat in the pews." She rested her chin on a palm. "Go on, go on. . . . What was that you said, getting 'con-veen-sed'?"

"Convinced," Elizabeth repeated, pronouncing the word carefully. "It's a change that comes over a person when they believe in the ways of *Friends*." She emphasized the word.

"That everyone has 'that of God' in them," added Richard.

Damaris immediately gave him her attention. "Any person? No matter what they've done?" She tapped her lips.

"Any person," confirmed Richard. "No need to have clergy take your hard-earned money."

"Now I like that," said Damaris, scratching at her side. "And you don't have to pay for it or do special favors for the men?"

"No, no," Elizabeth assured her, her forehead lined with fatigue.

"Well, maybe one day," Damaris said finally, as if she'd better things to do. "You two sure are serious sorts, ain't you?" She rose to get their sup. "Make ideal companions for an invalid."

Chapter 24

Elizabeth and Richard arrived to Chester a couple of monotonous days later. They found their way to the home of Edward Morgan, as Thomas had directed.

The wedding the following day was a modest affair, held during a meeting for worship. No one gave anyone away. No rings were exchanged. Thomas sat beside Richard. Elizabeth sat with Lizzie. The Morgan women had fixed her clean hair up into a neat bun and her outfit was clean and mended. She seemed pleased to have Elizabeth at her side.

After a good bit of quiet, a man rose to speak. "We are, by nature, all equal and alike in power and dignity, and so it's right and good that two so identical might be together always."

Elizabeth opened her eyes to see Lizzie and Thomas rise in unison and face each other. Thomas announced that he was commanded of the Lord to take Elizabeth Leavens to be his wife. "I was assured of it in the Light," he proclaimed, should anyone doubt it. There was a poignant, intimate Silence, and then Lizzie spoke as well. "We are to support each other in our work," she said easily.

Elizabeth quietly watched the couple until a man stood, shook Thomas' hand, and asked those present to sign a paper in witness.

It was done. Thomas and Lizzie were married in the manner of Friends. Lizzie went with her husband to greet their guests and Richard went to current news from Chester Friends. Elizabeth found her way outside for some air.

As she lingered near a well-kept flower garden, a young woman about her own age, but taller and better outfitted, came over to her. She had a full, dimpled face and wore a spotless white bonnet. Her dress was forest green, the sleeves of which came only to her forearms, boldly revealing her wrists. "Elizabeth Morgan," she announced, playing with the large, starched bow of her stiff bonnet that seemed to poke under her chin. "But they call me Bette. Sounds like Betty but spelt with an 'e,'" she explained eagerly. "I'm niece to Edward Morgan. He and Thomas met in jail."

Elizabeth returned a polite smile. "Elizabeth, as well. Elizabeth Fletcher. There seemed to be a lot of us named as we are. . . . Lizzie, too, of course."

"As well I know it," agreed Bette with a laugh. She straightened the narrow, white apron that went from her waist to her shoes, contrasting smartly with her outfit. "Can't go to any function without meeting another 'Elizabeth.' My fadder says it's from Hebrew and means 'God's promise.' For surely we weren't named after Queen Elizabeth."

She's educated and well-spoken, thought Elizabeth, taking in the information "What's promised?" she wondered aloud.

"Hmm, not sure," Bette considered pensively. "Satisfaction, devotion . . ." She shrugged.

"Would you like some cake?" Elizabeth asked to change the subject. The two women went to get a slice, then sat on a garden bench to enjoy it. Bette was enthusiastic to know about Elizabeth's convincement and ministry. Still, after a while, Elizabeth excused herself to find Richard. She was feeling the fatigue of the day; the uncertainty of her next steps.

"I've some news of Edward Burrough," Richard announced immediately when the two were together again. Elizabeth held herself tightly, trying not to look too eager. "Oh, you'd be proud, if we're permitted to boast," Richard went on. "Guests to the wedding are filled with talk of our quick-witted and zealous minister."

"Not a surprise in that," smiled Elizabeth. "And travels alone?" she asked innocently.

"Sometimes with John Audland, but rumor has it that he's now with Francis Howgill, headed for Ireland."

"Ireland?" Elizabeth had never thought of the place. "Are there Irish Friends then?"

"William Edmundson is there," nodded Richard. "He's English, though. Very charismatic. Working alone and by sheer determination to establish meetings all about the north." He handed Elizabeth several copies of pamphlets he'd been given to distribute as they traveled.

Elizabeth repeated the name *William Edmundson*. Before she could ask any more about him, she was interrupted by the commotion of Thomas and Lizzie's leaving. She went to them, an animated Lizzie hugging those who were standing around her and Thomas. She seemed ready to fly off into her new and coupled adventure. "His abilities will be put to good advantage in Wales," she was saying, her arm hooking into Thomas'.

Wales? Elizabeth was caught off guard. She knew of no one working in Wales. *I'll never see her again*, she worried. When it was her turn, she gave Lizzie a careful embrace, able to feel her shoulder blades through her wedding outfit. "I give you my love, dear Lizzie . . . Lizzie Holme." She stood back to see her beaming face. "When you look at a scar from Oxford, be reminded that I'm in the world, too, and that I love you."

Lizzie pulled back. "Oh, silly goose. We'll meet again." She nuzzled into Thomas' arm. Neither of them asked her plans.

After they were off, Bette found Elizabeth again and brought her to meet her parents, Matt and Rosie Morgan. "Your bravery is admired among Friends," Matt told her straightaway. He wore a dark waistcoat over a simple linen shirt atop dark breeches and high, polished boots. Rosie sat beside him; legs demurely crossed. She had a kind, inviting face. "Let's sit for a bit, shall we?" she suggested, a hand to the front of her modest gown. "Bette, would you fetch another round of drink?"

Elizabeth was grateful for the suggestion. She was beginning to droop, both from the recent travel and the emotion of seeing Thomas and Lizzie off. She sat to the one side of Matt and Rosie on a little stone wall. They reminded her of Kelsey and Hannah Leavens — unassuming and authentic in their manner. She was happy enough to listen to their cheerful banter, telling her of their time as Seekers before they heard Thomas preach.

A carpenter and heavily involved with his guild, Matt had been arrested for repeated failure to attend church. He'd befriended Thomas in jail. "We've lots in common, Thomas and I. Both in the trades, him willing to leave the family's business to travel and preach. Inspired me."

Rosie put a hand on his knee. "We heard you that day, too. . . ." she added, trying to direct the conversation to Elizabeth. "But we couldn't find you or the others after Thomas was arrested." She adjusted the drape of scarf around her bodice. "Bette and I were already visiting Matt. We worked for the both of them to be released."

"When Richard Farnsworth came through, he helped us to organize Friends to pester the judge," interjected Matt. "Finally, we were out."

Betsy was back with the drinks, distributing the mugs. "Richard and Thomas used our horses to ride to you and Lizzie — and Thomas and Lizzie stayed with us when they returned for the wedding," she explained. "They told us some about Oxford then."

There was an awkward pause, the Morgans waiting to see what Elizabeth would say about the ordeal.

"Got plenty of room for you, if you'd want to stay in Chester," Rosie offered finally. "Our other children are married and gone. The house is rather empty."

"Our little meeting could learn much from such a seasoned Friend," Matt urged. "Thomas gone now."

Bette raised her eyebrows and beamed hopefully at her. It seemed they'd be honored to have her.

Elizabeth mulled over the proposal. Fall was almost upon them. Winter was long off. She didn't feel well enough either inside or out to go on alone in ministry. If she returned to Kendal, she'd be tempted to stay there and she didn't want that.

When Richard was told, he seemed much relieved. "You're in capable hands," he said to the fifteen-year-old. He put a hand on Matt's shoulder. "Gives me peace of mind to know you're with this fine family of Friends and have Rosie and Bette to help with your healing."

Elizabeth was familiar with the goings on at the Morgan farm. With each day, she felt more at ease and began to assist with the milking.

"I could make some salve from nettles to lessen that scar," Rosie offered one afternoon as the two sat with Bette shelling peas. "I've dried fennel and feverfew from the summer, too."

Elizabeth nodded her permission. "You'd enjoy my Auntie and Lizzie's ma, Hannah," she suggested. "Well-versed in herbs." She told about the women and their relatives oft accused of being witches.

Over the next months, as the colors outside dulled and the first leaves fell, Elizabeth and the various members of the Morgan family learned more about each other. Elizabeth told of the circumstances surrounding her birth, her Da's leaving and his death in the War, and about the families at the farmstead. She shared about Moe coming to live with them, too. By flickering fire light and in the heavy scent of tallows, Matt, Rosie, and Bette told of their convincements and how important Meeting was to them. They told of the risks they took to try, as others, to be examples, models, as was the way of Friends.

It's good to be among them, Elizabeth decided. *Almost like family*. There were days when she was able to walk with Matt out to the sheep and watch them for a bit, her breath visible in the cold air. Her monthly returned and she put some weight on.

It was about the time of the first snow, when the dancing students wouldn't leave her, that Elizabeth finally confided to Rosie that she was plagued more by an unyielding misery in her heart than by the receding ache in her belly. "I struggle to find that of good in the ones who hurt me in Oxford," she explained, worrying one thumb with the other as she sat with Rosie and Bette on a gray afternoon. "I work to find the Light within them, but, but I can't," she choked. "How can I go on in service if I can't believe the Light shines on them? How can I talk of peace among others if I can't find it in myself?" There. She'd told them. Her secret was out. In the creak of the beams and the grumble of the wind, she heard the whispers of the college lads mocking her.

For long hours, Elizabeth sat by the fire or walked about the property, thinking of Christ on the cross and the inner revelation of his death. She longed to find the power within and be lifted, as Christ had been, to a new and different purpose, to find a way out of her self-absorption. *If I could but give myself over to that power, that is the resurrection*, she thought. After all, she'd known that preaching would come at a price. Hadn't she been told of Mary Fisher's public whipping before she herself was scarred from it? Hadn't Jane Waugh given her detailed descriptions of how Anne Askew had been martyred, of how her sister had been molested? It had been those tellings that had fueled her desire to be the first to preach in Oxford. *But did Mary Fisher and Dorothy Waugh feel ruined and ashamed, lost and unsure?*

"You're not yourself as yet," consoled Rosie, interrupting the whirl in her head.

"'Tis only been a few months," whispered Bette earnestly. She twisted the ring she wore, nervous to give her opinion.

Elizabeth considered Bette's fresh face, her innocence reminding her of how she'd felt "before."

"Can you not give yourself this respite? This time with us to heal in all manner?" asked Rosie earnestly. "No worries for a while of where you'll eat and sleep."

Elizabeth slowly wagged her head. *How would it ever be so?* "Perhaps," she allowed. She crossed her arms across her chest, rubbing her sleeves as if she was again without them.

"You have a right to feel angry," Rosie tried. "Go into it and let it have its say."

Elizabeth met her eyes, wishing the face were Auntie's. For a moment she was on an inner trail, disoriented. "Perhaps I did something to deserve it," she mumbled. "Perhaps I'm too ruined, too impure now for the work. . . ." Her stomach churned.

"You did as you were led," said Rosie firmly, tilting towards her and fixing on her eyes. "Accepted what was asked of you with your whole being and went forward into it."

"Those boys groped me for the sport of it," Elizabeth whispered, in anger as much as shame. "Not a thought to how their hands would assault my soul, challenge my faith." She glanced at Rosie and then away again, relieved to be sharing aloud more of what was affecting her. "And now I'm unable to feel any hint of Light. It's abandoned me. . . ." She slumped back, her head hanging low to her chest. "Or I it."

She wagged her head again. "I call, I wait but I don't hear or feel that wonderful holiness. I'm empty, alone in the darkness without a way to find direction."

The room stayed very quiet. After a time, Rosie came over close to Elizabeth and took her hand. "You're healing, healing from your deepest wounds," she said softly, searching Elizabeth's eyes. "Give yourself time to be strengthened by what has occurred, to see the good of it."

Elizabeth snapped her head up. "The *good* in it?"

"We endure, Elizabeth. We pick ourselves up and go on."

When Elizabeth bit her lip, Rosie gave a little squeeze to the hand she held. "I've heard you speak of George Fox, Firbank Fell and the wonder of the 'Quaker boy, James Parnell,'" she began slowly. "What's your favorite telling?" She knew the answer.

"George Fox . . . on Pendle Hill," replied Elizabeth almost immediately.

"Yes, and why?" Rosie prodded, her voice low.

"Because . . . because people tell about the glory of his vision but not about the hardship it brought him. Good days but hard ones, too. Pelted with stones. Beaten. Jailed. Time and time again. Yet, he didn't sway off course but went on and on. Continued to do as he'd been asked." The phrases fell out of her. "Steadfast in the work. Sure in his faith."

"And do you not suspect that it often happens like that?" Rosie asked. "That anything worthwhile includes untold sacrifice?"

Elizabeth tried to absorb the query, a hand to her scar.

"Don't let the college students stop you from your leading, Elizabeth," Rosie urged. "You're strong, powerful. I've heard you. Use what has happened to connect with others . . . for you are loved, Elizabeth. You are loved, and we don't get anywhere in this world without each other."

CHAPTER 24

It was over the course of the ensuing evenings, as Elizabeth concentrated on the upward, crackling dance of the fire, that she opened herself to answers. At first, she saw only the indistinguishable mob of students and professors, hot and quick. She wanted them to be remorseful and tormented by what they'd done. But then, as winter wore on and the licks of flame jumped, she saw the ghost lads and the constables and the man with the whip — separated. She began to surround each attacker with a white shield of healing, holy Spirit, moving the heat of the fire into each one as she'd once brought the blue sky above the River Kent into her own aching self. She soothed each person, listing as many as she could remember, and asking each of them to accept her ministry that day. She began to pair a flame with a loved one — a lonely, ostracized lad with Moe, a tall constable with Thomas, the Vice Chancellor with Auntie, the mayor with Rosie. She herself held the hand of the woman in the graveyard.

"You seem at peace, Elizabeth," Rosie observed one evening. "And I'm glad for it. It's a lifetime's work, a thousand little moments of awakening, for the desperation and doubt to vanish." She leaned over and hugged the preacher into the crook of her neck. "Trust holy Spirit. Way will open."

It was the next morning Elizabeth raised her head abruptly after worship and asked Bette if she'd like to serve as her companion to Ireland. "Should it be the way of things, perhaps you'd consider accompanying me?" she asked with a smile, ready, finally, to resume.

Bette was delighted, Matt and Rosie thrilled. "We might individually, and with our Friends, worship on it," advised Matt, but Elizabeth could see his willingness. "I'd pay a coach to get you to Kendal if you were wanting to see your loved ones there before you go."

Chapter 25

It took but three days to bump and jostle up the rough trail Elizabeth and the others had walked for more than a week almost a year earlier. The coach Matt found for hire had seen better days. The benches were hard, the compartment tight, and there were small holes in the weather-beaten roof. Still, Elizabeth was happy not to be walking or riding a horse. The driver seemed kind enough. He gave them blankets to cover themselves before climbing up above the front wheels to direct the four-horse team.

They passed through Frodsham, Warrington, Newton, Wigan, and Preston all in one day, stopping only to deliver and retrieve mail, to eat, and for visits to whatever privy was available. The horses were changed out in Lancaster where the driver and the women spent the night in an inn. Bette complained about the quality of the food and the lumpy bed, but Elizabeth was grateful for the hospitality. She wasn't thinking as clearly as usual and seemed to have the sniffles. By the time they were through Buron, Preston Patrick — where Edward had given her one of his reading lessons — and then to Oxenholme, she was wiping at her nose constantly. Her belly ached, too. There was nothing wrong with her heart, though. It beat faster and faster with anticipation as they approached Kendal.

The driver left them off in front of Moot Hall, not wanting to brave the narrow muddy ruts that barely continued north. Bette rented them a horse with money her Da had given her and they rode together sidesaddle past the Fleece Inn, through the Serpentine Woods, and out to the farmstead.

"Auntie?" Elizabeth puzzled when she saw a bent figure raking in Hannah's yard. She wiped at her nose. A willow of a child, golden hair long and floating behind her, came running towards her. *Moe? Indeed!* No longer at all frail but taller, stronger, she bounded like a jackrabbit towards her.

Bette helped her to dismount just as the child reached her and Elizabeth and Moe clung tightly to each other, Moe squealing in her odd way. Then her hands began to fly, the meaning of the signs lost to Elizabeth in their newness and rapid succession. When the child finally stopped, Elizabeth crossed her arms over her heart slowly and then put a finger on Moe's chest. "LOVE, LOVE YOU," she smiled solemnly.

"LOVE YOU," Moe repeated, wiggling her torso back and forth and laughing. She kept her fists snug in place, LOVE, LOVE, LOVE, nodding her head. YES, YES, YES. Then she broke away, jumping up and down, and snorting and gasping with the uncontainable thrill of the homecoming. She took Elizabeth's arm and, oblivious to Bette and the horse, who trailed behind them, pulled her toward the Leavenses'.

"Oh, me! Oh, Elizabeth!" Auntie exclaimed as they came closer. Her hair was grayer and she wore a blouse Elizabeth didn't recognize tucked neatly into a high-waisted skirt she didn't remember either. "'Tis a miracle!" Auntie moaned, stretching her knobby fingers out toward Elizabeth.

Elizabeth reached to take them, pulling Auntie as close as she could with Moe between them. Auntie tenderly took her beloved face and ever so gently placed a kiss on the pink scar of the whip wound.

"Auntie, Auntie," Elizabeth marveled as she tried to maneuver around Moe. She patted the top of the little head and pointed to where they'd dropped her bonnet. "HAT, GO," she signed, the gestures coming easily back to her. When Moe left her, Elizabeth introduced Bette.

Kelsey came running from the barn, seizing up Elizabeth. His whoop brought Hannah tumbling out the cottage door.

"Welcome home, Elizabeth! Welcome home!" she cried. She introduced herself gaily to Bette "And this is Kelsey . . . Leavens. And Moe." Back with the hat, Hannah took her hand so she'd let Elizabeth be for a while.

Tipping and swaying like drunks, everyone kissed everyone. "Good to be here!" Bette laughed. Elizabeth could see she was caught up in the gaiety. Kelsey left the clamoring huddle to take the horse from her and tie it.

"We came from Chester by coach!" explained Elizabeth. "Took only three days," she marveled. "Driver was afraid to risk coming out this way." She sniffed loudly, a hand to her nose, and glanced across the lane. A pricking sensation went down the back of her neck. There were no fowl strutting about the cow barn but she saw sheep out beyond it. "Is there a reason you're working at the Leavens'?" she asked Auntie tentatively, her head cocked.

"Ah, word didn't reach you then?" queried Auntie. Her face fell. "Wold was only waiting for his excuse to reclaim the Fletcher property after the group of you left. Said you and Lizzie had quite forgot your place, going off with unmarried men. Quakers at that," she quoted.

"Took whatever they wanted," Hannah interjected. "Come, let's sit, and Jane can tell you." She pointed Bette to a bench.

Moe climbed up on Elizabeth as she sat down, wiggling around until she straddled her lap facing her. She gently patted Elizabeth's scar and shook her head, her lip pushed out.

"But we were able to stock some of the vegetables and apples away in *our* root cellar," explained Kelsey, trying to lighten the insult. He stroked the horse and then came back to the women.

"They made sure I wasn't able to sell whatever I had extra in the market and harassed anyone who tried to sell to *me*,"

Auntie continued when Moe was still and she thought Elizabeth was listening again. "It wasn't long after that a constable confiscated almost the entire garden harvest. Clearly in league with Wold. . . . My debts amassed when I couldn't sell my vegetables and apples, and Wold demanded I move out in exchange for his new, trumped up taxes. What could I do? Only worse for all of us out here if I argued with him."

Moe opened and closed her mouth soundlessly, pretending she was a part of the conversation.

"Faced it with dignity, she did," added Hannah, looking fondly to Auntie.

"Oh, I'm so sorry to hear it," Elizabeth murmured, her belly uncomfortable with Moe's weight on her lap. She peeked again at the cottage she'd grown up in. "Your cross to bear because of me."

"Ah, and the fines continue," Hannah sighed, "for they know us to be Friends now." She gazed out at the greening folds of the hills and the grazing sheep. "There's a fair number now in Kendal. Folks have rallied around us to assist when they can."

Moe poked a stubby finger into Elizabeth's chest. "YOU," she signed, competing for Elizabeth's attention. She traced the scar with a finger and then drew her thumb down her own cheek. "YOU SCAR YOU," she signed. She repeated the whole sequence and gave Elizabeth her impish grin.

"Moe has a name for me," Elizabeth realized. "Scar-on-face." She gingerly put a thumb to the spot and moved it down the length of the wound. "ELIZABETH?" She raised her eyebrows and held them there. Then she touched a finger to her breasts. "ME?"

Moe grinned. She lifted a fist to mimic the movement of her head. "YES."

"ELIZABETH LOVE YOU," sighed Elizabeth, using the new gesture. She hugged the gift of a girl. "YES," she copied. "ELIZABETH LOVE YOU, YES." She pushed the child slightly back and examined her. "She looks so well. Smells so good."

"We've been well cared for," Auntie assured her. She smiled over to Bette and nodded several times to confirm it.

"Ah, well. Jane's like a sister to us," Hannah granted. "Never ignores a job needs doing."

"So we live here now," Auntie announced, as if it wasn't obvious. "And hope they don't confiscate the harvest or animals on *this* farm, too."

"We've moved Queenie and the fowl to our barn," said the kind-hearted Kelsey. "To at least give the thieves a bit of a challenge," he tried to joke. He didn't seem worried to Elizabeth, just the same good man, modest in his protection of them.

"I go over to the stump you love every morning to worship," Auntie said solemnly. "You've been held, dear one."

"And that one here's been a *big* help," Kelsey grinned, his eyes loving on Moe. "We need her, too. Any farmhand who asks about work out this way tells us they're threatened with jail. It's only us three to do it — ah, four."

Moe saw him watching her and giggled.

"What kinds of things does she know now?" Elizabeth asked, beginning again. She guessed Moe helped in all the ways she had herself when she'd been six or seven — fetching water from the well, gathering eggs, sweeping, learning to milk. She rubbed at her temple for the dull throbbing starting up there.

"She seems like such a smart little girl," offered Bette.

"Oh, she is," agreed Auntie. "Can learn most anything, though at least some in Kendal say her soundless chattering and the odd sounds that come out of that perfect little mouth are proof she's a witch. Can you imagine? This sweet girl?" She reached to tussle Moe's hair.

"The ministers are as daft as ever," Hannah agreed. She scrutinized Elizabeth. "They tell us that Moe's state is a punishment. Say it's on account of sinful parents. Don't want her in church but then badger your Auntie for not attending."

Auntie dipped her chin to confirm the contradiction. "Call her an imbecile and say she can't be educated."

"Not that she'd ever have the chance," Elizabeth scoffed, her voice gravelly. "Oh, Auntie!" she burst out. "I can read now . . . and write some, too."

"Learned in a jail cell?" It was Mary Fisher's story.

"No, no, a bit from Edward Burrough when we rested in the afternoons when we left here. Then from others along the way. A kind man in Birmingham gave me ink and a quill." She caught Bette's eye — willing her not to mention the reading she'd done while recovering at the Bettrises' house. "And Bette and I have been at it this past winter."

"Oh, child," Auntie cut her off. "You're shivering. Let's get you two inside."

In the next days, it seemed to Elizabeth that the wind found its way through every chink in the door and windows. Her mind filled with overly complicated bits of information and stories, but when she tried to tell of them, she'd forget her point. She was so chilled that her teeth rattled and her cough worsened. She rubbed constantly over her belly for how it bothered her.

Sometimes after a fitful nap she'd tell Bette of her constant dream. Her essence was in the center of a great bird. She remembered the feel of the huge, broad, angulating wings as she flew high above the countryside.

"Are you searching for Lizzie . . . or Edward?" Bette guessed, trying to be helpful.

After a week of struggle, Bette couldn't get her to dress in the morning, Elizabeth only wanting to lie limp, curled in a fetal position on the bed they were sharing. Her pallid face shone with sweat and she was warm to the touch.

Moe invented a sign for "SICK," touching her forehead with the fingers of one hand and her tummy with the others. Then she flicked them forcefully out, as if she could whisk the discomfort away. Like a loyal dog, she spent long hours lying beside her hero, Elizabeth rolling her head back and forth on the pillow, seeking a cool spot. She saturated sheets with her sweat.

"No . . . no . . . leave me be," Elizabeth sputtered, protesting the herbal drinks and cooled soups that Auntie and Hannah tried to force down her sore throat during the short periods she was awake. She covered her colorless lips when Bette tried to spoon watery broth in her mouth and wouldn't keep a cool cloth on her burning forehead. When Bette emptied the bed pan of urine, the liquid was the color of acorn squash.

Elizabeth's coughing fits and cries disturbed everyone's sleep. Even Moe, who wouldn't leave her bedside, was awakened by the violence of her tossing. Pretending to understand Elizabeth's infrequent gestures, vague and incomprehensible, she'd pull an adult into to room and over to her. "ELIZABETH SICK. ELIZABETH HOT. SICK," she'd sign, as if they were unaware.

About a week later, Bette came into the back room to change from the clothes she'd worn to the market and found Auntie with Elizabeth. She was sitting up in bed, pale, her hair matted, but she was alert and talking. "Oh, Elizabeth. Better?"

"Fever broke, cough's less severe," reported Auntie. "Telling me of Ireland."

"Head not so foggy," added Elizabeth, her voice raspy.

Bette came to sit on her bed. "Heard word of Mary Fisher from Friends in Kendal," she offered.

"She's not in Dublin, is she?" quipped Elizabeth, straining a bit.

"No, no, we'll have the place to ourselves," Bette chuckled, glad for the humor. "She's sailed for the colonies, funded by Margaret Fell's Kendal Fund." She watched Auntie put a veined hand to Elizabeth's cool forehead and tenderly smoothed back her hair.

"I should write Swarthmoor Hall for the same," decided Elizabeth. She asked to dress, telling them she was hungry. The next afternoon she went outside and the day after that she walked with Moe across the lane to the Fletchers' old vegetable garden. Each successive day she improved in stamina, appetite, and desire. She went down to the Holmes' place and told Thomas' parents all she knew about their son. It was hard to read Charles' expression, guarded as he was, but Jennifer didn't hide her relief in knowing Thomas and Lizzie were alive, married, and preaching in Wales.

Bette and Elizabeth began to repair their travel clothes. The Kendal fund bought them a horse and they began to ride around the farmstead for short stretches. "GO HORSE," Moe signed when she saw Kelsey bring the gelding out of the barn. She used a reverse of her sign for 'come' to indicate 'go' and two fingers tapping on either side of her head like ears for 'horse.'

"HORSE GO, YES. ME. ELIZABETH. ME. ELIZABETH. ME GO HORSE." She strung the gestures together, the meaning clear.

The girl's antics pulled Elizabeth into acquiescing. Kelsey

would lift Moe up and she'd insist on holding the reigns, grinning ear to ear, as they went for a cautious ride down the lane a bit and back again.

Moe wasn't so pleased when on a bright, sunny day, she watched Kelsey lead the horse from the barn and went over to it for a ride. She took one look at Bette and Elizabeth's traveling outfits and packed bundles and started yelling.

"ELIZABETH, NO, NO, NO," Moe complained, stomping in place. "NO GO. NO GO." She clamped her eyes shut, her face red with anger.

"What's all the fuss?" Auntie asked, coming to where Elizabeth was unsuccessfully trying to appease the child. She knelt down. "YES," she countered, calmly. She wiped at the tears that streaked down the sad little face. "ELIZABETH GO. YES." She stood up again, took the girl's hand, and pointed down at the ground in front of her and then to herself and Moe. "HERE. ME. YOU. We'll stay right here and be fine." The message was as much for Elizabeth as for Moe.

Kelsey fastened the women's bags and then held the reins as each of the women stepped up on the block and squeezed into each other on the saddle. Elizabeth gestured down to Moe from her perch. "YOU LOVE AUNTIE. YOU LOVE HANNAH, KELSEY. YES. YES." She pointed to each of them. "ME ELIZABETH, LOVE YOU," she signed tenderly as she leaned back into Bette to reference herself. "Farewell, farewell," she called as she and Bette rode away.

Chapter 26

Elizabeth was only in mild discomfort as the women trotted toward what had been called "Swarth Moor" for almost a hundred years. She couldn't figure out why her grave marker injury hurt on some days and not others, but she was encouraged that the distance to the manor was short and Bette had agreed to go with her to Ireland. By late afternoon the women were riding through Ulverston. Not long after that they spied the dour outline of Swarthmoor Hall. It sat high on a mound of grass and shrubs.

Larks sang as they rode through the gate of the property, Elizabeth craning to survey the three full stories, each with its own row of glass windows. A polite boy came out from the barn to take the horse and then Elizabeth and Bette followed a little lane between the garden beds to the elegant pebble-dashed manor. The luxury of the place was intimidating.

Margaret Fell herself opened the carved wooden door when Elizabeth knocked. She was Bette's height but heavier, with neat brown hair swept up in a bun. "Greetings," the grand woman welcomed them. She offered her hand, adorned with a single, gold wedding band, for a handshake to each. "We've been expecting you," she said warmly as she closed the iron latch behind them. "Come. This way," she invited. Her skirts, plentiful and of quality linen, swished as she moved down the long hallway, ushering Elizabeth and Bette into the front room.

We're lucky to have her among us, thought Elizabeth as she surveyed the parlor. It was a large space, neat, but not fussy, with a flagstone floor, stone fireplace, and a grandfather clock as its centerpiece. The Fell daughters were strewn about like fall leaves, the four older ones dressed in somber-colored dresses, all of the same design, with plain collars and simple lines. The younger ones were in undecorated white smocks. They all gazed up in unison at Elizabeth and Bette as the women entered the room, their faces lit amber by the afternoon light that came through the stained-glass windows. The whole of the scene completed the picture Elizabeth had imagined, a pious family, welcoming of traveling Friends.

The children began to introduce themselves: young Margaret, the oldest, then Bridget, Isabel, and Sarah. Mary was but a little girl, Suzanne younger yet, and Rachel, a toddler. "Our brother is with his tutor," the young Margaret explained, as she rose and came to them. She guided them to two elegant red velvet chairs, the air puffed with a perfumed smell as she did so. "That's where George Fox usually sits," she pointed as Elizabeth sat down in one. Bette took the other.

"Tea for our guests, please," Margaret Fell instructed a servant as she seated herself on a nearby short sofa, a sewing basket near its leg. She placed gold-rimmed spectacles on the bridge of her nose and picked up a rumpled dress. She was replacing brightly colored buttons with less attractive ones. "Tell us about yourselves."

Elizabeth complied, giving an abbreviated version of her life before her convincement, how it was when Edward Burroughs and then George Fox came, and some of the more interesting parts of the walk from Kendal to Oxford. When the servant girl returned with a tray of delicately painted, porcelain teacups, she sipped at hers for a moment, trying to decide what to say next. She continued then, talking of Lizzie's courage in Oxford.

Margaret interrupted her. "She's displeased me," she scowled.

"How so?" asked Elizabeth, the veins in her neck stiffening

with the change in the woman's disposition. Images of Lizzie, beaten and whipped floated in her mind's eye.

"She shouldn't have married. 'Tis not the work she was sent to do," came the hard retort, "but to be above the need for human love. She and Thomas Holme off now, singing their way through Wales, and writing for funds to buy shoes, a bonnet, stockings — breeches for Thomas."

"Lizzie is a most earnest minister in Truth," Elizabeth defended. "Excellent in her preaching. She wouldn't ask if there wasn't need." She sipped nervously at her tea again, trying to calm herself, her eyes on the matron over the rim of the fragile cup.

"We thought as much," interjected young Margaret. She smiled warmly at Elizabeth. "It's that the meetings in Wales are new and unable to support the couple as yet is all. I sent the money." She sat back, eyeing her mother.

"The Holmes won't disappoint," Elizabeth assured them both. "Lizzie was a loyal companion, sturdy as Mary Fisher, Anne Audland, Mabel Camm, Dorothy and Jane Waugh, and others unknown to me. Valiant sisters all."

"God put no difference between male and female," Margaret announced, then attended to a button for a moment. "Tellings of women, as well as men in the Bible. Does the verse not read, 'I will pour out my Holy Spirit upon all flesh; *your sons and your daughters* shall prophesy?'"

"Yes, yes it does," Bette answered. If she was intimidated by the matron, she gave no evidence of it. When Elizabeth started to cough, she flicked her eyes subtly at her, trying to let her know she wouldn't say anything about her recent illness. She knew Elizabeth wanted to be seen as she'd been in the last days before Oxford — a confident preacher, filled with faith and vitality.

A hired man was shown into the room and came hastily to

the senior Margaret's side. He bent to her ear and Elizabeth heard "struggling calf" and "immediately" as their hostess stood and followed him out.

"She manages a great deal here . . . and in Ulverston as well," offered Bridget. She checked with her older sisters as if asking for permission to speak. The young Margaret smiled warmly in return and then rose, returning to her place with the large family Bible. She positioned it across her lap and began to thumb through it, the other children turning to her attentively.

Elizabeth supposed the late afternoon reading was a family habit, transitioning the flock of them from their distractions to a thoughtful time before the evening meal. She relaxed back on the cushioned red chair and listened attentively to the lilt of young Margaret's voice as she read from Psalms and then the New Testament. Elizabeth found her faith in the phrases, more poignant to her now than when they'd been read during the dull steeple house services of her youth.

Chapter 27

Elizabeth and Bette met the only son of Margaret and Judge Fell, thirteen-year-old George, when he and his tutor came loudly into the richly paneled dining room with its massive table and sparkling chandelier. Elizabeth had never been so close to such fine clothes. George wore an elegant, dark blue velvet suit and hip boots with shiny silver buckles. Will Canton, the tutor, wore a pressed linen shirt, satin breeches, and polished heeled shoes. She recalled that Edward had said he'd been the one to first tell George Fox of Swarthmoor Hall and the Fells.

Maybe fifteen? she guessed of Will as the lads set their hats — Will's a flat, floppy affair and George's velvet and plumed — onto the massive sideboard that occupied one of walls. George seated himself at the head of the table, Judge Fell out of town. Will pulled out the ornate, high-backed, spindle chair next to Elizabeth and gave her a kind greeting as he slipped into it. He'd just begun to inquire about her travels when Margaret came back into the room. She reminded the children to hold their chat for the silence before the meal, but George ignored her. He loudly bellowed what Elizabeth assumed was the former family grace, and his mother didn't reprimand him.

Three servant girls brought great bowls of pottage to the nine of them. The rich concoction of bacon, jelly and egg was new to Elizabeth. This was followed by individual salads of mixed cooked and raw vegetables — leeks, onions, radishes, and cabbage — all of it on matching china plates with a simple, blue swirl on the rim as decoration. Elizabeth demurely watched Bette unfold her napkin and choose from the several pieces of silverware as they waited to see how the older Fell daughter, seated across from them, would begin eating. After two platters of freshly sliced ham, topped over with boiled carrots and herbs were set at each end of the table and the beer was poured, the servant girls took places at the table as well and joined in the conversations around them.

Elizabeth picked up her exchange with Will. He was a serious but friendly lad, happy to answer any question she had, but also interested in her work, too. Still, it wasn't long before George competed with her for his tutor's attention, not wanting talk of Friends around him. Elizabeth turned to Bette rather than to try to rival him and talked quietly with her until the end of the meal. Then Margaret and one of the servants took the littlest children off for bed and she and Bette were directed along with George and Will to a sitting room for dessert.

Elizabeth let the enormity of her meal settle, wrapped in contentment as chatter filled the room. A dessert of yogurt was served and when it was finished and the servants had collected up the bowls, the Fell daughters took up knitting or mending.

"You feel the need to fix that skirt, do you?" George chided Bridget, interrupting Elizabeth's serenity. "For you can certainly afford a new one."

His sister pretended not to hear him. "He's saying it for my thrift," she informed Elizabeth and Bette, loud enough for him to hear. "He's not of the faith."

Elizabeth didn't comment. Apparently, family relations could be strained when some were convinced and others not, no matter one's station in life. Had it not been so for George Fox himself, Thomas Holme, Edward Burrough, Richard Farnsworth and James Parnell? There were as many tellings of divided households as there were of convincements of whole families. She counted herself, Lizzie and Bette, too, lucky to have the support of their loved ones.

The elder Margaret re-entered the room and came to sit by Elizabeth, gazing fondly at her son and Will as they sat by the fire. "Will Caton will soon travel to Holland," she remarked as she sat down.

"The first," Will said when he heard his name. "A preacher in my own right."

Elizabeth turned to Margaret. "Is it you who decides where to direct Friends and to send them in waves?" asked Elizabeth. "For it works well, to have first some go and then others visiting after them — watering the new growth."

"Watering the new growth? I like that," Margaret smiled. "Sometimes, yes, I suggest who might join another. George Fox and I confer, although more often Friends preach where they are led. As you to Oxford."

"Yes. Lizzie Leavens and I to Oxford, surely," agreed Elizabeth. She thought back on it. "George asked us to consider our first travel to Chester, but we sat in Silence to season the idea of Oxford." She rubbed a palm down her skirt. "Would you tell of when George first came here?" she asked politely.

"Well . . ." Margaret collected her thoughts. "Will had given him directions knowing I enjoyed hosting interesting guests."

"It was thundering and lightning the night he came," Will jumped in, his eyes dancing. "When I opened the door to him, water was dripping mightily off that wide-brimmed hat he wears."

"Addressed us as commoners," interjected young George with a huff. "Though I'd have thought that he'd have known better from the grandness of our manor. When Will commented on the torrents of rain he'd come through, he said that he was 'surely in *the power of the Lord*.'" George gave the quote a sarcastic twist.

"He'd preached at Firbank Fell not long before it, yes?" Bette asked. She knew the telling from Thomas Holme.

"That he had. He spoke of it to my daughters that night," explained Margaret. "I was out, but the next morning he told me how he'd stood up on the ridge, so many gathered below, and he repeated much of what he'd preached. I was so touched by his words that I invited him to our little St. Mary's in Ulverston. 'Tis just down the road. He agreed to it for the next Sabbath and came when the service was ending — the law allows that. He stood among us, saying, 'Christ is the Light of the world, shining on every person.'"

"Our priest, Lampitt, tried to stop him," explained young Margaret, "but mother, mother gave him but a glare and he was at it no further."

"He called our attention to Lampitt then." Her mother took back the telling. "Called him 'a hireling,' serving for mercenary motives." She clasped her hands tightly and held them to her heart. "I was much taken by his way and his words. 'You will say Christ says this and the apostles say that, but what can you say?' he asked us. 'For aren't you a child of Light and haven't you walked in the Light, receiving messages inwardly from God?' His words opened me so. I saw in them that we were all wrong in our church doings and I cried bitterly. 'We are all thieves,' I said aloud to my daughters. 'We have taken the scripture in words but know nothing of them in ourselves.'" She paused, appraising her conduct. "I oft' say, he opened us like a book that first time, a book we'd never read or heard but that was our duty to consider. I stood and turned to him, asking him to say more . . ."

"You're allowed to speak in the steeple house?" interrupted Elizabeth, thinking the matron had risked arrest for it.

"Yes, yes, of course," chided Margaret. "I've oversight for the physical and spiritual welfare for my children, servants, and the local poor. I own the dairying and iron smelting businesses in Ulverston. None would protest my speaking." The candid retort was given without boast. "And on that day, that glorious day, George Fox touched me to core," Margaret finished. "His words made me weep."

"He made *me* ashamed I'd done so little with my life," young Margaret blurted.

"No, no, no," protested Elizabeth. "You care for Friends who seek your hospitality and your letter writing is a ministry in its own right. I know the truth of it from my own experience." She caught young Margaret's troubled eyes. "It's important work that you do, conveying and recording the stories and sufferings. Your descriptions encourage Friends all over England; tell us of the work of others. Truly. Your letters are kept and read over and over. Years from now, they'll inspire your little sisters, too — unaware now in their childhoods of the doings of the first Friends."

"I feel compelled to write," young Margaret relented, accepting Elizabeth's authority on the matter. "To put our doings into words — and to mark especially our experiences as women." She swallowed. "A voice comes up in me often. 'Write,' it says. 'Write.'"

"Then you must obey," said Bette solemnly.

A servant came to into the room and to young Margaret then, and who turned from Elizabeth and Bette to speak to her. They whispered to each other and then young Margaret shooed the young maid toward the staircase. She faced Elizabeth again.

"When George Fox came that day into the steeple house, he was so bold and sure. I felt my soul moved, moved deeply, when he spoke. My tears were steady and my heart beat so fast. My sisters were bewitched as well. It was a gift he gave, as a man to a woman, but a gift more becoming than pretty words or meadow flowers." She flattened her fingertips into her cheeks and gave her head a little shake. "When we walked outside with him and gathered around, he looked each of us over in his powerful, overwhelming love and told us to 'mind the Light in your conscience.' Then he left us, no word of where he was headed."

"That night, we began regular worship — in this very room," added the senior Margaret.

"And all attended?" asked Bette.

"Not William — and my husband wasn't home — but everyone else of our household, and a few of the neighbors who were in church that morning."

"Wasn't but a few days later, different neighbors came to us with their concerns of it," sighed Bridget.

"They heard of our silent worship; our attempts to remember to address the servants as equals and asking them not to use titles with us," explained Margaret. She stopped and looked carefully at Elizabeth. "You're exhausted, aren't you, dear? We've carried on so."

Young Margaret rose abruptly, as if commanded. She kissed her mother's cheek, said goodnight to her sisters, then asked Elizabeth and Bette to follow her. "Come, let me show you upstairs to your rooms." She took up a candle in its pewter holder and led them to the stairs.

No rushlights here, thought Elizabeth as she and Bette bid the other Fells "good rest" and dutifully trailed after young Margaret. She started up the stairs, considering the large, oil portraits that hung above them in the shadows, and running her hand briskly over the edges of the books shelved in the case on the first landing.

Young Margaret noticed. "Would you like to pick one tomorrow to take with you? Or a tract by Hester Biddle?" she urged. "Do you know of her?"

Elizabeth and Bette said they didn't.

"Oh, my goodness. She's so prolific," marveled young Margaret. "Writes that she found peace when she joined with Friends. And 'woe to Oxford and Cambridge for their financial and ideological domination,'" she quoted. "Suffered at least six arrests that we know of . . . beaten and imprisoned for preaching in public in defiance of the law. Continues to produce a string of pamphlets. 'We are not like the World,' she advises in one of them, 'who must have a minister to interpret the Scriptures to them. . . . We Friends, we have the Lord speaking to us in our own language and we hear him perfectly." Young Margaret paused, catching herself with her ramblings. "She was convinced by Edward Burrough," she finished, indicating that they should continue down the second-floor hallway.

Elizabeth halted. "Edward Burrough? Have you any news of him?"

"Ah, Elizabeth, he's a weighty one, isn't he?" teased young Margaret. "And but my same age. Clever. Have you heard of him in London at the wrestling match?"

"No," Elizabeth allowed softly, trying not to sound too eager.

"Francis Howgill wrote to us of it, that London was full of pious people, teeming with all sorts of religious ideas. . . ."

Elizabeth tapped at her leg impatiently. She knew these things.

"A large crowd of them were at the match and the wrestlers had finished. Edward made his way into the ring. Of course, people assume it was a challenge to the winner. . . ."

Elizabeth smiled weakly. She could see his handsome face before her.

"But it was a ruse," whispered young Margaret, her voice low and mysterious. "So that he could preach — and he was so effective and persuasive that they left him to it, the champion wrestler included."

"Remarkable," Bette snickered.

"A keen mind and a ready tongue," agreed young Margaret, matter of factly. "It's said Edward Burrough is responsible for the conversion of thousands in London. One of the best loved Friends."

"He is that," agreed Elizabeth.

"Come, let me show you your rooms," directed young Margaret, dropping Bette off at the first door. From where she stood, Elizabeth couldn't see much into it. There was a poster bed, the mattress of it held above the floor by a web of ropes, a nightstand with a lit candle. She supposed a servant had already been there. "You'll find a chamber pot under the bed," young Margaret whispered to Bette, Elizabeth grateful for the knowing. "Just replace the lid when you're finished and we'll deal with it in the morning."

She gestured to Elizabeth to follow her down the hall. "And this is where you'll sleep." She entered another candlelit chamber. It, too, was a practical room, with a small bed and nightstand. Elizabeth spied a mug of malt and noticed rose petals floating in the bowl on the table positioned along one wall.

Young Margaret set her candle by the one already flickering on the nightstand. "You'll sleep here." She patted the curtained bed. Elizabeth sat down beside her and let Margaret rub her back, telling her more of Edward and his companion, Francis Howgill. They'd been arrested after the wrestling match, sentenced, and allowed to go alone through the busiest streets of London, from Newgate to Bridewell, trusted with no keeper to arrive at the cells.

"It's our way," said Elizabeth soberly. She wondered if their lives were something of a game to the wealthy, inexperienced young Margaret who had plenty to eat, wore nice clothes, always slept inside, and certainly had never been arrested for a night in a stinking cell. She suspected she knew nothing of the dangers the rest of them faced.

"I have a surprise," tittered young Margaret, sliding off the bed and pointing to a partially hidden tub on the other side of the bed. "One has been readied in Bette's room, too." She went over to remove the cover and sprinkle lavender, rue, and rosemary stems that lay on a plate atop of nearby dresser into the steaming water. "Here, let me help you," she offered, coming back around to Elizabeth. She stepped behind her and began to untie the back of Elizabeth's traveling outfit. Elizabeth slipped off her shoes and stockings. "Step in . . . step in," young Margaret mumbled, trying to hide a gasp. A multitude of raised scars crisscrossed the pale, bent back. She stooped in excuse, hanging Elizabeth's clothes on the wall pegs.

In the moment of privacy, Elizabeth went to the tub, stepped carefully over its edge, and sunk into the warm, aromatic water. She stayed modestly bent forward until Margaret left her. Then she leaned back, letting the warm and bubbly bath overtake her.

Elizabeth soaked in the tub for a long, lazy while, letting all that had happened in the day float away. When she finally stepped out, the scents faded and the water cooled, she stood before a full-length mirror to towel dry. For the first time ever in her life, she examined her full self. "I give you this," she whispered, her eyes moving to the rafters. Then she looked again at the reflection of the sallow face and thin torso. "I give you this," she repeated. She took up the night gown that had been wrapped around a warming pan and left for her. The fine linen was the color of dust. She slipped it on, the sleeves to her wrist, the length to the floor because of her short stature. She took a sip of the malt and crawled into bed, her belly catching with the movement. She reached to the candle and snuffed it out.

The next morning over breakfast Elizabeth asked Margaret for her support. "Perhaps you might be guided to sponsor my leading . . . my continued work . . . in Ireland." Her stare was steady, her lips thin.

Margaret took no time to season the request. "We need more preachers there," she allowed. She traced the rim of her mug with the tip of her finger, took a sip, and slowly set the cup down. "The Kendal Fund will cover your horses to the port and your fare to Dublin. We'll write ahead to James Smith, a Friend. He'll let William Edmundson know, too." She gave her eldest a worried glance. "But, oh, it's a wild place."

Chapter 28

A sharp wind was howling on the day Elizabeth rode with Bette to the port near Chester. They'd decided not to stop at the Morgan farm, Bette thinking she'd find a second parting more difficult than the first and Elizabeth excited for the work in Ireland.

Elizabeth could smell the tang of salt and seaweed long before she caught sight of the ocean. *Eternity*, she thought, the white of the water merged with the pale sky, the ocean and sky one when she first saw it. She squinted at its vastness, her bonnet doing little to protect her eyes from the brightness, and stopped her horse to take it in. Then she held out her arms in the warmth of the sun. Always in the sky, aglow and consuming, even if hidden on a cloudy day. Auntie had said that. And the ocean, lapping at the edges of England, Auntie had said, too, even if Elizabeth hadn't seen it until this day. She took a jasper out of her pocket, given her for its properties of peacefulness, happiness, and completeness. "*Have faith*," she'd said. "*Listen*." She pressed the stone to her heart. Bette guided her mare up beside Elizabeth, gazing at the vastness, too.

Elizabeth was mesmerized by the frosted crests as they rolled in, soaking and darkening the sand. "*I saw that there was an ocean of darkness and death, but, too, an infinite ocean of Light and Love that flowed over.*" They were the words of George Fox when he'd been in despair. *Had he ever actually seen the ocean?* she wondered. She watched crash after crash of the replicating waves and the receding of the water on the sand. *Second chances*, she thought.

Eventually, the women guided their horses down the beach and slid off them to make their way through a swath of rounded stones, a garden of smooth, hard rows. They tied them to the jagged white limb of a bleached log that had washed high up on the sand and sat down on a smooth driftwood throne.

Elizabeth bent to untie her boots. She pressed a stockinged foot carefully into the sand and considered the imprint. *Cruelty and despair will not have the final word*, she vowed, letting the abuse disappear along with her footprint in the wind. *Oxford won't take all that I hold dearest*. No. She stood up, Bette watching her. "I will serve," she yelled into the rushing of the gusts and the thunder of the waves. "I will serve and my life will matter."

At the Port of Chester, Bette took the lead in asking dockhands about passage to Ireland. Sweat poured from beneath the caps of the men who bothered to look at her. Their pay depended on the volume of timber, flax, and rice they moved on and off the boats and they'd little time to offer suggestions to girls. Not dissuaded, the women rode to a stone wall that bordered the port area, tied the horses, and sat down to enjoy the meal the Fells had packed for them. A stocky old captain strode over their way. He was wearing a square-shaped cap, the likes of which Elizabeth had never seen before, and a red kerchief double-wrapped around his neck. "Where you headed?" he asked, regarding their plain dress.

"Dublin," Elizabeth told him, her eyes on his large gut, held with a wide black belt.

"Would ya be willin' to swap the horses for the ferrying on me boat?" he asked. "Leavin' soon though," he warned. "I could have the both of them sold, take the earnings for your fares, and give you the rest."

"How long will it take?" Bette asked.

"The horses but a minute, the sailin', well now, that depends on the wind," the captain laughed. "A couple of days at the least. . . ." He waited to see if they were going to change their minds. "Tie your tresses in braids and re-tie those bonnets tighter," he advised. "It's choppy out there. We'll be leavin' soon. Name's Cap."

Elizabeth and Bette followed him to a boat he called a dogger. It was a short, stubby fishing vessel, with high sides, a main sail and a smaller one. A much smaller open boat was attached to one side. Cap handed off the horses to another fellow for their selling.

"'Tis the bait you're smellin'," advised a young sailor, Maurice, who took their bundles. Another, Galen, held each of their hands in turn as they went from the dock to the boat on a wide board that he called a gangplank. He helped them each to step down onto what he called the "deck" and gestured toward a bench on one side of the dogger. "Port."

The women sat like nested birds, Elizabeth scrutinizing the faded and peeling paint all around her and the short, wooden patches on the sides of the little cabin that stood high in the center. The boat was more weather-beaten than the cow barn back home. She turned to watch the "deckhands" as they moved around her, attuning to their accent and the vocabulary they used. The "galley," the area for cooking, that was near to where large barrels were being rolled for loading to the "hatch." Elizabeth watched as a barrel was lifted down to where she saw only the stubby dirty fingers of another sailor from below. Still other men were busy tying down the largest bundles on the deck. The effort they put into it made Elizabeth nervous for the rough weather she imagined lay ahead.

When it was time to set sail, two men untied the boat and jumped aboard in succession. Bile rose in Elizabeth's throat as the dogger began to fight its way through the open, emerald sea, and she imagined the whole of the vessel, like some huge bird, taking flight over the waves. Tendrils of her hair blew about her face and she tried to hold down her skirts as they swelled in harmony with the wind when the boat tacked in one direction and tried to fly up from her legs when it turned in the other.

After a while Bette wanted to go exploring. She convinced Elizabeth that they should grab round each other for support and walk the deck to get their sea legs. "No, no," a young man, Michael, ordered when they stood. "Back to ye bench, out of our way."

It was late in the afternoon before some of the men set about to lower the main sail and others uncoiled a massive rope that'd lain like a giant snake on the deck. Maurice untied the lashing ropes that held a large iron anchor, and Galen stood at the ready with a hammer to release the jammer of it. Elizabeth jumped at the clang when it was dropped with a jerk to disappear in the green water.

Michael came to invite them to come closer, to watch how the men caught and stored the hake cod, eel, and pilchard herring they took in. "Was originally a Dutch name, the dogger," he explained as the men trolled. He was something like an Irish version of Will Canton, the tutor they'd just left at Swarthmoor Hall, though dressed quite differently for his work. Elizabeth found him charming. "Name was given to the trawlers that were common in the North Sea," Michael added with a sheepish grin. He pulled at the scarf he wore around his neck to protect him from the sun. Like Maurice and Galen and most of the other men, his shirt was open at the neck, his breeches loose for the work about the dogger, and he was barefoot. Elizabeth found his dirty banged up toes quite ugly and tried not to stare at them.

Sup was cooked by a man, of course — there were no women except the two of them on board. Hardly anyone ate together. The deckhands came to the galley when duty permitted and grabbed what they could.

The first night, after Elizabeth and Bette had eaten, Cap invited them to his cabin. They squished in around a little table there, a map of Great Britain loosely scrolled out before them and held in place with three heavy seashells and a pocketknife. Cap tapped on the drawing, the land colored brown and the sea blue. "This is where's we're bound." He traced the route from England to Ireland. "If there were glory days, the 40s were them," he groused, tapping the depiction of Ireland again. "When the Catholics rebelled against the English and their Protestant faith." He leaned back and held a match to his wooden pipe, waiting to see if the women were interested.

"How does the Catholic way differ from Presbyterian?" Elizabeth asked, resting her elbows on the table and tenting her fingers.

"Oh, we Catholics, whether here or in England, think the Pope grander than Christ," Cap grinned. One of his lower teeth was missing. "Love our traditions and statues at least as much as the Bible."

"The Bible *is* an important book," Bette allowed, her voice a bit of a reprimand, "but Friends believe that it's the Holy Spirit, alive and present, who inspires what is written there."

Elizabeth held her lower lip with her bite and waited for Cap to say something. She worried that he'd see a debate from them and end the session. "Know nothing of your kind," he nodded to Bette, "but if I've learned anything from all the fighting we've endured, it's that what others believe ain't nothing to me."

"Wish there could truly be an end to the warring," offered Bette humbly.

"Doesn't seem possible in Ireland," Cap sighed. "Always been fighting. Vikings at the Celtic people. English on us since the Norman invasion." Elizabeth lost some of what he was saying because of his accent but she got the gist of it. "In my younger days, I was all in, lured by the commissions and the challenge. Ya needed a skilled captain for battles at sea. In 1649, it was the Catholics against the Roundheads."

Only six years ago, Elizabeth quickly calculated. *Me ten or eleven*.

"Cromwell came over with his thousands of troops, righteous and believing himself to be called by God. Lots of shipwrecks when those vessels of yours sailed into stormy weather — your crews unfamiliar with our coasts."

Elizabeth cringed at the reference — *yours* — but she didn't interrupt him.

"We seized hundreds of ships in those years," Cap continued, waving at his puffs of smoke. "Cromwell was a genius with the cavalry but not at sea. Those who made it ashore were half froze — then massacred. We're still being punished for it — have no share in how we're governed, can't serve in Parliament."

He stood to reach for a small, dirty bag that held his tobacco. "Can't live in town or marry a Protestant — though some do in places." He gave a flimsy smile. "Cromwell came back at us with huge ships, he did." He stretched the word. "We'd never seen the likes. Brought heavy artillery. Marched his men through the settlements along the coast. Not heard of the Massacre at Drogheda?" He saw they hadn't. "Cromwell claimed he was persuaded by God to spare neither troops nor citizenry, the Royalist leader beaten to death with his own wooden leg — the Roundheads, the troops supporting Parliament," Cap explained as if they wouldn't know. "Told it hid gold. Ha! Over 3,000 killed. Not thirty escaped the whole of it."

Cap came out of his memories and scooped his pipe into the bag. He puffed rapidly as he lit a match to the bowl. "War's a wicked thing. You English seized livestock, burned villages, ravished and butchered without regard for sex or age. Called it a '*Holy War*,'" he added sarcastically.

"I'm sorry for it, Cap," Elizabeth stopped the diatribe. "But they weren't *our ships* and we didn't do those awful things. Friends work against warring, will take no part in it."

"No, no. Sorry, Miss. Of course not," apologized Cap. "I get carried away. It's that Ireland was ripped up — still is. The survivors were shipped off to Barbados as slaves to the sugar. Any Catholic clergy who were found were clubbed to death. Landowners were forced to Connacht on the west coast . . ." He tapped on the far side of Ireland on the map. "Their farms scorched." He caught her young eyes with his old ones. "Ya should know about it. Ya'll face it. Half the country has no one living on it. By 1653 we were crushed."

The year of my convincement, thought Elizabeth.

"But you've kept your faith?" asked Bette kindly.

"As much as possible," agreed Cap. "Fortified by monks who move about disguised as shepherds, cattle herders, ploughmen and the like." He extended a hand warmly to each of them, not wanting them to worry. "You'll be fine in Dublin. Mostly English there."

"I'm not sure why I'm going there, Cap," Elizabeth clasped the wrinkled hand. "Or what it is that I'm to do when I arrive." She found his small, gray eyes. "But I go as an instrument of peace."

Part IV

Ireland

1656–1658

Chapter 29

For the entire four-day voyage to Dublin, Elizabeth felt better than she had since Oxford. She thought it was the salty, cold air that cleared her thinking and she stopped wrapping her chest because, even with the constant dodging of the dogger, the pain in her belly only stabbed infrequently. She spent much of her time perfecting the knots that Michael showed her and trying to use the sailors' terminology in her exchanges.

Bette wasn't as content. She sat on the bench, nervously twisting the ring she wore and feeling unwell. Elizabeth wasn't sure if it was seasickness or homesickness that bothered her most. When Maurice, Galen, and Michael came excitedly to them, yelling that land was sighted, Bette didn't go to the bow with her where the deckhands were pointing to a faint outline of Ireland. They'd made it safely.

"Just there. Rinn-Ann," Michael hollered above the wind, pointing to a dip in the landscape. Dolphins led the way and sea gulls swooped and cawed as the dogger came into the harbor. "Look, see?" Michael pointed as they came closer. "That there's what's left of Howth Castle.

"'Tis the Liffey River there, where it dumps into the sea," Michael pointed again. Cap had told the women of it the night before. Either they could take a smaller boat up it to Dublin proper or go by land. "The weather will be colder than you're expectin'," Cap advised. "Coach will be faster," he'd said by way of his goodnight.

Next morning Michael worried over them like a brother. "If no one meets you and you're unsure," he told them as they prepared to leave the dogger, "ask to be taken to Deer Park. Was once the Earl's estate, a beautiful place. You'll find lots of English there and surely someone to help you." He handed over their bundles, stooping to make eye contact past the brim of each bonnet.

Elizabeth thanked him and extended a solemn hand to Cap. "I apologize for what my people have done to yours."

"You'd no control over it, lass," the old man replied, holding her fingers gingerly. "Never shook hands with a woman." He took his hand back and wiped it inattentively on his breeches.

"May you not be homesick," Michael grinned at Bette as he pushed the dogger away from the dock and into the awaiting current. "We graze sheep here, too, ya know. Ya'll see them on the way into Dublin."

The women stepped in turn onto the wide walkway of the jetty, Elizabeth surprised by the wobble of her first tentative steps. Their arms around each other for support, the two of them maneuvered like drunks over ropes, around crates, and toward an expanse of solid ground where the trees had been cut back to create the harbor.

"Elizabeth Fletcher? Elizabeth Morgan? Elizabeth Fletcher? Elizabeth Morgan?" an approaching voice called at them. Elizabeth found its source, a sturdy, red-head about their same age coming quickly towards them, hands waving. "Come to fetch ya," the young woman puffed, stopping in front of them. "English Friends, no?" Her green eyes sparkled like the sea and a trail of freckles was sprinkled across her nose.

"Friends, yes," Elizabeth answered cautiously. "But should we be declaring it so loudly?"

"Elizabeth Smith. Betsy, then." The robust young woman threw out a hand, ignoring her worry. "So pleased to have finally spied ya on this go of it!" She laughed gaily. "Someone had it on when they sent one Elizabeth to find two others!" Red frizzy bangs peeked out from her handsome bonnet. The harbor breeze colored her cheeks a rosy pink.

"Are we that obvious?" asked Bette.

"Two dark wrens arriving on a fishing dogger?" Betsy laughed again. "Ya." She grabbed their bundles from them without asking, one in each hand, and started up the hill. A carter came past them and stopped to ask her if she needed his assistance but she shrugged him off. "Mam and Da will be so pleased," she said to them instead.

Elizabeth and Bette followed the back of Betsy's cloak as she trudged ahead to where a line of brightly colored coaches waited. Elizabeth had only ever ridden in the raggedy, country coach from Chester to Kendal. The one Betsy flagged was elegant. It was hitched to six horses, ribbons tied in their bridles, and came with a handsomely clad driver whose black hat never tipped from his head as he took their bundles and secured them to the rooftop of the carriage.

"Climb in, misses," he welcomed, straightening his coat with its rows of shiny buttons. He turned the latch on the odd-shaped door, a window as its top half, and stood at attention, holding it for them.

"Your family is English, then?" Elizabeth asked when she was settled comfortably on the cushioned bench across from Bette and Betsy.

"Do I have an odd look about me, then?" Betsy teased as the coach started off with a jolt. "Red hair and a couple of odd expressions?" She didn't wait for an answer. "It's that my Mam is Irish but my Da keeps an English home. My brother and I were born here."

"Your Da came a long time ago then?" asked Bette.

"Ya. When he was a boy. Parents recruited along with some other weavers. Hardy folks, they were, with no strong family ties to England. Little attachment to the Crown or Cromwell."

As Betsy and Bette talked on, Elizabeth took in the

scenery out a window. She caught glimpses of the narrow, snaking path they were following alongside the River Liffey, a few men passing on horseback and another coach, passing them for the docks. There were large expanses of budding fields and she saw the sheep that Michael had promised. *Not so different from home*, she decided.

The dirt tracks turned to cobbles when they reached the gates of Dublin and, after a bumpy bit of travel, they arrived to a brick home with other similar dwellings beside it in a row. Elizabeth had never seen houses so close together. "We live round back," Betsy explained as they collected on the slim garden footage at the front. Elizabeth and Bette followed her around the side of the rectangular structure, Elizabeth craning her neck to consider the three rows of matching windows that ran across a second story.

"Mammmm," Betsy called, shooing Bette and Elizabeth through the back door. "The men will be busy upstairs with their woolen affairs," she explained as a handsome woman came towards them in the hallway. "Mam — Peggy Smith," she announced formally. "This is Elizabeth Fletcher and Elizabeth — Bette — Morgan. With us at last!"

"Welcome, girls," Peggy offered warmly. "My, three Elizabeths!" Her green eyes sparkled and she sported the same sprinkle of freckles as her daughter. She had the same striking red hair, too, hers pulled into a long, thick braid that flowed down her back. Wild curls trimmed her temples as they did Betsy's. Peggy reached to take their cloaks and shuffled them to the parlor.

It wasn't until the evening meal that Elizabeth and Bette met the men. When James Smith came stiffly to the large oak dinner table, Elizabeth didn't think he seemed 'hardy and independent' at all, but pudgy and self-consumed. He wore the tailored shirt of a businessman, linen beeches, and evenly knit stockings with a narrow top welt. When he sat down, he looked as if he were readying to preside over a meeting.

The women chose to sit all on the same side of the table and were seating themselves when Betsy's brother came in. He was tall and slender, older than Thomas Holme, Elizabeth guessed. He had his mother's fair skin and flaming red hair, with a mustache and preened beard the color of rust. He slid sullenly into a chair opposite the women and beside his Mam, barely acknowledging Elizabeth and Bette.

When he didn't introduce himself, James gave his name. *Dáibhí. David*, Elizabeth repeated to herself for the practice of it. She looked past him to a painting of his younger self with Betsy in one of the few family portraits that hung on the nicely painted walls.

James called for silence and Elizabeth settled into it. She gave thanks for their safe voyage and the Smith's hospitality. She hoped Bette would feel better. She opened her eyes to Peggy quickly touching her forehead, chest, then left and right shoulders in efficient succession.

"Sign of the cross," she explained in response to Elizabeth's stare. She left the table to serve the food.

"English Friends, then . . ." proclaimed James before Elizabeth could ask about the mix of religious practices that seemed at play. "Not many of you brave enough to come this way . . . or stay long when you do." He began cutting the wedge of ham on his plate. "Tell us about yourselves," he asked, not looking up.

Elizabeth took the lead in telling of the Kendal farmstead and of the Holmes' weaving business, thinking it'd be of the most interest to James.

"Friends, too, are they?" James asked before anyone else had a chance to comment.

"The son, Thomas Holme, definitely," said Elizabeth,

picking up a cake of oats. "Walked with Lizzie Leavens and me from Kendal to Chester. . . ."

"Not the Thomas Holme who rankled the prison guards by singing at midnight in the jail there?"

"You've heard that story?" Elizabeth asked incredulously, with a crooked smile of confusion. "But how?"

"I exchange letters with Swarthmoor. Easy enough to send messengers with our shipments of wool, silk and poplin. The Fells are much interested in our work here and have asked us to keep records of the sufferings of Friends — but it's the unusual events that are most eagerly retold across the sea."

"For who wants to read of the constant arrests for the interruptions of church services or the bore of the frequent fines for refusing to doff a hat or give a curtesy?" Dáibhí grouched.

"Thomas is married now," Elizabeth offered after an uneasy moment. "To Lizzie — Elizabeth Leavens."

"Not in a church, of course," Bette added. "In my uncle's home."

"'Tis similar for us," said Peggy. She'd returned to set the food on the table. "Neither the church nor the government recognize our love." She reached to touch her husband's hand. "We've adapted an ancient ceremony, handfasting, for our own, binding our hands with pretty twine and ribbons and saying our own vows before our community of friends."

"Acting as if it's legal," muttered Dáibhí, not looking at anyone. "Without much thought for the product of . . ."

James cut him short. "More of us than the government would like to acknowledge — English and Irish married. Plenty of mixed children about and no shame in it." He stared severely at his son. "We've carved out a good life here, Dáibhí. Let's not pretend we've suffered, shall we?" His jollity was forced.

"Well, Mum's people did." Dáibhí turned to his Mam and then glanced across the table. "You were but babes when it was happenin'. Whatever ya have suffered over there — that put that scar on your cheek," he caught Elizabeth's eyes, "it weren't nothing compared to the atrocities committed here."

Elizabeth stared down at her food, a knot at the base of her neck. *Why is he so rough with us?* She wondered if he'd somehow been caught between the two cultures, unable to find his place in them.

"That's enough now," said James sternly. "People from both sides are scarred, for the English have their complaints, too. . . ." He looked vaguely around the table. "Children forced to listen to mass when we came. People speaking Gaelic all around us, though they knew we didn't understand it."

"And your parents grabbing up land," sighed Dáibhi. He stood and stalked out suddenly.

No one said anything for a while, James taking noisy bites in quick succession to finish his food and Peggy quiet, unable to mend her son's disruption of their first meal together.

James put his napkin over his plate. "It's true that the abandoned land was offered to the adventurous English who were willing to give it a go over here," he explained finally. "The crown and then Cromwell thought we'd bring the Church faith here and their empire would be expanded. Didn't count on William Edmundson."

His expression softened Elizabeth. "Yes?" she encouraged.

"Oh, he's mighty, that William Edmundson." James snapped his fingers. "A charismatic speaker, with a reputation for sincerity and integrity, and for having the courage of his convictions. He's expected soon. Always stays here when he comes. He'll tell you all about it."

"Yes? The George Fox of Ireland?" Elizabeth raised her

eyebrows. She hadn't known whether she'd meet the preacher or not.

James rubbed at his chin and chuckled. "Yes, I supposed he's that. About the same age, with equal zeal . . . both with a mighty measure of good."

"You've known him a long while, then?" queried Bette. "William Edmundson?"

"We met in York when he was apprenticed out . . . but yes, before he joined the Army." James stood, his pipe in hand. "He'll tell it himself." He went off to smoke in his study.

"Might you two enjoy a bit of fresh air?" Betsy offered, rising, too.

It felt good to be outdoors in the crisp night and away from the tension of the supper table. "I've never had to contemplate being more Friend than English," Elizabeth admitted, pulling the collar of her cloak tighter around her neck.

"'Tis new to me, too, to think of my composite parts," Bette agreed. "Look," she pointed into the dark above them. "The Starry Plough."

Elizabeth floated her eyes into the night sky. The Plough was one of the few constellations she knew by name. She took in the brightest light of the otherwise dull formation, connected and needing one another. "See the North Star there," she reached towards it. "It shines so brightly."

"The Light touching us," sighed Betsy. "We who are making the world anew. . . ."

Elizabeth dropped her hand to flatten her skirts against her legs. "I am glad to have you both with me on this journey, sisters.

Chapter 30

"Elizabeth Fletcher," William Edmundson called out as he came with Peggy towards her in the parlor. His dark, straggly hair danced on his shoulders. He *did* remind Elizabeth of a younger George Fox, in his wrinkled shirt and mud stained breeches. Elizabeth watched him size her up, perhaps comparing her to the two other young women beside her, all dressed in muted colors, neat in their appearance. She was the shortest, of course. She hoped he saw her well and ready.

She stepped forward with an outstretched hand. "Greetings, William Edmundson. Happy as well, to meet the preacher who has done much good work here. And this, this is my companion, Elizabeth Smith. Bette."

"Come, come," James beckoned the little group of them, Peggy and the Elizabeths. "We've all afternoon." He guided William from the parlor and its unadorned plaster walls to the inviting dining room. "Tea, Peggy?"

"James Smith," his wife chided him, her hands clamped on her hips. "Let the man catch his breath." She left them to fetch drinks.

"Had a letter about you," William hedged as he sat down. He pulled a folded paper from his pocket, the wax seal visible, as the three women took their places from the night before so that they were sitting across from him. He held it up and squinted.

Bette leaned forward. "From my Da?" she asked, her pitch unusually high.

Still homesick? wondered Elizabeth, hoping it wasn't so.

"Hmmm, no," smiled William. "Edward Burrough. Dated in this year, 1655. Seems he knows Elizabeth's here and is worried for her."

Elizabeth's eyes widened. "Edward?" she asked, her heart hammering. "He's not here, in Ireland, then?" she managed. She could feel the blush crawl up her cheeks. It was all she could do not to reach for the page.

"No, no." William fumbled with the letter. "Margaret Fell enclosed his letter in the one she wrote to me so I'd know you were coming."

Peggy returned with a tray of mugs and he waited while she passed one to each of them and then took the empty chair between him and James.

"It's only a small bit," William started up. "Let me find it. He laid the letter out before him and scanned it with a finger until he came to the part he wanted to read aloud. "Little Elizabeth Fletcher is in Ireland, but I do not know how long she will stay. Her dear love is to you and to all the flock of God. Truly I suffer for her, since she's all alone and has no other woman with her in that ravenous nation where I'm told it's very bad traveling every way by foot and dangerous. If it were the will of the Lord, that any woman was moved to come over to her, I would be much relieved."

William's eyes rested on Elizabeth, slumped to her bad side. She straightened with his gaze. "*Truly I suffer for her . . . I'd be much relieved,*" Elizabeth repeated to herself. She bent to Bette and found her hand. "He doesn't know that you've accompanied me," she said generously, feeling her tremble. "*In this 'ravenous nation,'*" she considered, worried for them both.

"We've a reputation," admitted William with a crooked expression. "But I'm grateful I was led to work here." He brushed back a lock of hair from his temple.

"Might you tell us of it?" asked Elizabeth. "How you were convinced and came here?"

"Well, it's a tale," shrugged William, obliging. "I'm from

a little mud and wattle cottage in Musgrave — northeast of Kendal. Orphaned when I was a child, my Ma dying when I was but four and my Da when I was eight. Sent to an uncle who was quick to apprentice me out as a carpenter and joiner in York." He sucked in a noisy breath. "A few years later I enlisted in the Parliament Army for some of the War. My brother, John, was already serving." He picked up his drink, obscuring the lower half of his face as he held the mug.

"You aren't the first Friend who served Cromwell before serving the Holy Spirit," offered Elizabeth kindly.

"Yes," he took a sip, "But what was it that George Fox said about war? And there I was partaking in it. . . ."

"'That we live in the virtue of that life and power that takes away the occasion of all wars,'" Elizabeth quoted. James cocked his head and stared at her. His expression was a mix of awe and curiosity.

"Yes, well, I came to that, to the peaceable kingdom . . . but not before I went with Cromwell to Scotland and I saw war for the truth of it." He set his mug down carefully and stared at a spot beside it on the table. "In the pubs and around the campfires, there's the boasting. Soldiers saying that they're serving for the honor and glory of the campaign, and wasn't it an adventure?" He wiped at his mouth and went on. "I was happy to be fed and paid, but we were a cold, miserable, rag-tag lot — instruments of so much cruelty and destruction. I was left with the trauma long after each battle." His eyes glazed over.

"It didn't take long to question it, us soldiers, sitting 'round the campfires. Most could read the different pamphlets that made their way into camp, plentiful as flies. Protestants and Baptists wondering for the first time in their lives about the tenets of their faiths. Levellers wanting an end to the classes." William cleared his throat and looked directly at

Elizabeth. "One night I was lying out on my bed roll and a question came to me: *If my kingdom were of this world, then would my children fight?* I thought about it for days and decided God was asking me to lay down my gun and face the enemy within."

"And you found Friends and came to Ireland," urged James, drumming his fingers on the table.

William wouldn't be rushed. "Yes. Was back in England in '52." He gave James a quick glance. "We defeated the Royalists, the allies to the Irish, and were rewarded with land here. My brother already had a store in Antrim and needed help with it." William considered Elizabeth and Bette. "It's north of here. I got a farm there, too." He twisted apologetically to Peggy. "I'm sorry for it. Understand the whole situation better now. We were pawns, we soldiers. Offered the chance to own land for the first time — in our names and legal. No worry that some lord would find some reason to snatch it back. Still, I had no thought about whose farms they'd been or what'd happened to the ones who'd worked them." He put a hand to his smooth chin. "I haven't resolved it still. Don't know how to make amends." He took another sip from his mug.

"Many'd be grateful you at least say so," said Peggy, a hand to his broad shoulder. "Tell the girls of your convincement."

William smiled at her, obeying. "I was the one to go back and forth to England to buy goods for my brother's shop. On one of those trips I went with relatives to hear 'a famous preacher,'" he said the last with a funny twist, his eyes twinkling.

Elizabeth flicked a look at him. She was the only other one of them that had heard George's ministry.

"You can well imagine, can't you?" asked William. "He's truly amazing, George Fox. The fire, the power, in those eyes! All of us convinced. *No trouble* remembering what he'd said."

He chuckled to himself. "His preaching stuck with me like clay on my boots. Immediately went to tell my girl about it, my Margaret. We married before I returned to Antrim."

William stretched back. "I stopped swearing any oath, bowing. Waited on the Lord almost daily with my brother's family and Margaret." William's eyes softened as he continued. "We moved to Lurgan and are living our lives to reflect our faith. Use words that speak our truth. We don't attend the local church — so, of course, we don't tithe and the authorities hound us, fine us, and steal our cattle in retribution. Still, our business is thriving. Most people appreciate that we ask a fair price for goods . . . but also that my Margaret is a good listener, willing to hear the burdens of those who come for a purchase. I think folks come in as much for her to listen to them as for our pricing. . . ."

"And they ask about the worship," Peggy nudged.

"Yes, yes surely . . ." William dipped his chin. "For, of course, we don't hide it. The first settled meeting in the country meets in our cottage, my Margaret the first convinced here in Ireland. We've eight or nine regulars now — mostly non-conforming English and Scots Irish."

"And you travel? Spread the word?" asked Bette.

"Oh, yes," praised James. "He's accomplished great things. Steadfast. Fearless."

William ignored the compliments. "I've gone out from Lurgan some with a John Tiffin," he said humbly, wanting Elizabeth to know the present situation. "I don't find the ground so fertile, many here are rooted in Calvinism."

"Calvinism," asked Elizabeth, she didn't think she'd heard of the sect. Under the table, she wiggled the fingers of one hand, thinking of Edward.

"Brought by the Scots about a decade back," James butted in. "Popular in all the North. Some call them Irish

Presbyterian." He gave William a look, wanting him to take the telling back.

"Mostly I made the rounds to the fledgling meetings," William continued. "Wouldn't be possible without Margaret managing the children and the Lurgan Meeting business while I'm away. Stands up against the mayor."

"And punished for it?" asked Bette, worried. She fiddled with her ring.

"Truly, yes," replied William, not denying it for her benefit. "Last winter when I was away, she was made to go naked in the cold. Still not completely recovered — yet goes on in faithful obedience. The Lord increases things beyond the ordinary under her hand," he added.

"We're ordinary people but in our hearts, we know extraordinary things." Elizabeth quoted in her head. It was what Edward had said a year ago when they'd parted.

"The 'valiant sixty,' is what Margaret Fell calls you . . . us," said Bette. To Elizabeth, she seemed guarded against Margaret Edmundson's ill treatment.

"But no Irish. No Irish." William took up Peggy's hand, resting between them on the table.

"It's difficult to move from the grand traditions of the Catholic Church to the stark way of Friends," she proffered.

"Well," William exhaled as if he were setting down a heavy feed sack. "I've tried to enlist George Fox for his assistance, but he's not come over as yet . . . and we're in such need of seasoned models." He turned back to Elizabeth. "'Tis good of you to've come."

"Because few others have?" asked Elizabeth. She wondered how she might best be used.

"Three men came last year and two older women, too," offered Betsy. "Stayed here, didn't they, mum?"

"Ya, ya they did," Peggy confirmed.

"But didn't last? Aren't traveling in Ireland?" Elizabeth asked.

"It's a dangerous place, our Ireland, just as 'ravenous' as Edward Burrough remarked in his letter," admitted William. "Wild. Treacherous. I worry constantly that my cottage will be burned." He looked straight at Bette and then to Elizabeth. "English Friends seem to come and go. Richard Clayton worked with me not long ago, us together at fairs and other public gatherings — north of here as well. Almost arrested for it and had to spend the night in a damp, abandoned mountain cabin to dodge the authorities. They wish me expelled, but I've managed to start meetings in Londonderry and Kilmore. . . ."

"Any women?" Elizabeth probed. *Room for me in the work?*

"Ann Gould and Juliann Wastwood came from London, separate from any men. They wanted to venture to Coleraine, northwest of Belfast, to the Scots Irish. Started off on foot on a muddy pack horse trail that winds through dense forest to Belfast. Wolves out there, too. They met hostile folks. Nearly froze. When I found them, Anne Gould had been confined to bed. She said she'd lost sight of God and wasn't sure anymore why'd she'd come."

Elizabeth followed a dark river of knots on the table. She knew that struggle; had lived in it herself.

"I brought them here to Dublin," finished William. He ran his tongue over his dry lips. "They were done. Sailed back."

"Told us they'd waded high rivers and dirty, miry swamps and lowlands to reach Londonderry, way in the north," sighed Peggy. She rose to refresh the mugs, her eyes steady on Elizabeth's own. "A leading doesn't always take you where you want to go."

Chapter 31

"Let's be doing," announced William, pushing himself up square from the breakfast table the next morning. He'd suggested that, it being First Day, they go to the market cross to preach and sell the pamphlets Elizabeth and Bette had brought from England. When the service at the ancient St. Audoen's, the wealthiest Protestant church in the city, was near to its end, they'd go there.

Elizabeth knew Dáibhí wouldn't be going along, but when Bette pulled her aside, she was taken aback. "I'm not feeling well," Bette told her, twisting her ring. "Peggy said she and James would keep me company. . . ."

Elizabeth suspected William's tellings had scared her, but she didn't pry. Still, she was disappointed. She'd thought the selling of the pamphlets would be a perfect first role for Bette and that she'd be excited not only to hear William's ministry, but her own as well. And she'd hoped Peggy would stand with them, too, an Irish Friend. She decided not to ask her why she and James weren't coming. The Smiths had offered her hospitality for as long as she needed it and she didn't want to question them right at the start. Each person had to decide for themselves as to how much they could risk. Elizabeth threw her woolen cloak about her shoulders, gathered up her skirts, and met William and Betsy by the door.

The preaching and the selling in the market cross went well. "People will take the tracts home and share them," Elizabeth explained to Betsy, pleased to have her at her side. Betsy was energetic and earnest in learning the ways of Friends. "They'll read them aloud to those who can't and Truth will be spread."

It wasn't a long way to where St. Audoen stood, in the

heart of medieval Dublin. William led the three of them outside the city walls, south of the river, to the church.

As Elizabeth entered, the first of them to start down the center aisle, she realized that the layout was similar to the church in Kendal—a large, square sanctuary and a congregation standing, packed together like herrings. She moved quickly, stepping up on the raised step behind the minister to face those in front of her. William went to the side, and Betsy followed him, quivering with equal measures of excitement and faith.

Throwing off her English bonnet, Elizabeth arched her back, and called out loudly, rhythmically, "I'm a Friend . . . from England. . . . And I urge you to go *silent*. Silent. Search within to see your evil ways. *Repent*. . . ." From the height of where she stood, she could easily see the slack-jawed nobility in the front pews. A rumble of awe, and then hostility, moved through the congregation.

It happened fast. A man came at her from out of the faithful and grabbed her up. "We'll not allow dissenters to disturb our worship here, you hussy!" he screeched. Another went for William and a third for Betsy. They were pushed past the noble men sitting feet from the ruckus and marched back down the way they'd come, taken immediately to the courthouse.

Elizabeth had contemplated this moment, worried that it might bring back debilitating memories of Oxford. Instead, she found herself filled with strength and conviction. She was able to infrequently make eye contact with Betsy as they were marched through the street, William farther back, and she smiled assuredly at her. When they stood before the judge, she was a model of trust — calm, centered, her expression a knowing smile. No questions were asked of her, the judge speaking only to William, but had they been, she would have responded with the authority her faith provided her. They were given but a night in jail, the judge's wig of silver curls bobbing as he exited the chamber.

A night. 'Tis nothing. Elizabeth decided. She'd assist Betsy though it.

"Now you'll see hell on earth," the court constable wheezed as he passed them off to a hunchbacked, hacking jailer. They were led to the "Black Dog" dungeon in Browne's Castle. Inside the daunting place, they shuffled through a dank maze of bare hallways of exposed and crumbling stone, the jailer's lantern casting an eerie oblique shadow that did little to assist them in finding their way down the rough passage.

Elizabeth, the last in line, moved like a mole behind Betsy who was in back of William. As they went down a set of slippery stone stairs and deeper into the bowels of the damp prison, she held the collar of her cloak to her nose to block the foul odor that assaulted them. Finding Betsy's hand in the dark, she gave it a reassuring squeeze as shouts for water and pleas for bread amplified.

They arrived at a row of cells in the basement, William handed off to a second jailer and taken down an adjacent hallway. Only a few feet further, the hunchback pushed first Betsy and then Elizabeth into a room the size of Queenie's stall back home. With a jiggle of his keys, he relocked the door and receded away.

Elizabeth was flooded with relief. There was no window and they'd been left no lantern, but they were together and unmolested. She slid down one of the cold, dank walls into straw that smelled like cat piss, and pulled Betsy down beside her. "Lizzie and I used to play a game," she whispered after a few moments. "Might we try it now?" She was unsure if Betsy could make out her face. "We could take turns to list what we're grateful for. . . ."

"Thank you, Elizabeth. 'Tis a good idea," agreed Betsy. She snuggled her shoulder against Elizabeth and began. When they tired of the game, they tried to rest.

Next morning, it wasn't one of the Smiths who paid their fine, but a Dublin tailor, Richard Foukes and his "second," Richard Field. Neither William nor Elizabeth refused it. Elizabeth was happy to stand with the kind men, clean and neat in their appearance, to have the payment recorded. She itched all over and felt a cough teasing in her throat. It was the chill of the cell, she figured, anxious for remedies to abate it.

As they walked, Richard Foukes explained that he and his mate heard William Edmundson preach on a previous visit to the city and had been captivated. He lived closest to the dungeon. Thinking it more dangerous for James and Peggy to be associated with the Quakers, the two came humbly to help when news of the arrest spread among the Dublin Friends.

"Going to our home for a nice breakfast," Richard Foukes explained.

James was awaiting them when they arrived. Betsy rushed into his arms and he kissed her warmly, then explained over her head to William and Elizabeth that he'd already sent Peggy to fetch fresh clothes. She'd bring William's horse on her return. "Bette's taken to bed," he informed Elizabeth. "Shaken, I think, by the arrest and news of the sentencing." He squeezed Betsy tighter to his chest and then, seeing the lice, released her.

Elizabeth followed Betsy, itching as well, to a back chamber to wait for Peggy while William joined the other men in the dining room. She wondered about Bette, waiting to talk with Peggy about the situation when she came to them not much later.

Peggy checked them both from head to toe, wanting to know the details of what had happened in the Black Dog.

Then she helped with the laborious delousing. She agreed with James that Bette was more distressed than ill. It was William's tellings of others who'd suffered for sure, but then, too, the arrest of the women that had sent her to bed.

Made presentable, Elizabeth and Betsy returned with Peggy to the chaos of the front room, the Foukes' daughters dancing excitedly about the table. They invited the women to sit and went immediately to bring them food. Elizabeth could hear Charlotte and Nicole, the older two, arguing as they went to the hearth as to who had cooked more of the eggs and bacon. When they returned with the plates, they served the women and then plopped down across from them on either side of their youngest sister, Grace, who, grinning and giggling, was talking constantly to Elizabeth. Within seconds, they started up arguing about who would fetch the drink, neither of them going for the mugs.

Elizabeth and Betsy weren't asked by the men about their jail experience nor did they interject comments to describe it. They'd spend a cold night in an awful cell and survived it — and for that, Elizabeth was extremely thankful. She told this to Peggy, sitting beside her and talking mostly with Betsy. She tried to hear more of the men's conversation, the merriment of the Foukes girls making it difficult. She caught that William was first hung from wall rings — he held up his cut wrists to show the deep, red splotches — then shackled. Late into the night, for reasons he didn't know, the jailer had come and released him so that he was able to lay with five other men on the one rotten mattress provided, "damp from water seepage." He, too, looked tired, but was determined to ride north to his family as soon as he'd eaten. Elizabeth felt suddenly exhausted. Her bones steeped with fatigue and her stomach ached. A bothersome cough wouldn't leave her alone.

The meal finished, the group of them accompanied William to his horse at the hitching post and gathered around him. Before he mounted, he walked Elizabeth a few steps away from them for a more private conversation. "Might you consider working in the southwest?" he asked. "No Friend has gone that way, to the coast. Lots of garrisons there. Soldiers and their families waiting. . . ."

"I will worship on it," Elizabeth promised, pleased with the idea.

Almost as soon as the group of them returned to the Smiths, Elizabeth went to Bette's bedside to talk with her. Eyes darting everywhere but on Elizabeth, she confessed that she wanted to return to England and hadn't been able to think of anything else for the last two days. The danger was all too real now.

"You've been a good companion," Elizabeth assured her, making no attempt to argue. "The work is not for everyone. You accompanied me to Kendal, tended me when I had the croup, escorted me here so I didn't travel alone. 'Tis certainly a different country than England, another life than yours in Chester. I understand that." She smiled sincerely. "You'll go back to make the Meeting stronger, that's important, too — to be a model for others, grounded in our ways, and welcoming of those who risk it."

Bette came into Elizabeth's embrace. "I've been thinking that I'd have a place in Chester. There is so much unknown here," she said honestly. "Thank you. Thank you for your understanding. . . ." She sat back. "And if I go now, I'll be home before winter sets in and the sea is rough."

To everyone's shock and dismay, Elizabeth took to bed herself soon after Bette departed. She remained there for most of the fall and into the new year of 1656, depending on the Smiths as if they were family. At first she complained that she couldn't move without a sharp pain from the one side of her belly coursing violently through the rest of her body, but what kept her suffering was the relentless cough that had started in the dungeon cell. Mysterious fevers took hold of her, too, for much of the day and night, and left her too weak to eat with the family, let alone go outside. When she described her disorders to the doctor, sent to her by the Dublin Meeting, he was as perplexed as everyone else as to what was the root of her ailment. He felt around the injury she'd sustained when she'd been thrust over the gravestone in Oxford but couldn't figure, if that was the cause of her present condition, why it hadn't put her down sooner. In the end, he ordered hearty soups for her stamina and mule milk for her cough and gave her care over to Peggy and Betsy.

On the occasional days when Elizabeth felt well enough for conversation with Betsy, the two friends told each other stories, the brown and red heads tipped together, and sipped on the herbal teas that Peggy brewed. Betsy read to Elizabeth, too, usually from the New Testament but sometimes from the book that young Margaret Fell had given her.

News spread among the ones who could be trusted in Dublin that a weighty Friend was among them and available, Peggy allowing only a few visitors at a time. It was mostly women who called. They were mesmerized by the young, unmarried preacher, who'd had such daring exploits. Pairs of them would sit about the bed chamber and listen attentively to Elizabeth's tellings of George Fox — his searching and his first experiences at preaching, the hundreds who had come to hear him at Firbank Fell, and his vision on Pendle Hill. Eyes on her pale face, the women would listen to her recount the stories, adding a truncated version of what James had recently calculated to be her 230-mile walk to Oxford. She emphasized how she and Lizzie had learned to preach and minimize the abuse. She had a way of signaling Betsy when she needed the sessions to end and the worship to begin.

Elizabeth no longer stood when she was able to dodge her cough and speak in Meeting. She found the Divine in the lessons of the past years — in the people she'd met and in the natural way of things. "Just as the roses and lilies grow among the thorns and the lambs skip and play in the rain on the hillsides, you will find Spirit everywhere," she counseled. It was something of what George Fox had told her when they'd been together. "You can find beauty in the challenge of your life. You needn't heed the tempest nor the storms, the floods nor the torrents. For Good is over all and reigns." Perhaps the message was for her, Elizabeth realized one day; that she was to accept her present state and find the lesson in it.

At the rise of most Meetings, Betsy would serve drinks and sometimes cake. There'd be a time of socializing, the guests would drift out, and she and Elizabeth would snuggle together, yoked as sisters, reviewing some of the situations about which Elizabeth had given counsel. Betsy, an eager pupil, was quick to see the importance of listening, asking what was needed, and using queries to find a way forward.

One woman, for example, told of her husband, who'd been sweet and attentive before her convincement, but now threatened to rip up the plain attire she wore on First Days. He'd forbade her to leave their cottage if she wouldn't dress to reflect her station. Elizabeth stayed quiet, a hand rubbing on her own plain top skirt.

"'Tis not the clothes that matter, though, is it?" the woman had said. She sat quietly for a moment, considering her realization.

"It is good you come, no matter how you are dressed," Elizabeth agreed. "And if you have to stay back, you might find a place in your flower garden to ease into the Stillness." She'd surveyed the others who were listening and told of the farmstead stump and how she and the others had worshipped — as George Fox had said — "in Spirit and in Truth" on the trail. "We, of course, wear the same clothes for years, dependent on our sympathizers to replace them or give the money for new." It seemed to Betsy that the woman had left bolstered with resolve.

Another woman had bragged about being forced to take over her husband's printing trade when they'd lived "up north" and he was absent to travel and preach for long periods. Fines had been laid upon the family for it, the woman needing to continue the work to pay them.

Elizabeth nodded, offering a thin smile. "And you enjoy it?" she'd asked.

"I am quite good at it," the woman admitted sheepishly. Found out, she couldn't hide her smile. Customers were steadily loyal, returning to her shop for a fair price, which she wrote on slips of paper and displayed by each item so there'd be no secret. Elizabeth told her of George Fox offering a fixed rate as a shoemaker's apprentice and praised the woman for her moral conduct. Over sup that night, Betsy asked her Da about his pricing, and they held a good discussion. As it turned out, James had long ago asked a consistent amount for his wares and saw to it that Dáibhí did as well.

Chapter 32

As spring approached, Elizabeth was improved enough to occasionally go with the Smiths to Meeting. It'd been moved outdoors to the Foukes' gardens, chairs set in several rows across from each other. Elizabeth sat bolstered with pillows and covered with thick blankets, amid the couple dozen others, inhaling the fragrance of the buds and manure. She let the songbirds call her down into the holy Truth.

During one of these times, she heard a familiar voice give ministry and popped open her eyes at the surprise of it. *Edward.* He'd come! In the silence of worship, he'd slipped into a chair across the way from her. His eyes closed, like all the eyes of those in attendance, and she studied him. He was fit as ever and sat solid and sure. It was only his unkempt curls, hanging into his eyes and his worn clothing, that gave any indication of the hardship of the last two years. *Oh, Edward.*

At the rise of meeting, when their eyes met, Elizabeth didn't know how to behave. She sat slack-mouthed and watched as he dutifully exchanged pleasantries with those around him. When he started toward her, her throat tightened. She lost her breath when he grabbed her up and pulled her in so tightly that she was lifted to her feet.

"Elizabeth. Elizabeth," he sighed into the curve of her neck. "How wonderful to see you again." He hugged her closer into his chest, starting up her cough. "You're but a willow," he whispered into her pasty face.

Self-conscious then, Elizabeth stepped back from his warmth. She stifled a cough and apologized for it, then introduced Betsy and her parents. Edward summoned his companion as well.

"Francis Howgill, 'tis an honor to meet you," Elizabeth tendered graciously when James and Peggy had left the four of them alone to talk. "I've heard about your good work in London." She met the older man's tired eyes, noticing his receding hairline.

Edward thanked Betsy for her willingness to serve as a companion to Elizabeth, telling them in a rush of his worry for her. He'd heard about Oxford and how she'd been injured. Elizabeth couldn't tell from his vagueness how much he knew. "Let's get away from all this," he suggested abruptly. He sanded his hands together, his eyes dancing. "We have a surprise, dear Elizabeth," he hedged, offering an arm.

Elizabeth couldn't shake her dizziness as Edward guided her, their shoulder brushing, to a thick tree away from the other Friends lingering about the garden. She sank down against the wide trunk, Betsy folding in beside her. Then they watched attentively as Edward and Francis stood a short distance from each other and began to exchange crisp gestures without speaking. Hands jerked with deliberate movements as they placed various handshapes on their faces or in the space in front of them. Some gestures involved both hands, others required but one or two fingers of a single one. It was like watching the wings of a captured bird, swooping and landing but for a moment and then off again.

"Yes, yes," Elizabeth called when Edward glanced over at her to see that she was watching. She was charmed by his want of her attention.

The two men continued for a few more moments, Elizabeth and Betsy giggling at some of their exaggerated facial expressions. "What are you doing?" Elizabeth finally asked, but then, suddenly, she knew. She knew. "A silent language?" The forms weren't single signs, like the ones Moe used, but a more complicated system of words and sentences.

Edward rushed to her and crumpled her fingers into his own. "Yes, yes!" he sang gleefully, his hair swinging at his shoulders as he knelt in front of her. "You can talk with these . . ." he pulled her up. "Just as you can with *this*." He kissed her parted lips. "You and Moe! Moe and everyone!"

Ocean waves crashed in Elizabeth's head. "My little sister," she mumbled to Betsy, still tasting the cool of the kiss. She was thankful that whatever her companion was thinking, she kept it to herself.

Edward didn't seem to notice her reaction. He began to explain in the truncated way he did when he was eager. "We were dining in London with a member of Parliament. Sir George Downing. Much interested in our faith. Took notes about us in his diary. And this servant boy came in to ask something."

"And this has something to do with talking on your hands?" asked Elizabeth.

"Oh, well, see . . ." Edward crackled at her. "The two used signs like the ones Francis and I were using — but much more quickly." He fluttered his fingers. "Able to talk about things that happened, things not present and future things. That we were Friends. And some about how we worshipped." He twiddled is fingers, rotating the thumbs around each other. "That's their gesture for 'Friends.'"

"George Downing called it Kentish Sign," interjected Francis. "He'd grown up near Maidstone, in the heart of Kent, not far from London. Deafness is widespread there — the deaf and hearing people marrying each other and having deaf children."

Edward took the lead back. "Everyone in Maidstone uses the manual signs." He collected himself to continue. "When I told Downing of Moe, he invited us to dine with him again, next midday. And of course, we went." He took a joyful gulp of breath, his color high. "And when we arrived, two other guests were there as well — a philosopher named John Bulwer and his daughter. It came out that Bulwer had seen two mute deaf men arguing in signs and he realized how capable the deaf were of *thought*, of thinking just as we do."

"The ministers in Kendal think Moe *incapable* of it," Elizabeth cut in. She turned to Betsy. "Although we all know better. She's so obviously clever." She covered her mouth, trying to stifle the harsh cough that wouldn't quit for her excitement.

"Well, it's an argument, surely in these times, whether the deaf can think or not," Edward acknowledged. "But isn't it *miraculous* that we found these people?"

"A miracle, yes," Elizabeth agreed. And divine intervention that Edward had brought the signed language to her. "Spirit," she confirmed. "As much as me finding Moe in the market cross or of her being raised by Auntie now." *Or you coming to find me*, she wanted to add but didn't.

"Or Bulwer adopting the deaf maiden," agreed Edward.

"Wait, wait." Elizabeth put up a hand in protest. "Bulwer's daughter was *deaf*?"

"Did I not mention that?" Edward tittered. "Bulwer's daughter, Chirothea Johnson, is deaf, and every bit as elegant and well-mannered as any duchess. Dressed in bright silk from head to heeled boots, with the hundreds of buttons that are the fashion in London. A flowing scarf wrapped about her perfectly curled hair. Intelligent, too." He clapped a single time. "Bulwer talked with her in signs to form whole, complicated thoughts . . . and he used an alphabet on his hands, too. Developed by a man named John Wallis, an Oxford professor." He peeked at Elizabeth, the irony of it not lost on her.

"And you've, you've learned the alphabet, too?" Betsy guessed the obvious. "The letters made of fingers?"

"Yes, yes!" Edward squatted down in front of the two of them. He caught Elizabeth's drooping eyes. "I've learned both signs for single words and the individual letters, too. Here, this is 'A.'" He placed the pointer finger of one hand on the top of the thumb of the other one. "A."

The women copied him. "Like writing letters in the air," Elizabeth murmured, thinking back on the time with Edward she'd written "love" with a smoking poker from the fire. She began to cough again, the sound like a stone caught in a wheel — repetitive, purposeless.

Edward looked carefully at her, past the ghosts of handshapes that hung in the air, and to her leaning flaccidly against the tree. "Elizabeth, Elizabeth," he pleaded, feeling in a pocket for a cloth to wipe the beads of perspiration from her forehead. "I should have come to you after London." He swallowed. "I, I was so caught up in all that was happening in there." He dabbed at the sweat, then dipped his head like a guilty child.

"No, no . . ." She wanted to tell him so many things. Instead, she reached a hand to his smooth, ruddy cheek, wondering how it'd have been if he'd found her then — after — when her breasts were pinched black and blue, her thoughts untethered, her faith challenged. "This is better, Edward." She cupped his chin, willing herself not to cry after all this time. "We rose above it, Lizzie and me, our faith strong there. And I'm past it now, led to, to something, something different," she finished. Life was love and Edward was here. A reward.

Much later in the day, after the four had eaten and Elizabeth had drunk a strong tea and napped, Edward told of James Parnell. "He was a charismatic minister," Edward began, looking over to Betsy to inform her.

"Was?" Elizabeth queried.

"'Tis not what you're thinking . . ." answered Edward. "But let me tell it in my own way. It's difficult." He let out a shaky breath. "You know, yes, that James Parnell was in prison?"

"I recall it now," replied Elizabeth, scanning her memory. She thought back to the men, the ones who'd come the night they'd had the delicious fish, when they'd been walking to Chester. James had been jailed in Colchester Castle then and George had left with Richard Farnsworth to go to him.

"Pulled fellmongers, staplers, and tanners into the faith. Wealthy ones in both Colchester and Coggeshall," Edward was saying. His gaze fell again on Betsy. "Continually disrupting services, climbing up high to be seen, and questioning the congregation. No one able to answer to his satisfaction so he'd embark on his persuasive preaching. The ministers feared they'd lose a good share from their coffers if they didn't find a way to stop him. Riots would break out in the pews, he was so powerful."

"And loved for it," interjected Francis. "In Essex they called him 'the Quaking boy.'" He checked with Edward to continue. "The tradesmen in Essex are protecting the whole of his generation. They take boys in as shop apprentices to learn skills when others won't have them."

"Because they're Friends," said Edward, wanting to make sure the women understood the discrimination.

"Grateful to James and wanting to honor his youth," added Francis. His forehead wrinkled. "Couldn't stay out of trouble, James. He was led to preach at a special service being held 'to pray against the errors of the people called Quakers' in Colchester," Francis quoted. "James was openly defiant there, preaching from a hayloft with boundless energy, addressing a thousand people."

"Was committed to Colchester Castle as 'an idle and disorderly person,'" managed Edward, wiping at his eyes.

"The cruel jailer and his wife put him in a cell hole," Francis interceded a second time. "So small he had to stay bent in it. It was high up in the cold, damp thickness of one of the ancient castle walls. Could only be reached by a ladder that was purposely six feet too short so for the last bit, he had to climb up and down a rope."

"And none came to his aid?" asked Elizabeth.

Francis shook his head. "They tried. Local Friends offered to give him a cord and basket so he wouldn't have to go up and down on the rope so often but the jailers wouldn't have it."

"When Friends went to the dungeon windows to try to talk with him," Edward forged on, "they could hear the other prisoners mocking and thrashing at him. Trapped by wolves, he was. And so weak from the lack of food and because of the climbing that one day he fell on the stone below and broke a leg."

"Oh, my Lord," whispered Betsy incredulously.

Edward exhaled loudly. "No doctor was allowed to see him but he was moved to a lower hole. Visitors called it 'the Oven,' it was so small and hot. In the days after that, he told Friends that he felt the power of the Lord God within him." Edward looked down for a moment. "Francis and I went to him then. They let us be with him and he told us of his gratitude for the life he'd had. The life. Ha. He was nineteen years old. . . ."

"Oh, no," whispered Elizabeth. She put a hand on Edward's back.

"I cradled him in my arms. Kissed and kissed him on his gray cheek, his breath rugged . . . shallow. And then, then stopped. And he was . . . gone."

No one said anything for a long while.

"I wish I'd known him, that our paths had crossed," offered Elizabeth finally. "I'm sorry for it, Edward."

"Oh, Spirit," prayed Betsy. "Holy Spirit. May we bring heaven to earth. May we find that of Good and Right in *all* people and be always in the Way."

"James Parnell . . . the first . . . martyr," whispered Edward, dragging out each word. He caressed Elizabeth's cheek with the back of his hand. "Only a year older than you, my sweet girl."

Chapter 33

Edward didn't plan to stay long — a couple of weeks at the most. Fall was coming and he and Francis thought they'd want to sail back to England before winter. The two of them had come to "prime the pump," as he put it.

Elizabeth wasn't invited to go with them. It hurt her feelings, though she knew well she wasn't the vibrant girl Edward had left on the trail in England. She could barely walk, let alone ride a horse and sleep in barns. Still, for the week or so that Edward remained in Dublin, Elizabeth found the strength to work long days, handing out tracts, encouraging people to come and listen to the great preacher, inviting those who desired it to experience silent worship.

Edward thought she should dictate a tract of her own and offered to record it. Elizabeth readily agreed. She didn't see herself preaching much longer if at all and she wanted her prophecy available to others. She titled the warning, *A Few Words in Season to All the Inhabitants of the Earth*. In it, she described herself as "a servant who knew the terror of sin." She invoked her wrath and indignation against "the proud and greedy." Edward, pleased with the strength and phrasing of her words, promised to take the pamphlet to London to see to it that it was published.

Elizabeth didn't doubt he'd do it. The twenty-two year old Edward was tireless and mesmerizing in any project he desired to accomplish. It was easy to imagine how he'd conquered London, convincing so many there, and earning the nickname, "Son of Thunder." In Dublin, Friends and sympathizers were grateful that he and Francis had left what they'd cultivated in England to come to them.

It was Francis who left first. He went westward with a new

convert, Cornet Cooke, on horses furnished by the Meeting. He sent back letters by courier to the Smiths, knowing Elizabeth and Edward would read them, too. He told of riding several days from Dublin, "through woods and bogs, and the most desolate places that I ever did see, without any inhabitants except a few Irish cabins here and there. Robbers and murderers live about in holes where none can pass."

Edward left soon after, on horseback as well, determined to stop at whichever garrisons he came to. His letters were about his arrests and examinations by mayors and former colonels. He was often turned out "violently," and always released at night, the city gates locked behind him. He had to watch constantly for robbers, though he carried nothing they'd find of value. He signed his name, "a poor Quaker," hoping it'd make Elizabeth laugh.

That autumn of 1656, Francis and Edward worked separately in the garrisons a day or so ride from Dublin and along the east coast where the countryside had largely been left in ruin. They circled southward to preach to soldiers and their families in Youghal, Kilkenny, Limerick, Bandon, Kinsale, and Waterford. Francis wrote to Margaret Fell of the convincement of former Baptists and Fifth Monarchs: "The Lord is among them and gives utterance."

Not staying long in any one town, Edward wrote that he was only wanting to set the groundwork for those Friends he was sure would come after them. He didn't suggest it'd be Elizabeth. "*Let's meet in Cork*," he scribbled in a short letter to her.

The invitation excited her. She'd find a way to get to him. Who knew what the future held, when they'd have the chance to be together again? When she asked Betsy if she'd accompany her, the young woman readily agreed. She'd never been much outside Dublin and wanted to serve. Besides, she was the logical one to go along. She cared deeply for the preacher, felt herself a sister to her, and was strong enough to aid her should her ailments worsen.

The Dublin Meeting took up a collection for the travel, and to Elizabeth's shock, Dáibhí offered to drive a cart for the women. He was bound that way for business reasons, he claimed, and had contacts for lodging. Elizabeth suspected he wanted to make sure his little sister was delivered to Cork safely. He engaged Elizabeth in their first civil conversation, asking more specifically of her plans and wanting her to understand how far and wild it was between Dublin and Cork. As Edward's letters had warned, there were highway men out there, harsh cart paths, and desperate people. The sweeping cold wind could be unbearable.

"I've a recent customer who barely made it to Cork," Dáibhí told her. "He lost the route just outside the city and led his horse through marshes for two days before finding the main way again. You'll get wet for sure. Pack extra shawls and coats and have them at the ready."

Peggy, Marcy Foukes, and her servant girl, Lucy, helped with the preparation of clothing and personal effects. It was only Betsy that needed supplies for her monthlies; Elizabeth hadn't had hers since Oxford.

On the day they left, James and Dáibhí worked together to maneuver an old straw-stuffed mattress into the back of a wooden cart to soften the bumping and then hitch a muscular work horse to it. Peggy and Lucy helped Elizabeth and Betsy to climb up and position themselves so they would be less apt to knock their heads against the backboard but could talk to each other. Then they joined Marcy in the packing of their personal bundles and the supplies they were taking around them for added protection. After that, the men spread a large piece of coarse hemp canvas over the top of them so that only their faces were visible.

"Keep ahead of that cough, Elizabeth," Peggy fussed. "Stay low and out of the wind."

They bumped off on a route, the axles moaning, that was in far worse condition than any Elizabeth had walked in England, her with her arms snaked across her belly, hoping she'd be able to guard her old injury from the jarring. Just as had been predicted, there were several times Betsy had to help Elizabeth climb down off the cart and hold to the horse's halter so it could be maneuvered across an especially muddy place. Head down, she watched little streams of water run under her boots and tried to keep close into the warm flank of the beast. Even so, Elizabeth found the wild mountainous sea cliffs and the beaches along the coast below breathtaking. She was sure she was not the first to peer over the edge at the sky and the crashing waves and wonder what it would be like to fly.

Betsy pointed out hawks, woodcock, osprey and kestrels soaring among the scrubby trees. Back in the cart, sitting upright, the two of them would list the birds they knew — then the trees, then the flowers — and when they tired of that, they hummed the Presbyterian hymns they could remember.

They stayed the first nights with Dáibhí associates, reaching the seaside hamlet of Youghal late on the afternoon of the third day. Elizabeth was chilled to the bone by the time the trio found an inn off the market cross. Still, she felt moved to preach outside it before she gave in to the day. After all, that's why she'd come, was it not? As she declared her truth, an Independent came at her from the little group that had gathered, claiming that God only called men into service. "What right do you . . ." he started his challenge, standing only inches from her.

It was a familiar refrain. Elizabeth didn't let him finish. She stood firm, legs wide and solid, and rapidly citing from

Timothy and Corinthians and then Joel, to argue that "God pours out his spirit on all flesh, *all* flesh." The man stepped back, stopped for a moment, seemingly shocked at her abilities. Then he came back into her, too close. He began to yell and find fault, his fists cocked and ready.

It was a captain, James Sicklemore, who came between the two of them, blocking the livid man from whatever he was planning to do to Elizabeth. "May Truth prevail," announced Elizabeth, turning from both men and letting the soldier carry on. She was weary with her effort and felt she'd already said all that was needed. As she started to the inn door with Betsy and Dáibhí, a second Cromwellian warrior came alongside her and offered an arm.

"Lieutenant Robert Sandham, at your service," he smiled, inviting them to sup with him inside.

"Done my job. Goods delivered," Dáibhí called out triumphantly as the cart rolled over a bridge on the River Lee and past the medieval walls of Cork. The arrangement of the town astonished the women. It was laid out on a marsh, close to the sea between a network of canals instead of streets.

Dáibhí asked directions to the house of Denise Cooke, sister to the man who was riding with Francis Howgill. The older woman met them at the door and showed them to their upstairs room, Dáibhí staying only long enough to secure a promise that the women would send letters home so his parents knew they were safe and being well-treated. After he'd left, Betsy transferred their things into the two small chests provided for the purpose while Elizabeth lay on the four-poster bed and stared about the room. The walls were shabby in places but there was a small table with a bowl for washing up and a little rug on either side of the bed. *Cold floors*, she thought, *but we'll be just fine here.*

When she'd finished, Betsy came to lie beside her, the two of them listening to the shiver of wind as it blew through the walls and trying to nap. Elizabeth's cough made it difficult. They gave up and readied themselves for sup, lured by the aroma of meat stew and freshly baked bread. Downstairs, chatting around a large table in the modest dining room, Betsy and Elizabeth met the others who were staying there.

The women had planned to go daily to the Cork market to preach — Elizabeth to give ministry and Betsy perhaps to try. However, the harsh weather wore at Elizabeth the few times they went out for errands, and Denise, seeing her condition was worsening, offered the large open parlor of the Cooke house as a place for meeting for worship. In addition to Denise and the roomers, those who attended were former Protestants who'd sought refuge after the Irish Rebellion of 1641 and Parliamentarian soldiers and their families. Betsy wrote home with a bit of pride, "*The Cork Meeting is settled.*"

Chapter 34

Finally, it was spring, the buds of hazel and rowan shining among chartreuse greens, and Edward arrived. He stayed with a man, fresh to the city himself, Thomas Loe, and found Elizabeth and Betsy the following day.

Elizabeth didn't miss the shock of his expression when Denise first brought him into the parlor or how he tried to hide it. Betsy jumped up to welcome him, but Elizabeth didn't try to get to her feet. "Tell us where you've been, what have you be doing," Betsy urged, covering for Elizabeth's sluggishness. Elizabeth wished she could muster an equal measure of enthusiasm. Instead, she kept her lethargic hands to one side in her lap, the pressure on her old gravestone injury a comfort.

Edward tried to include Elizabeth in his conversation. His brow furrowed, she felt like he was testing her — checking her memory, seeing if her comments fit the topic, grimacing with discomfort when the word she was wanting vanished like a dream. "How about some fresh air?" he asked only shortly after he'd arrived. He wanted out, out of the parlor, out of the awkward exchanges. "I passed a lovely pond on the way here. Would you go with me?" He considered only Elizabeth, moving abruptly to take the blanket off her lap and help her to her feet.

"Well, yes. Yes, of course," Elizabeth agreed, leaning heavily on his hands to stand. She knew him well enough to know there was a reason for it.

Edward did the talking as they started off. "There's to be a Meeting of Friends in Westmorland," he blurted before they were barely out of sight of the Cooke home.

"Yes?" Elizabeth asked hesitantly, trying to keep up with his strides. "Wonderful." The pain hurled from her belly. It took all her effort to not let it stop her, to focus on something ahead on the path to keep the spinning in check. She blinked rapidly to find her focus, thinking her legs wouldn't hold her much longer.

"Isn't it? Friends from all over England are invited. Ireland, too, I suppose," Edward continued, tittering nervously. "Coming together to worship as a whole and conduct business." He bent to her, to see her colorless face behind her bonnet.

"A meeting of the whole," Elizabeth repeated, avoiding his glaze. "To see all those Friends." She'd brought a limp hand to her mouth as if it helped to stop her cough.

"Maybe Thomas and Lizzie Holmes. . . ."

"Oh, Lizzie," sighed Elizabeth. Her mind slid back to the chilly night that she, Lizzie, and . . . and . . . someone else . . . had slept like worms in a castle garden. She didn't think Thomas was with them, but she couldn't recall why not. She put a finger to her scarred cheek as if it would help her lucidity. "In Wales, are they?" she suddenly remembered.

"Yes, they are," Edward chuckled in relief for it. "Maybe Jane and Dorothy Waugh, as well . . . at the meeting in England . . . and those you know only by name from tellings and letters, yes?"

Friends will be annoyed with my coughing, thought Elizabeth. *Edward's exasperated now. Even if Betsy went with me. . . .*" She didn't have the stamina to make another sea crossing, let alone ride a horse to the Meeting, she concluded, surveying what she could see of the pond. Ducklings and a swan swam noiselessly among the loosestrife and cattails and she felt a bit restored. "And Mary Fisher?" she asked, coming back into the conversation. *Oh, to meet Mary Fisher.* A pheasant flitted past in the shrubbery.

"She's in the colonies," said Edward. He spread the blanket at the water's edge and helped Elizabeth to sit down. Leaning on his shoulder, she watched the sunlight change the colors on a patch of ground beside her. *A clue, a message*, she considered. She waited for him to tell her what was on his mind.

Edward reached to pick up two long, slender twigs. He fit one in her hand before leaning forward to poke a leaf under the water. "Might the water be love?" he whispered, holding the leaf just beneath the surface.

Elizabeth leaned forward, barely able to copy, and submerged a second leaf.

"And we the leaves, surrounded in it, precious in our different shapes and colors," finished Edward. He dropped his stick and found her brown eyes. "Divine love like this water, all around us, available always." He pushed carefully against her shoulder. "Always, if we but allow ourselves to go into it." He took the twig from her hand. "You are so precious to me, Elizabeth Fletcher."

"I want so much to be your helpmate, Edward," she whispered back, his smooth white neck a blur. She met his eyes, seeing her face reflected in them, wanting the days back when they'd walked together for endless hours. "Heaven" was the only word that occurred to her as she kissed the soft lips. For just a moment, she mourned another life, a different future. "Must you go?" She shifted the tiniest bit to press her cheek into the hollow of his, engulfed by the love she felt for both the man and the faith.

Edward searched the wells of her eyes. "Yes. Truly I must. I am called." Elizabeth understood that he meant more than to the Westmorland Meeting. "Will you instead go back to Kendal?" he asked, his face set. "I could get you that far by coach. Home to the farmstead." He took her by the shoulders and moved her back so he could see her full face for her pledge of it.

"Yes," came the single, husky syllable.

The deed done, he stood and pulled her gently to her feet. "I have a surprise for sup," he winked, cheerful again. He'd said what he'd come to say. "We've been invited to dinner where I stayed last night. 'Tis not far."

Over plates of roasted ham cut in thick chunks and buttered potatoes, Thomas Loe told of how, until recently, he'd been an Oxford tradesman. "I was absent the day you and Lizzie Leavens preached," he explained to Elizabeth, holding a piece of the tender meat in his fingers. "When I returned, all talk was of you and your preaching, your bravery with the flogging — of how you called out and were a model even as you were wronged."

Elizabeth couldn't think of anything to say.

"The Meeting at the Bettrises' is a strong one now," Thomas went on, wishing she'd say something. "Though it's often bothered by rude and abusive students." He moved his fork around his plate. "John Audland came through just a few months after you, a boost to Meeting. 'Twas him I heard and was convinced." He paused, waiting for her again, some acknowledgement of the important event. "I wager you were in Dublin by then. . . ."

Elizabeth felt so tired, wracked by the hurt of Edward wanting her to go home. "We were but a step to the Meeting surviving," she muttered, her fists tight on her bosom in a failed attempt to quiet her sputtering cough. She was hot and uncomfortable. "A holy mission. . . ." She licked her dry lips. "To be sure."

"I've tried to make something good come from your mistreatment, to honor your sacrifice," said Thomas. He poured her more drink. "I've only just arrived at Cork myself, to work here and strengthen what you've started. . . ." He looked away from her.

"Ah," nodded Elizabeth. He was stepping in for her, was he? Defeated, she left the conversation to the men and wandered into herself. Perhaps if she and Lizzie hadn't gone to Oxford or had gone with another pair, maybe things would be different now. Maybe if that woman hadn't pushed her so hard over the marker, her belly wouldn't spew the giant spider of pain that crawled relentlessly through her. Still, she'd done as she'd been led.

She lost her train of thought and then found it again. *If it hadn't been Oxford, it'd have been something, someplace, else.* Hundreds of them were being beaten and imprisoned. And hadn't she wanted just this? A faith that mattered, a life with purpose. She'd been happy; she'd loved and enlightened countless people. Even this man here, this Thomas Loe, had been influenced by her work. Elizabeth looked over to him, his head tipped to Edward as they talked. She saw the future as she watched them. Saw that the work would go on. That Friends would continue.

"Touching lives with your own preaching?" Edward was asking Thomas as she resurfaced.

"Perhaps," Thomas allowed. "One especially — a remarkable boy. I'll have you meet him at Meeting tomorrow. Quite something."

"There he is," Thomas pointed as they entered Cork Meeting the next day. The lad was sitting across the room dressed in a brown satin shirt with a wide, white collar and breeches cut from the same cloth. He reminded Elizabeth of George Fell. *Probably not as unpleasant*, she guessed.

"A regular attender," Thomas was saying as he, Edward, Elizabeth, and Betsy found places. "The family is from England. His Da served in the Navy and Cromwell rewarded him with Catholic land here. Retaliation for the failed Irish

Rebellion. The boy comes with neighbors, drawn to the Truth."

It was the last Elizabeth heard as she closed her eyes and was carried off on the imagined waves of the Irish Sea into the Light. Betsy needed to nudge her awake at the rise. Then she moved off with the men to socialize while Elizabeth sat slumped in her chair. She followed the aristocratic boy about the room, watching him engage easily with the adults. "They say you're from England," he started up bluntly when he came beside her.

"Yes, yes, I am." Elizabeth snaked a hand slightly forward on her lap. "Elizabeth Fletcher."

"William Penn," he introduced himself. He took the offered hand gently in his own and held it as if she were an old woman. "But you've been working in Ireland of late?" he asked. His expression suggested he questioned the truth of what he'd been told.

"Yes, couple of years now. Ireland, yes," said Elizabeth, fever flushing her cheeks. "Dublin . . . now Cork." She worked to look alert, blinking to focus on the pink, smooth cheeks.

"They say you walked *days* from Kendal to Oxford," said William, skeptically.

"I was younger then," Elizabeth quipped. She was only eighteen now.

"A weighty preacher?" the lad queried, his head cocked. Perhaps he'd overheard the description and was trying to match it to her sickly appearance.

"Do they say that about me?" Elizabeth asked modestly.

"I plan to go to college in Oxford."

"Ah," sighed Elizabeth. She was charmed by the boy's respectfulness as he continued to keep hold of her hand. "Know some fine people there. The Bettrises." The name came suddenly to her, a surprise. "Hold Meeting regularly in their home." In breathy spurts she told the story of Oxford.

"I'm sorry for it, Elizabeth Fletcher," William said earnestly when she'd finished. He rose and stood directly in front of her. "I detest all Presbyterian practices."

"Not expelled from school if you don't attend steeple house services?" Elizabeth probed tenderly.

"I might be," said William, puffing his chest, and starting to move off. "But it's no matter. My Da will simply have me go elsewhere."

"Ah," was all Elizabeth could manage. When she brought her hand down from yet another cough, there was blood in it.

Chapter 35

Edward wrote a letter to the Smiths before he set out to preach his way back to Dublin. He told them about how Elizabeth continued to decline and that Betsy was serving well in her role as companion to her. His plan was to meet the women at the Smiths and take Elizabeth back to England. He told Elizabeth he'd write to her when he'd arrived and was ready for them to come.

As things turned out, when a letter arrived, it wasn't from Edward but a Munster sympathizer. Betsy broke the seal and scanned it. "He preached to a great multitude, the people trailing behind the two of them — Francis Howgill, too — as they rode through the city." She paused, smiling, then read on. "He's jailed," she said with worry. "The both of them. Awaiting a warrant from Dublin to be returned there."

"We must get there, too, then," whispered Elizabeth. "To be there when he's jailed." Her heart was pounding.

The Cork meeting found the funds for a coach, Betsy worrying over Elizabeth for the almost week of travel. She complained to the old driver that they could've walked faster. As chance would have it, or perhaps Divine will, they arrived late in the afternoon on the same day that Edward and Francis were incarcerated in the Black Dog in the castle.

Peggy and Betsy were just settling Elizabeth into a chair and catching up on what had gone on in Cork when James burst into the room. "It's serious," he puffed. "I've just come from the castle." He gave Betsy a quick hug and went to kneel at Elizabeth's feet. He searched the vacant eyes, so dark they looked bruised.

"Tell," Elizabeth entreated. She tried feebly to rise.

James flapped his hands at her to stay still. "They're in

that filthy pit of a place. You've been there, you know what it's like." He stood, turning to Betsy. "I went immediately to the mayor when I heard. Paid for a cell with a window. Might keep them alive if they have to be there long. He's allowing us to visit if we hurry yet this evening. . . ." He went to her, hugging her tightly. "I'll flag a coach."

Peggy grabbed a blanket and a lantern and then she and Betsy all but carried Elizabeth outside. When they arrived at the castle, Elizabeth leaned heavily against James as they searched to find the right cell window.

"Ah, here," Betsy announced, her face pressed against the bars. "Edward, Francis. we've come." She quickly spread the blanket out on the hard ground for Elizabeth, and James moved around to stand behind her as a brace.

"Dear Friends, dear Friends. Thank you for coming," Edward praised, coming close to the bars so he could see the Friends. Peggy lit the lantern and handed it to Francis.

"Elizabeth!" Edward called, reaching through the bars toward her.

When she said nothing to him, Peggy broke the awkwardness. "We can't stay long tonight, good preachers, but we'll come back tomorrow with food, ale . . . whatever it is that you're needing."

"Elizabeth," Edward called firmly, shaking her cold fingers, wanting the once brilliant eyes. Elizabeth rose up a bit out of her cloak collar. A gray fog drifted in her head. "I see God in your face, Elizabeth," Edward told her. "I see Love."

"For heaven's sake, what's happened to her?" Edward pleaded when Betsy came alone the next day to bring the promised supplies. He turned his hat over and over in his hands.

"No one knows," admitted Betsy, her tone dull with

anguish and her own fatigue. She watched him pace the cell like an untamed stallion, tied firm. "Whatever started in Oxford worsened this last year. You saw it for yourself. She eats like a bird and her energy spurts and goes. We can't keep her warm and she coughs and coughs."

Betsy saw nothing to be gained in telling Edward that once he'd wanted Elizabeth to go back to Kendal, she'd completely given in to her affliction. They'd tried bloodletting, her arms now blotched black and deep blue from it, and concoctions of mercury and salt. Friends in Cork had fashioned every herbal remedy without result.

"They're going to deport us back to England. Banish us," Edward interrupted. "I can no longer take her."

"I can try," Betsy pledged. "As soon as things for you are decided."

The verdict was announced without a hearing after Christmas. Edward and Francis were never to return to Ireland. On a cold day in the new year, 1658, they were roughly escorted to the docks, James, Peggy, and Betsy walking a good distance behind to witness it. For most of the way, especially when he passed a grand tree or heard a sparrow call, Edward thought of Elizabeth. He imagined her almost weightless on his arm, the winter breeze coloring her cheeks a delicate pink and tousling her chestnut hair. Surely holy Spirit would give her peace. She deserved as much.

"We need to get you back as well, Elizabeth," Betsy told Elizabeth shortly after Edward and Francis had been deported. They couldn't afford to all go, so Betsy would have to make it alone. Spring ripened the shrubbery of Dublin. The seas would be calming, the roads clearer. If they waited much longer, it'd be impossible to get her home.

James had messengers take a letter to Jane Fletcher. A reply came a couple of weeks later from Kelsey, but Hannah and Auntie had made their mark on it, too. They were heartbroken and planning for the worst. If anything happened en-route, Betsy got lost or Elizabeth worsened, Betsy was to take her to the Morgans' in Chester — Bette's home. If she could get her further, then to Kirkby Lonsdale and the farm of Wendy Hampton and her husband, Ben. They were Friends and hosted a little Meeting in their cottage. Jane Fletcher's people, the Mansergh, could help as well, if Betsy needed assistance. They were near a well-known landmark in the area, Devil's Bridge. At any rate, Kelsey wrote, the trail to Kirkby Lonsdale would be a better route than the muddy one to the farmstead. Betsy was to send a message when they arrived and then Kelsey, Hannah, Auntie and Moe would come to them. Lizzie, Kelsey wrote, would be with them, too. He didn't explain why.

A week later, James and Peggy went with Betsy to settle Elizabeth on a boat, the four-day trip from one country to the other uneventful. Elizabeth tolerated the travel better than Betsy had expected. She lay in her bed most of the time, staring at nothing or sleeping. If she said anything, it rarely made sense.

Betsy left her for short periods. She'd found the pleasant company of a linen merchant who knew her father. He took meals with her and engaged her in small talk and, at one point, unpacked his samples for her to examine — flax and hemp from Russia, fine Irish linens, coarse material for bedding from Germany, and muslins and calicoes from the East Indies. When they docked, the kind man paid for a coach for the women and one of the crew carried Elizabeth to sit inside it, sagging beside Betsy.

The driver got them to the Hampton farm by evening. Wendy, in plain dress, greeted Betsy's knock. Her eyes were full of concern, her expression kind. Ben, her husband, came up behind her and introduced himself as well. He could have been Dáibhí, her brother, Betsy thought. He was at least as tall and sported the same short beard — brown, not red, but trimmed as neatly. Betsy followed his long, hurried strides to retrieve Elizabeth and wave the driver off.

"You're home. You're home," Ben muttered as he slid his arms tenderly under Elizabeth and held her like a sleeping infant to his chest. He meant England, of course, not Kendal. He carried her into the cottage and to a back, sparsely furnished room where he laid her out, fully clothed, on a mattress plumbed with straw. Wendy fixed a pillow of chaff husks under her head so that it was raised only slightly. Then she covered the preacher with a light blanket, more to hide her immodest position than for warmth. She tapped Ben and they left Betsy to remove Elizabeth's bonnet, an act that seemed almost sacred.

When there was nothing more to do, Betsy left the almost lifeless Elizabeth and gathered with Wendy and Ben around a writing desk. Ben composed a message to be sent to Jane Fletcher and then rode into Kirkby Lonsdale to find a runner. Meanwhile, Betsy and Wendy returned to Elizabeth's bedside to undress her. They pulled a clean shift over her limp head and tucked her in. Betsy saw Elizabeth weakly palm at the blanket, the closest she could get to the fabric of her shift. She'd seen Elizabeth run her hands down her skirts many times in the past two years. She knew the gesture held meaning.

When Ben returned, he moved chairs into the space from the front room and for large portions of the next day, the three of them worshipped beside the dying Elizabeth. They arranged themselves to form something of a circle — Ben beside Wendy, a hand reaching across the narrow bed to Betsy, and Betsy touching Elizbeth's hand.

Wendy left at one point to gather wildflowers from the garden and set a vase of them on a table that Elizabeth might see if she opened her eyes. Betsy told her that Elizabeth had always loved anything from out-of-doors and that her ministry was grounded in flowers and animals and birds. "If she could see the arrangement, she'd be grateful for it," she assured Wendy. Then she rose to go outside herself. She bent to collect a few smooth stones and came back in to put them beside the vase. It was then, staring at the ashen face and listening to the occasional garbled word, that she realized she hadn't heard the wretched coughing for days.

"Light. Spirit," Elizabeth moaned between her uneven breaths. Several times Betsy thought she whispered "James Parnell" with a pitch of wonder and Betsy took comfort in the idea that the "Quaking boy" was beckoning her to come to him. Betsy lit a single rushlight in the darkened room to guide him to her.

When they took a break to eat, Betsy talked to Ben and Wendy of how honored she'd felt to serve as Elizabeth's companion. She told of their work in Dublin and Cork and of Elizabeth's walk from Kendal to Oxford — how she had long said that her injuries in the graveyard there were the cause of her demise. Betsy wasn't so sure, she admitted. A relentless cough and fevers had started after they'd been imprisoned in Dublin. Elizabeth worsened when they'd made the trip to Cork and by the end of it, she was coughing up blood.

As she talked, Wendy regarded the young Betsy carefully. "You've been a faithful companion," she counseled, taking note of the dark circles under Betsy's eyes. "Have you any idea of what you might do while you're here in England?"

Tears welled up in Betsy's eyes as she began to talk of a future that wouldn't include Elizabeth.

Finally, those from Kendal arrived — Auntie and Moe, Hannah and Kelsey, and Lizzie with a small daughter. Betsy felt like she knew them all.

"ELIZABETH, ELIZABETH," signed Moe, the gesture much exaggerated as she came cautiously into the room. When Elizabeth didn't move, her chest lifting, her breath jagged, the girl went to her side and stretched out beside her on the mattress, just as she'd done when she'd been so ill with the croup.

"Moe," Elizabeth whispered. She moved her chin to rest on Moe's head.

Moe, not able to hear her, turned her face into Elizabeth's cool neck and slung an arm across her chest. No one tried to tell her that Elizabeth knew she was there or suggested that she move off the bed.

It was a miracle, Betsy thought, when Elizabeth opened her eyes a short time later. "Lizzie," she smiled. Her voice hushed. "Auntie?" she asked with great effort, unable to see that her aunt, Hannah, and Kelsey were standing around the bed as well.

"Yes, dear one, right here, with Hannah and Kelsey," whispered Auntie, gently touching her shoulder. Kelsey and Wendy supported the old woman so that she could bend low to kiss Elizabeth's cheek. Then they stood over her and watched her face for a few more minutes, Hannah moving a strand of stringy hair back and away from the smooth forehead.

"We'll come in to see you in a while," she whispered as she gave one of the clawed hands a gentle squeeze. "Come, sweetie," she said to her granddaughter, taking the little hand and leading the group of them out. Betsy went, too, wanting Lizzie to have Elizabeth to herself.

Sitting gingerly on the edge of the mattress opposite

Moe, Lizzie didn't know how much Elizabeth could understand or what to say. "Oh, Elizabeth, I've missed you so. There's so much to tell you. . . ." Her voice wobbled. "It's been so fulfilling to preach with Thomas. The Meetings in Wales grow and grow." She fiddled with an edge of the blanket. "Oh, and that Mary Fisher. She went to a place called Turkey and then with Elizabeth Hooten to the colonies. Remember about Elizabeth Hooten?" She leaned back, wishing the wise Mansfield elder was with her now. "We, we Friends are all over the world, hundreds of us, Elizabeth." She searched the sunken, half-closed eyelids, and the matted hair. She let images of others, broken from whippings, arrests, imprisonments, and banishments, float through her mind. Still, she'd not seen anyone die. She'd only heard about James Parnell, the first martyr. "We endure, Elizabeth," she whispered into the precious face. She moved her forehead down to rest on Elizabeth's temple.

"Good life, Liz . . . zie?" Elizabeth mumbled, her eyes closed and the words barely audible.

Lizzie sat back in disbelief. "Yes, oh yes, dear one," she answered. It was something of a lie. She was broken herself from the cold, wet days in Wales, too many nights in dark, damp prison cells. She'd come home recently to live again with her parents and rest from the rigors of the work with Thomas and life with a baby. "You'd adore little Elizabeth . . . my, my daughter," she tried, realizing Elizabeth would never know the child. She went on, wanting to believe that Elizabeth understood they'd named the child for her. "Ah, yes, dear Friend. Came to us in Meeting." There was no response. "I love you, Elizabeth Fletcher," Lizzie whispered, praying it wasn't too late. The weight of what was happening descending on her and she pressed her cheek back into Elizabeth's.

In the holy moment the two companions created, Elizabeth submerged into a pond, Edward's pond. The water cooling her back and legs. She felt her hair released to float out from around her head.

Lizzie kissed her cheeks and forehead. "I love you," she said again, fixed on the gaping mouth. She reached her arms under the pillow that held Elizabeth and pulled her close.

Elizabeth unfolded her arms, her dress twisting and rolling gently into the Water.

"You loved. You are loved," Lizzie repeated. It was all that mattered, all that was the work of this life. "You loved. You are loved."

Elizabeth arched her arms wide and then back flat against her thighs. She glided forward, her mouth loose.

"Heaven's inside you, Elizabeth." Lizzie reached a thumb to close the eyelids and didn't wipe away the tears that rolled down her cheeks. She was unsure how long she sat there.

It was sometime later that the others came back into the room. Hannah touched Moe's shoulder and the girl sat up and stared at Elizabeth. She kissed the cold lips and slipped off the bed to cry into Auntie's skirts. Ben brought in a bench and they sat in prayer, no one moved to speak. Then Wendy rang a bell one time and passed it to Lizzie who was sitting beside her. She rang it one time, too, and it was passed around from one to another until it had been rung nineteen times. Moe was the last. She clapped the bell and brought the metal to her cheek to feel the vibration.

Chapter 36

A year after Elizabeth died, Friends gathered at the farmstead to celebrate her life. Although there were 60,000 Friends in England, and Friends were active in their meetings, preaching and writings, due to changes in the laws, they were punished more harshly and in greater numbers than even in the first days. Dangerous as it was, several of them laid aside the struggle to come to Kendal for the memorial.

Margaret Fell, eldest daughter of the Swarthmoor Fells, now twenty-five and recently married, joined George Fox and Edward, Rosie, and Bette Morgan in the worship. Jane Fletcher was supported on either side by Kelsey Leavens and Thomas Holme, caught up in the thought that she was breathing the air that her niece had once breathed. Thomas' parents and Hannah stood nearby.

Moe, the deaf orphan, clung to Auntie. She pointed to the coarse ground where the body had been buried a year before and drew a line slowly down one side of her face to indicate the scar on Elizabeth's face. "ELIZABETH," she mourned, rubbing her eyes with the heel of her hand. She clenched a small quilt in the other that Lizzie had fashioned for her from the dress that Elizabeth had worn last. The thread color of the embroidered edges was muted, the stitches the ones she'd learned from the women who'd provided them hospitality as they'd walked from Kendal to Oxford five years earlier.

Edward Burrough stood among them, too. He'd see to it that the tract that Elizabeth dictated while he was with her in Ireland was published two years later. Three years after that, he'd be arrested and imprisoned in London, martyred himself by a raging fever.

This day Lizzie stood beside him. She'd be whipped in Wales while clutching a nursing infant and would die the same year as Edward. Thomas stood on her other side and held little Elizabeth, their daughter. Thomas would die a year after his wife and be buried as they all would, in unmarked graves. This was the practice in the mid-17th century.

Out of the silence, Edward stepped forward. "I thank you all for coming to honor our dear Elizabeth." His voiced cracked. "I believe Jane and Dorothy Waugh are here with us in Spirit, too. Dorothy sailed to New York to protest the treatment of our ministers by the authorities there. We've heard recently that she was arrested and banished but we know nothing more. Jane Waugh, her younger sister, has been imprisoned in Chester."

Edward paused, a hand over his heart. "I see the depth of your sorrow for Elizabeth and I am led to bring this message." He took a slow deep breath and then started.

"Once you were lonely and confused in your purpose, in how to live your life, waiting and searching for guidance. A person crossed your path and confirmed the possibility of a direct, Spirit-filled relationship if you were to but sit in Truth and go inward. That preacher might have been nineteen-year-old Elizabeth Fletcher or a poor maidservant the likes of the Waugh sisters or the bold Mary Fisher. It might have been a man — George Fox, Thomas Holme, or myself — untrained in ministry at college. Still, you were drawn in by what was revealed. You paid attention to the images, felt the nudges, and were counseled. A tender transformation began to transpire in your soul. . . ."

"It might have been that your relatives disowned you, or at the very least, misunderstood. It might have been that your peers didn't care to know your faith or your commitment to it. It might have been that you didn't have the words to explain what you knew to be true in your heart to anyone else. No matter how uncertain, how confusing, how uncomfortable, you took up our faith and are here today, plain sparrows who worship here in England but around the world, too. You continue to dedicate yourselves to honesty, equality, community, and peace-making. You are Friends, those envisioned on Pendle Hill, for we are a people gathered of good faith and valiant. Who speak from experience, embrace the equal treatment of all people, stand up for the measure of good in each one, and share our tellings. We seek that holy connection again and again. For in it, we are home, we are saved. This is heaven. My gratitude to you Friends. Go out into this world and love. Let your lives speak."

Biography of Elizabeth Fletcher

Elizabeth Fletcher (October, 1639–1658) was born in Kendal, Westmorland, England. Penney (1907) stated that she was "a virtuous maid of considerable family" (p. 258) and Mack (1992) also described her as a woman "of means" (p. 145). However, in my research I found no primary source to verify this status and Brailsford (1915) documented in *Quaker Women: 1650–1690* that according to the account books kept at Swarthmoor Hall, Elizabeth's "means" did not allow her "to travel upon her own purse." A hat and shoes were provided her by the "Kendal Fund." In my novel, she lives on a farm north of Kendal across the lane from Elizabeth Leavens (whom I call "Lizzie") and near Thomas Holme. In real life, Elizabeth, Lizzie, the Waugh sisters, and Mary Fisher, as documented in my novel, were "ordinary people," not ministers with any special training, who wanted to share their "new awareness" (Vipont, 1976; p. 114).

Elizabeth was convinced by George Fox when she was fourteen years old and began preaching when she was fifteen years old. Penney (1907) wrote that John Camm, John Audland, Edward Burrough, Thomas Holme, Elizabeth Fletcher, and Elizabeth Leavens came into Cheshire in 1654 (p. 16). They were zealous and often under strange workings of "the power," the people rude and violent, the authorities alarmed at what they could not understand. "Not surprisingly," wrote Mack (1992) considering their youth, ". . . sadism towards Quaker women was laced with sexual innuendo and public frivolity" (p. 248).

According to Besse's (1753) *Book of Sufferings* (pp. 562–654), Elizabeth and Lizzie went of their own authority by the leading of the Spirit (Grubb, 1917; p. 181) to Oxford, the first to bring the Quaker message to where young men were trained to become ministers of the Church of England. That they were influenced by Mary Fisher, who went to Cambridge months earlier, is my own invention, though highly probable.

According to Penney (1907), the two women arrived in Oxford on June 20, 1654, and "went through the streets and into the colleges and steeple and tower houses, preaching repentance and declaring the word of the Lord to the people" (p. 210). Five days later they were moved to go to Martin's at the Crossroads of Cornmarket Street to the north, High Street, to the east, Queen Street to the west, and St. Aldate's to the south.

Penney (1907) stated that "at the backside of the city, the women met 'a black tribe of scholars' and spoke to them" (pp. 210, 258). The students "fell on them very violently," and the women suffered "as is almost a shame to relate, considering the place and persons that acted upon the two innocent, comely, young maids" (p. 258). They dragged them through a dirty pond or pool and afterwards tied them back to back, their mouths held in an endeavor to pump water into them until they were almost dead (Penney, 1907; Besse, 1753; Chapter 29). Besse (1753) reported that the students inhumanely dragged the women up and down near St. John's College in what Thomas Ellwood (Sewel, 1722) described as "a disgraceful riot" (v. ii, p. 227). Vipont concurred: "two Kendal girls . . . suffered savage treatment from the authorities at Oxford and the most inhuman mob violence from the students" (Vipont 1976; p. 44).

The author of the Kendal Chronicle as recorded by Penney (1907; pp. 210, 258) wrote that, "free from all restraint by the magistrates, the students, backed by the townsmen, abandoned themselves to an orgy of horse-play and shameful abuse." Wagstaff (1845) wrote that the women "were cruelly and shamefully beaten and mistreated in every manner" (p. 48).

"A few days after this," reported Besse (1753), "the same women went to one of the places of public worship, and after the priest was finished, one of them spoke something to the clergy and people gathered there. A woman named Ann Andrew thrust Elizabeth Fletcher over a gravestone in the yard outside St. Giles Church, "where a corpse was to be buried" (Penney, 1907; p. 258).

Penney (1907) concluded that the gravestone event "bruised [Elizabeth Fletcher] so sore that she never recovered but complained of it as a principle cause of her lingering weakness," a "hurt she felt until her dying day" (p. 258). Thomas Camm blamed the "schollars and rable" who attacked her for the fact that she "was never so well againe in health" (Penney, 1907; pp. 259–60).

Besse (1753) reported that two justices of the peace were present at St. Giles and "because of the tumult," they ordered the women be immediately sent to the Bocardo Prison where felons and murderers were housed (also reported in Penney, 1907). The bridge that held them was in a fortress that formed part of the North Gate of the city. It attached to the Tower of St. Michael's. Today, the prison is no longer there but the tower of the church still stands.

According to Besse (1753), there was a hearing for Elizabeth and Lizzie the next day. The women were asked their names, places of abode, and made the proper answers:

- Why were they in Oxford? "They were commanded by the Lord to come thither."
- What did they come to do? "To declare against sin and ungodliness, as pride, lust, and 'all manner of

self-righteousness, and failed worship, which both priests and people live in, contrary to the commands of God.'"

- How did they know they were called of God? One of them replied, "They knew the Voice of God, and that they were called of him."
- The Vice Chancellor said that they had blasphemed the name of God and asked whether they read the scriptures. One of them said, "They did."
- Then he asked if they were obedient to the power of the magistrate? One of them answered that they were obedient to the power of God, and to the power, as it was of God, their souls were subject for conscience' sake.

The Vice Chancellor declared that the women profaned the word of God and that he feared they knew not God, though they talked so much of him (Besse, 1753). Besse (1753) also reported that it was the custom that before any sentence or corporal punishment was executed, the mayor had to sign the petition as well and put the seal of his office on the order. In this case he refused to do so. "But so eager were the Vice-Chancellor and some others that they told him [that] if he would not sign their sentence, they would execute it without him" (p. 563). The mayor did not sign it but offered the women food and money if they would leave town. They refused.

The next morning, Elizabeth and Lizzie were whipped out of the city. "The consciousness of their innocence did so move the hearts [of the people watching], even of the executioner," that he performed his job with reluctance. As the women were whipped, "many of the sober inhabitants, who, observing the innocence of their testimony, acknowledged them as servants of the living God, and in much love a tenderness accompanied them out of the city (Besse 1753; p. 563). According to Penney (1907), the women "were received by Mary Clewer, Elizabeth Digby, and Jane Bettris, some of the first to be convinced in Oxford, being honorable women, faithful to the truth" (p. 258). Jane Bettris' husband was a doctor and the first Meeting was held in their home.

At some point Elizabeth Fletcher went naked through the streets (Penney, 1907; pp. 258–59). Barbour and Roberts (1973) reported that although she was "a very modest, grave, young woman, yet contrary to her own will or inclination, in obedience to the Lord, she went naked as a sign against the hypocritical profession they then made there, being then fledgling priests — Presbyterians and Independents. She told the students that the Lord would strip them, so that their nakedness should appear, which shortly after, at the return of King Charles II, was fulfilled" (p. 593). The act of "going naked" is based on a passage in the Bible ("Then the LORD said, "My servant Isaiah has been walking around naked and barefoot for the last three years. This is a sign — a symbol of the terrible troubles I will bring upon Egypt and Ethiopia." Isaiah 23:10, New Living Translation). Brailsford (1915; p. 151) suggested that it indicated that Friends were willing to proclaim Truth at all costs.

Thomas Holme and Lizzie Leavens were married in Chester shortly after Oxford. From jail, Thomas wrote of the two Elizabeths: "They are such as the like of them I know not. By their ministry Friends grow exceedingly and meetings are kept up gallantly. Friends are kept fresh and green here always."

Although it is unclear how much after Oxford it occurred, Thomas Camm (his account mentioned in Brailsford, 1915) wrote that Elizabeth's mind was unhinged for a while by her cruel sufferings. She brooded over the hypocrisy of the students of religion who had abused her.

Elizabeth Fletcher was never well again, through for some time after she did travel according to the ability of her weak and bruised body (Penney, 1907; p. 258). Thomas Camm claimed also that her "childish body was so weakened and injured by the rough handling in Oxford that the remainder of her short life was one of struggle with pain and weariness" (Penney, 1907; p. 259). Yet, Brailsford (1915) wrote elsewhere that with "the marks of her brutal flogging in the market place yet fresh upon her, she set out upon her mission to Ireland" for the three years prior to her death. "With a mind smarting under these indignities, and a body unhealed of its wounds, little Elizabeth Fletcher crossed over to Dublin in early 1655" (Brailsford, 1915; p. 179).

Elizabeth Fletcher preached and was arrested in St. Audoen Church. By order of the Lord Mayor (Brailsford, 1915) she was imprisoned in Newgate Prison. Newgate was located on Cornmarket Street on the south side of the Liffey River and was originally the site of one of the city gates.

Elizabeth Fletcher was with either Elizabeth Smith or Elizabeth Morgan. As was Quaker practice, the women refused to pay the rates for bed, food, and drink. Those who could not pay were stripped and beaten and kept on a side of the building that only had "loopholes" for lights. Brailsford (1915) wrote that "the friendship of the women sustained them and that upon their release they stayed a while to preach" (p. 180), "spreading their message, perhaps in less obtrusive ways" (p.179). Wright and Rutty (pp. 83–89, 92) concurred, reporting in a *History of the Rise and Progress of the People called Quakers in Ireland from the Year 1653 to 1700*, that the first Quaker Meeting was in Dublin with ministry from the women at the chamber of Richard Fowkes, a tailor in Polegate (a part of Dublin). There might also have been a Meeting in the home of George Latham near Polegate (Myers, 1902).

It is unknown whether Elizabeth Fletcher met William Edmundson, the first Friend to preach in the country.

Brailsford (1915) stated that "Francis Howgill and Edward Burrough came over from London and worked in Dublin for three weeks" (p. 180). It seems they crossed paths with the women, Edward Burrough writing to Margaret Fell (in January, 1655), "Our dear sisters Elizabeth Fletcher and Elizabeth Smith are also in the west [Ireland], valiant for the truth" (Brailsford, 1915; pp. 181–82). Braithwaite (1912) noted that the men were helped in their work by "little" Elizabeth Fletcher of Kendal" (written in a letter by Howgill to Margaret Fell, p. 214). Brailsford (1915) added that "their ignorance of Gaelic might have presented an unsurmountable difficulty, but they seemed to have felt no desire to reach out to the unhappy natives who were casually stigmatized by Howgill as being 'robbers and murderers'" (pp. 181–82). According to a manuscript written by Edward Burrough (Swarthmoor MSS III. i6, as recorded in Brailsford (1915; p. 182)), after three weeks, Francis Howgill and Elizabeth Smith left Dublin to work elsewhere.

Once Elizabeth Fletcher was without a companion, Edward Burrough sent a "forlorn letter" to Margaret Fell (Swarthmoor MSS III. i6) stating that, "little Elizabeth Fletcher is at present here, but I know not how long she can stay; her dear love is to you . . . truly I suffer for her, she being as it were alone, having no other woman with her, in this ruinous nation, where it is very bad travelling every way on foot, and also dangerous (but we are much above all that). If it were ye will of ye lord and any women were moved to come over to her. There's at Dublin six of our brethren and sisters, in bonds [four men, whom he names], Elizabeth Morgan and Rebecca Ward, taken without anything being laid against them" (in Brailsford; p. 182).

It seems that at some point Elizabeth Fletcher and Elizabeth Morgan were joined by Burrough and Howgill. It is true that Howgill and Burrough were forced out of Dublin shortly thereafter. Brockbank (1949; p. 75) noted that they went on a vessel bound for the port of Chester and it took them two or three days to sail there.

Roberts (1973; p. 593) recorded that Elizabeth returned to Ireland in 1657 and was with Elizabeth Morgan there (Braithwaite 1912; p. 388). This is reported to have been when Francis Howgill recommended her to Friends: "I am glad that my dear friend and beloved sister, Elizabeth Fletcher (who is a helper and worker in the Lord's vineyard) is moved to come to you again, who is found honest, precious, and of good report in the family of God, who I know will be serviceable to the Lord and to you, in this his day, wherein he is spreading his name throughout the nations."

Brailsford (1915) noted that from Dublin Elizabeth Fletcher and Elizabeth Morgan traveled south into Munster, holding meetings in the towns through which they passed. Declaring Truth in the marketplace at Youghall, a large and satisfactory meeting was held (Wright & Rutty; 1751). As is stated in the novel, among numerous converts were Captain James Sicklemore and Lieutenant Robert Sandham, two of the Cromwellian soldiers stationed in that town. "The young girl, still only 18 years of age, spoke . . . from the text in the Prophet Joel, which is so familiar to all leaders of revival: 'Your sons and your daughters shall prophesy . . .'" (Wright and Rutty, 1751). At the close of the service, an Independent teacher stood out from the crowd and began vehemently to oppose the preaching of women. "The girl preacher listened without reply, weary with the effort of addressing that great company, and conscious that she had already said all that needed to be said in pounding her own text. The two men began to argue on her behalf, carrying the meeting with them and 'Truth prevailed'" (Wright and Rutty, 1751; pp. 93, 120–21 from Edmundson's Journal, reprinted in Wright and Rutty). Elizabeth was recorded as the first Quaker to preach in Cork and was well-received there.

At some point Elizabeth authored (wrote or dictated) one tract, *A Few Words in Season to All the Inhabitants of the Earth . . . to Leave off their Wickedness* (1660). It was a warning in which she described herself as "a servant who has known his terror for sin." The text gives a flavor of her hortatory [strong urging] skills as she invoked the wrath and indignation against the proud and greedy, whom she believed were to reform immediately or suffer for all eternity.

Several authors reported that Elizabeth was sent back to England in 1658 and constrained to stay at her Aunt's, Elizabeth Mansergh, in Kirby Lonsdale as her health was failing (Penney, 1907; p. 259). It is my invention in the novel, the idea of it being from my childhood friend, Bette Cox Gray-Fow, that Elizabeth contracted consumption.

She was visited as she died by many Friends and she enjoyed their company, glad and resigned in her decline. It's reported that she was "much at peace and contentedness of mind, blessing the Lord that had raised her up to bear testimony to his name and truth; that she was counted worthy to suffer for the same" (Penney, 1907; pp. 259–60). In her dying days, Elizabeth was reported as saying that "it was that crush that she got upon that gravestone that was the ground cause of her illness, praying that the Lord might forgive and open the eyes of all her blind persecutors" (Penney, 1907; pp. 209–11). She died on July 2, 1658 and

Friends accompanied her body to Kendal, eight miles away. She was buried two days later in what is believed to be the Birkrigg Friends burial ground in Kendal, as Quakers were forbidden burial in "consecrated ground" or in church-connected graveyards. Her grave is unmarked as was Quaker tradition at the time. The gravesite in Kendal is in a little walled, rocky enclosure that can be found two miles southeast, towards Kirby Lonsdale. It is neither in Sunbrick where Margaret Fell is buried near Swarthmoor Hall nor in the Sepulchre Lane Quaker burial ground.

Elizabeth Fletcher was nineteen years, nine months old at the time of her death. "Her life counted as dear," and her loss was lamented as she "was so young and so excellently qualified, affected with testimony that made her service great and greatly valued, but filled with wisdom to divine the word aright and greatly exemplary in her virtuous innocence and chaste conversation" (Penney, 1907; pp. 209–11).

Brief Biographies of the Young Quakers Appearing in this Novel

Many of the characters in *The Kendal Sparrow* were real first Friends. Books and journal articles tell the stories of the men, but in most cases, little is known about the women. In the information below, I use the names for the Elizabeths that I used in the novel.

Anne Newby Audland (1625 or 1627–1705). As the young wife of John Audland, Anne Audland was associated with the Westmoreland Seekers and entertained George Fox at her home after he spoke at Firbank Fell. She was born in Kendal but lived in London as a preteen before coming to Crosslands and marrying John Audland. Listed as one of the Valiant Sixty, she traveled in ministry with great capability (Emmott, 1916) and was a leader among those imprisoned with her. Christine Trevett (1998) noted that Anne Audland had been an uncompliant female and a troublesome prophet (p. 90). She detailed her life in *Women and Quakerism in the 17th Century* (York, 1991; 47–48). Anne died in 1705 and is possibly buried in Kendal.

John Audland (1630–1664). As one of the Valiant Sixty, John Audland was one of the first Quaker preachers. Born near Camsgill, Kendal, in Westmorland, John worked as a linen draper and farmer, living at Crosslands, near Preston Patrick. He was associated with the Westmorland Seekers before convincement. Here, in approximately 1650, he met and married Anne Newby. According to his personal testimony, he was twenty-two years of age when he and

Francis Howgill were preaching "to a seeking and religious people" at Firbank Chapel on the day George Fox preached at Firbank Fell. When he heard him, he was immediately convinced and invited George to his home. Brailsford (1915; p. 162) wrote that John Audland was "made at once to taste the fruits of his convincement," preaching among Baptists and Independents. He often traveled with his neighbor, John Camm, who was older. In 1653, he was imprisoned in Newcastle for preaching, and in the same year, he was in York Castle, a fellow prisoner with Mary Fisher and Elizabeth Hooton (Brailsford, 1915; p. 162).

Apart from a visit to London, Audland's ministry concentrated on Bristol, where he and Camm were repeatedly imprisoned, and parts of southwest England. Brailsford (1915; p. 162) wrote that when Camm and Audland arrived in Bristol they met a community of Seekers, "humble and tender" souls who were praying and fasting for guidance. That this group was so receptive gave a "power to the two missionaries," and within but a couple of days their ministry outgrew the private cottages. Villagers and the garrisons left by Cromwell flocked "like an army" to meetings in the open fields outside of the city. By November, Camm wrote back to Swarthmoor Hall that they had "most commonly 3,000 to 4,000 at a meeting." Threatened with their churches quickly emptying, the ministers and magistrates of the city "began to rage, but the soldiers kept them down."

Audland's preaching was powerful, appealing to all sorts of people and hundreds were convinced by him. He also published many tracts. He died on January 22, 1664 at only thirty-four years of age and was buried at Birkrigg Park (Westmorland) in the Quaker burial ground of Preston Patrick near Kendal, Westmorland. (This is a different burial ground than the one at Swarthmoor Meeting, near Ulverston,

Lancashire North of the Sands; now Cumbria). It's believed that his early death was a result of his many sufferings.

Edward Burrough (March 1632–February 1662) was born in Underbarrow, England. At age twelve, he became a Seeker. Convinced by George Fox in 1652, he became an itinerant preacher at twenty years of age and was disowned by his parents. One of the Valiant Sixty, he mostly traveled with Francis Howgill, who was an older Friend. Edward was a noted leader and controversialist who authored many pamphlets and was known for his wit and poetic style. In his clear, logical, and carefully constructed writings he showed "a deep love and knowledge of the Lord, conveyed with clarity, brevity, eloquence, power, and authority; his sentences are surely aimed arrows, reaching both the tender hearts of the saints and the hardened hearts of their persecutors" (http://www.hallvworthington.com/Burrough/Memoir1.html). He was an extraordinary servant, serving "magnificently" in Northern England, London, Bristol, and Ireland, being "the spiritual father to thousands" (http://www.hallvworthington.com/Burrough/Memoir1.html) despite his young age. As is described in the novel, he was nicknamed the Son of Thunder, the name Jesus gave to John and his younger brother James. He was cheerful and gentle, and although he wrote fondly of Elizabeth Fletcher in letters, the romance between them in the novel is invented.

It is true that Edward was in Dublin in 1655 where his presence in towns was of great annoyance to the Cromwellian authorities, who feared that the promotion of egalitarian principles would cause unrest amongst the troops and Irish. Edward stated in a letter to Margaret Fell: "Our service lies only in the great towns and city, for generally the country is without inhabitant, except for bands of murderers and thieves, and robbers, who wait for their prey and devour many, from which yet we are preserved" (Brailsford, 1915; pp. 181–82). He and Francis Howgill were arrested in Limerick and sent back to Dublin under armed guard (Harrison, 2018; p. 5). Edward never flinched from fines, imprisonments, or any species of personal abuse or violence, but prison quarters undermined his health. He was illegally arrested in 1662 and sent to Newgate Prison, London. Although Charles II signed an order for his release, local authorities ignored it. He died "of a raging fever" (Vipont, 1954; p. 87) on February 14, 1663, at thirty years of age, and was buried in the Quaker Burying Ground at Bunhill Fields, London.

Mabel Benson Camm (1627–1705). As the wife of John Camm and mother of Thomas Camm (born in 1641), Mabel Camm was good friend with her neighbors, the Audlands. She hosted George Fox after he preached on Firbank Fell and before he went to Swarthmoor Hall for the first time. When her family and two maidservants (Dorothy and Jane Waugh) were convinced, Mabel was about twenty-eight years old. She stayed back with her son for at least a time while the servant girls and John Camm (and John Audland) set off to travel and preach. She's listed as one of the Valiant Sixty, serving locally, and did later also travel, often with Anne Audland. Her burial site is unknown.

Thomas Camm (1641–1707). Born at Camsgill, Westmoreland, in 1641, Thomas Camm was the son of John and Mabel Camm and was convinced with his parents when he was twelve years of age. He began traveling to preach at a very young age and is listed as one of the Valiant Sixty. By 1666, he was married to Anne Audland, who tended to him faithfully in his repeated imprisonments. In 1674 he was sued by John

Ormrod, vicar of Burton, near Kendal, for small tithes, and in default of payment was imprisoned for three years. In 1678 a magistrate broke up a meeting of Quakers held at Ackmonthwaite, committed several Friends to prison, and seems to have fined them, since Thomas Camm, who had been the preacher at the meeting, lost nine head of cattle and fifty-five sheep. Shortly after, another fine was made upon his property by warrant from the same justice. Somewhat later he was imprisoned for nearly six years in Appleby jail, most likely for some offense against the Conventicle Act.

Camm did much to prevent the growth of the schisms to which Quakerism seemed liable. He wrote considerably. It is unknown whether he knew Elizabeth Fletcher. He died after a short illness in 1707 and is buried in the Friends' burial ground at Park End, near Camsgill.

William Canton (dates unknown). Serving as a tutor to the youngest children of Judge and Margaret Fell, Will Canton was a young teen when he heard George Fox preach at Firbank Fell. He was friends with William Fell who rebelled against the Quakerism of his family. Will truly was the one to give the directions that brought the preacher to Swarthmoor Hall for the first time. Listed as one of the Valiant Sixty, he acted as Margaret Fell's secretary and wrote many letters to inform Friends of the work of others. He died in Holland at but twenty years of age after serving as a Quaker preacher, always homesick for Swarthmoor Hall.

William Edmundson (1627–1712). William Edmundson was born in Little Musgrave, England and reared by an uncle. He was apprenticed out as a carpenter's assistant when he was thirteen years old and eventually joined the Parliamentary army under Oliver Cromwell. When he'd served out his term he went with his new wife, Margaret, to join his brother, John, in Antrim, Ireland. He frequently travelled back for trade to England to buy supplies, and it was on one of these trips that he attended a Quaker meeting. In 1653 he heard James Nayler, a noted Friend, preach, and was transformed. William became a significant minister in his own right, a charismatic speaker with a reputation for sincerity and integrity. In 1654, he and his wife moved to Lurgan, where they founded the first Meeting in the country. The Edmundsons had seven children and lived last on a farm at Tineal, Rosenallis. William continued his work in Barbados, Jamaica and various parts of the colonies, returning home in 1672. He died in 1712 and was buried in the Quaker Burial Ground, marked as such today, at Mountmellick, Ireland.

Richard Farnsworth (1637–1666). Richard Farnsworth was born in Tickhill, North Doncaster, England. At about sixteen years of age he experienced a spiritual awakening and began to doubt the teachings of the Church of England. In 1651, now a yeoman, he was convinced by George Fox and was one of the Valiant Sixty. As is told in the novel, he traveled with George Fox to Pendle Hill, but a bad knee prevented him from ascending it.

Richard primarily preached in the East Midlands and held meetings that attracted hundreds. He prolifically wrote thirteen pamphlets in 1653 alone, as well as a brief biography in 1654. In *A Woman Forbidden to Speak in the Church* (1655) he defended women's preaching and might have been the first to record the story of Elizabeth Fletcher in his letters.

Richard died in 1666 at twenty-nine years of age of a "fever" and was buried in the Checker Ally Burial Grounds, which is now lost below the present Broad Street railway station, London.

(Young) Margaret Fell (1633–?). Margaret Fell was the oldest daughter of Judge and Margaret Fell. She was nineteen when George Fox first came to Swarthmoor Hall. Her siblings were Bridget, Isabel, George (b. 1639), Sarah, Mary, and Susanna, and Rachel (b. 1653). Her personality and role of letter-writing are completely fabricated in this novel. Her younger sister, Sarah, was much more involved in the movement.

Mary Fisher (1623–1698). Born in north Yorkshire, at Pontefract, England (Brailslford, 1915; p. 107), Mary Fisher worked as a housemaid for Richard and Elizabeth Tomlinson. As such, she was at Selby in late December 1651, where she, at twenty-nine years of age, was convinced by George Fox. She was released to preach, an extremely active and daring Quaker, and was one of the Valiant Sixty.

As is told in the novel, Mary Fisher accompanied Elizabeth Williams to Cambridge in December 1653, as part of the Quaker drive to bring Quakerism to the south of England. Vipont (1954; p. 44) wrote that the women were "greeted with jeers and catcalls," and were arrested and sentenced by the mayor to be "stripped to the waist and brutally flogged at the market cross until the blood ran." It's recorded that the unresisting women never opened their lips except to pray for their persecutors.

In 1655, Mary Fisher and Ann Austin set off to the New World to spread the Quaker message. They first sailed to Barbados in the Caribbean where they were well received and where they converted the Lieutenant Governor of the island. In May 1656 (Brailsford, 1915; p. 109), Mary Fisher and Ann Austin became the first Quakers to arrive in the colonies when they docked at Boston in the Massachusetts Bay Colony. News of the heretical views of the Quakers had preceded them and on arrival they were taken ashore and imprisoned.

They were forced to undress in public and their bodies were intimately examined by a "female" dressed as a man for signs of witchcraft. Finally, after five weeks of imprisonment, the women were forced to return to England. In 1658, at thirty-five years old, Mary Fisher felt prompted to travel in a group of six Quakers to the Mediterranean. She alone visited the Ottoman Empire and the Sultan Mehmed IV.

Mary Fisher married at least twice and had several children who emigrated with her to South Carolina. She was reverently referred to as Mother Crosse, dying in 1699 at about seventy-five years of age (http://esrquaker.blogspot.mx/2013/11/preaching-truth-and-listening-for-truth.html). In her will, she bequeathed to her daughter, Mary Basden, "one Indian Girl slave named Rayner." Mary Fisher Bayly Crosse is buried in the Quaker burial ground, Charleston in Charleston County, South Carolina (located on Meeting Street near Broad Street, on the right when traveling west, in Lawrimore Park).

For more information:

- Sylvia Brown, "The Radical Travels of Mary Fisher: Walking and Writing in the Universal Light," Sylvia Brown (ed.), *Women, Gender and Radical Religion in Early Modern Europe* (Leiden: Brill, 2007), pp. 39–64
- There's a detailed section on Mary Fisher and Quaker ministry in Barbados in Stephen W. Angell, "Early Quaker Women and the Testimony of the Family, 1652–1767," Michele Lise Tarter and Catie Gill (eds.), *New Critical Studies on Early Quaker Women, 1650–1800* (Oxford: OUP, 2018), pp. 50–68
- Althea Stewart, "Public Justice and Personal Liberty: Variety and Linguistic Skill in the Letters of Mary Fisher," *Quaker Studies* 3 (Liverpool: Quaker Studies Research Association, 1998), pp. 13–159

- Mary Fisher is one of four Quakers discussed in *Four Early Quakers* (London: Friends Education Council, 1978). The book lists no author.

Thomas (1626/27–1666) and **Elizabeth (Leavens) Holme** (1624?–1665). The Holmes were both born in Kendal, England. Both were convinced in 1652 and listed as among the Valiant Sixty.

Penney (1907) described Lizzie Leavens as of more humble parentage than her companion Elizabeth Fletcher and it is unknown what she was called to distinguish her from Elizabeth. According to Wright and Rutty (1751), Thomas was of an impatient character and posed as a martyr in the whole tenor of his life. Brailsford (1915; p. 103) described Lizzie Leavens as "a most attractive personality, affectionate and impulsive to a degree which called for censure from her grave superiors in the work."

In October 1653, Thomas visited Durham (an area also known as Bishopric; Braithwaite, 1912; p. 114), as is described in the novel. He worked as well in Cumberland, Westmorland, Lancashire, and Staffordshire. Allen (2004) wrote that he occasionally met violent opposition (also recorded in Braithwaite, 1912). According to Braithwaite (1912; p. 125), Thomas, Lizzie, Elizabeth, and Jane Waugh went together to Cheshire and South Lancashire in November 1653. Braithwaite (1912; p. 125) wrote that, "The Friends were zealous and often under strange workings of the power, the people rude and violent, the authorities alarmed at what they didn't understand." Braithwaite also wrote that Thomas was a man of little judgement and was imprisoned for going naked through the Cheshire streets as a sign.

Braithwaite (1912) also reported that a Quaker meeting was held and people returning from church looked in at it and saw those gathered were trembling and crying (p. 125). They told the mayor who sent an officer. It is true that when he arrested Thomas, he fainted. Later, in prison, Thomas lay on the floor of his cell saying that he was commanded by the Lord to refuse his bed. Then at midnight, he claimed the Lord came upon him and he was compelled to sing. The same thing happened the next night and, in the morning, he sang again and was crying with "unspeakable love of God" (Braithwaite, 1912; p. 126). Much of this history is told in the novel.

Trevett (1991; p. 24) wrote that a 1654 pamphlet noted that in the towns of Kendal, Hutton, and Kirby, eight people came naked. Thomas Holme was among them. Also in 1654, Lizzie Leavens walked with Elizabeth Fletcher to Oxford. The degree of her suffering there is not recorded.

Thomas was in jail while the women were in Oxford. From there he wrote of them: "They were such as the like of them I know not. By their ministry, Friends grow exceedingly, and meetings are kept up gallantly. Friends are kept fresh and green here" (Brailsford, 1915; p. 150). After such enthusiasm, Thomas felt a "sweet melody within" (Brailsford, 1915; p. 150) and decided he was to marry Lizzie. "Upon the 13 day of the 8 month (October, 1654), the same day we were set free from outward bonds, being in Chester at Edward Morgan's house, and she with me, and many more other Friends, I was immediately commanded of the Lord to take her to wife that day, having before seen clear in the Light eternal, and had a vision of it long before, as likewise, she'd had. So in obedience to the command of the Lord, I took her to wife contrary to my will before diverse friends and I would have you send word to him who hath joined us together [in convincement], George Fox, for it will stand before him, and so before the eternal God" (Swarthmore, MSS I, 195).

Brailsford (1915) stated that by Thomas' asking that George Fox be informed of the marriage, he was indirectly asking for his approval as there was no lawful way for Quakers to marry at the time (p. 150). Mack (1992) stated that although Margaret Fell thought the marriage divinely willed, she was displeased with the couple. Quakers were supposed to be focused on experiencing the deepest, most hidden authentic aspect of self and be above the need for human love and sex (Mack, 1992; pp. 145, 183). It is unknown whether Elizabeth was in attendance.

In 1655, Lizzie was whipped for nudity in Chester (http://www.holytrinitybickerstaffe.co.uk/wp-content/uploads/2016/03/Bickerstaffe-New-Text-Quakers-1-PDF.pdf). Thomas was "settling Knowsley Meeting at the time," Brailsford wrote (1915, pp. 150–51). The first year of their life together was an idyll of mutual help and childlike happiness as Thomas' "brave" friend (Brailsford, 1915; pp. 150–51).

Thomas and Lizzie are said to have gone singing through England together, both "being much exercised by the power of the Lord in songs and hymns and prayer" (Brailsford, 1915; p. 151). This behavior made some doubtful of the wisdom of their words as singing wasn't typical of the "serious Quaker." "When the unconventional services of the young Holmes came to Fox's ears, he wrote in his journal with board-mindedness" 'Your life was raised thereby and refreshed by many in your meetings but some did worry — the singing muddling your enticing, wise words." (paraphrased by me from Brailsford, 1915; p. 151; Fox's journal, vol. 1, p. 326).

Brailsford (1915; p. 151) described Lizzie Leavens Holme as a diligent, faithful, and zealous laborer and a faithful and constant sufferer. In January 1656, she and her companion, Alice Birkett, joined Thomas to preach in South

Wales (p. 207). Musical and enthusiastic, their style was particularly appealing to the Welsh nature, wrote Brailsford (1915; p. 151), and by April they were able to report almost a dozen small meetings had taken root.

In June 1656, Thomas traveled back to England to meet with George Fox, who counseled him about the arrangements for their first child so they could continue to serve in ministry. Margaret Fell was not sympathetic, refusing Lizzie shoes and other necessities. She regarded the couple as an improvident pair who should have concentrated on their missionary work rather than producing a baby for other people to look after (The whole story is told in Swarthmoor MSS I, 197, 202–3, 238, 304]. "It's difficult," wrote Mack (1992), "to imagine the maternal and emotional suffering implied in these bare facts, although some historians insist that the traveling Quaker women didn't allow themselves maternal feelings."

In 1658 George Fox came to Cardiff and found a separation among Friends (Braithwaite, 1912; p. 270). An attempt was made to stop Thomas' work. People came to Meeting and fell on the floor singing and sat in haircloth and ashes.

The couple hadn't been married seven years before the health of Elizabeth Holme began to fail due to the strain of travel and hard imprisonments, complicated by the frequent separations from her husband whom she held dearest to her (Brailsford, 1915; p. 155). In 1662, Thomas wrote to George Fox that she'd been very sick for more than ten days with a body that was all out of order. "Her love is dear to you and she salutes you" (Besse; pp. 741, 748). Three years later Elizabeth died at her home in Kendal on the 10th day of the seventh month, 1665. She would have been in her late twenties. A year later in 1666, Thomas Holme died at St. Faganns, Cardiff at thirty-nine years of age and was buried at Point-y-Moel Burying Ground, Pontypool in Munmothshire,

England. It is unknown where Lizzie Leavens was buried. The couple left three children behind, two of whom grew to adulthood. None became Quaker.

Elizabeth Morgan (nd). Elizabeth Morgan was from Chester, the daughter of Edward Morgan. It is true that Thomas Holme and Edward Morgan were friends but the story in the novel of how Elizabeth and Elizabeth (Bette) Morgan met is fabricated.

Braithwaite (1912) wrote that Bette "bred dissension in Bristol meeting in 1655 by her unwise conduct and exalted spirit" and led a man "astray for a time. . . . [She] came among Gloucester Friends and in her ecstatic way declared her message to the people very boldly" (p. 389). It's recorded that she was with Elizabeth Fletcher in Cork in 1657. Little else is known about her.

James Parnell (1636–1655). James Parnell was born in East Retford, Nottinghamshire, the son of Thomas and Sarah Parnell (Davies, 2004). He was reported to be of small stature and physically weak but possessing a precocious intellect. When fifteen years old, he left home against his parents' wishes and traveled north to find Seekers. It is true, as is described in the novel, that those he met told him of George Fox and that in 1653, he walked over 100 miles to Carlisle to visit Fox in jail. After the two talked, James was convinced and began to preach; he is listed as one of the Valiant Sixty. Because of his youth and slight appearance, opponents nicknamed him the "Quaking boy" (Davies, 2004). James eventually returned home, and at sixteen years of age authored many pamphlets and books. When he was eighteen years old (1665), he visited Essex and settled Meetings in Cambridge, Felstead, Witham, Colchester, and

Coggeshall, often the first Quaker preacher in these areas and very loved by the people there. James was arrested several times and eventually sentenced to Colchester Castle. As reported in the novel, he was forced to climb a rope to the window of his cell to receive food and that he weakened over time, being kept in the damp cell. He eventually fell, broke his leg, and was moved to a cell called "the Oven" by his cruel jailers. He died in prison in May 1656 at nineteen years of age. While it's true that two Friends heard his last words, Edward Burrough was not with him. His body was kept from Friends and buried in the Colchester Castle yard.

William Penn (1644–1718). The son of Admiral Sir William Penn and raised with wealth and privilege, William Penn was born in London but lived in Ireland on an estate that was awarded to his father, a naval figure, for service during the Civil War. When there, he attended a Quaker Meeting with his father at the home of Isaac Pennington where Thomas Loe was preaching. Other than that he lived in Ireland as a young boy, the story of him in this novel is completely invented. He'd have been about twelve years of age at the time Elizabeth Fletcher was in Cork, but it is unknown as to whether they met.

It's true that William Penn left Ireland to attend college in Oxford in 1660 when sixteen years of age. There he refused to go to Church services and was expelled. He later studied law.

Penn embraced the members of the Cork Meeting in 1667 when he returned to Ireland to manage his father's estates. "As a member of the small and despised religious sect, Penn was persecuted and imprisoned in an era when religious toleration was virtually unknown" (Bronner, 1975, p. 6). In the next decade, Penn traveled to Dutch and German states to visit Quakers. By the time he was thirty years old, he was seen as a spokesman for an important group of at least fourteen substantial Quaker merchants based in London. This gave him access to Quakers across England. Penn married the daughter of Isaac Pennington and became a leading advocate for tolerance and complaint against harsh laws penalizing Quakers. Worried for him, his father sent him to govern Pennsylvania where he assisted in applying Quaker principles to rules and regulations. He died in 1718 and is buried in the Quaker Burying Ground beside the Meeting House and Quaker Center at Jordans in South Buckinghamshire, England.

Elizabeth Smith (nd–1668). In 1655 Elizabeth Fletcher and Elizabeth Smith traveled to Dublin and were imprisoned there for a short time. She's called Betsy in *The Kendal Sparrow*. When Brailsford (1915) wrote of Francis Howgill and Edward Burrough coming from London to work in Dublin "for three weeks" (p.180), he stated that they crossed paths with the women. According to a faded manuscript written by Edward Burrough (Swarthmoor MSS III. i6, as recorded in Brailsford (1915; p. 182), after three weeks, Francis Howgill and Elizabeth Smith left Dublin to work elsewhere. I also found that Miles Huberstie (also spelled, Hubbersty) of Underbarrow, married a virtuous maid, Elizabeth Smith, who was endowed with a large gift of ministry, and had before her marriage, traveled to preach in several parts of west England as well as Ireland (briefly with Elizabeth Fletcher). According to Brailsford (1915), Betsy died a young woman in 1668 in Kendal (perhaps about twenty-eight years of age).

Dorothy Waugh (Lotherington) (nd–1666) Dorothy Waugh was probably born in Hutton, Westmorland and was sister to

Jane Waugh (later Whitehead) [From Catie Gill (no date) http://www.oxforddnb.com/view/article/69140.]. Dorothy was fifteen when she and her sister were maids in the home of John and Mabel Camm in Preston Patrick. They were convinced by George Fox in 1652 and are listed as among the Valiant Sixty. Both were released to serve as itinerant preachers in the fledgling movement and shunned by their relatives for doing so (Mack, 1992; p. 245). Trevett (1998) wrote that the Quaker tenet of equality enabled the women an unexpected freedom (p. 14). Dorothy had little or no education, but she had enthusiasm and energy, and like her sister, she was described as having "intense sincerity of Quaker purpose" (Barbour & Roberts, 1973; p. 94).

Initially Jane and Dorothy traveled with John Audland and John Camm but later with Anne Audland and Mabel Camm in ministry. According to Gill (no date), Dorothy was imprisoned in Kendal in 1653 and spent another four months' detention in Norwich in 1654. She subsequently preached in Buckinghamshire (1655), Cornwall (1655), and Carlisle (1655). Penney (1907) described Dorothy as bridled after preaching in the streets on a market day in Carlisle. One Peter Norman, who was the mayor at the time, asked her "from where she came" and her answer greatly angered him. "His wrath was so kindled against truth and her that he caused a bridle to be put upon her, which is said to be a stone weight. . . . She was sentenced to Mute-Hall until his heat was abated" (Mack 1992). Mack added that Norman thought Dorothy's preaching against the citizenry's "deceit & ungodly practices" might "spoile a whole Cittie" (Waugh, 29–30 in Mack, 1992). Dorothy described the bridle as "on her head with a stone eight and much iron in her mouth like an egg" (Mack, 1992; p. 248), providing one of the few firsthand accounts of being bridled that has survived from the seventeenth century. Sometimes when a woman was bridled, she was led about the town on a chain and whipped so that people could mock her, throw trash at her, or even urinate on her.

Penney (1907) wrote that in 1654, Jane and Dorothy Waugh, Anne Audland, and Richard Farnsworth came to Oxford after Elizabeth Fletcher had been there. Apparently, "they had great success in 'the building of Friends and [the] establishment of Meetings.'"

According to Trevett (1998; p. 25), Dorothy Waugh was with some other women in Malton where they burned "silk ribbons and fine materials" as "a witness against pride and injustice," to the anger of shopkeepers and woolen drapers. She may have been with other women who, according to Trevett (1998; p. 25), held meetings at strange times, sometimes in the middle of the night, which disturbed families. So compelling were the meetings that the mayor couldn't keep his wife at home.

Dorothy preached in Reading (1656) and journeyed to New England on two separate occasions (1656, 1657). After her return, she married a Friend, William Lotherington (d. 1674?) of Whitby in Yorkshire. The couple settled there and became members of the Pickering meeting. Dorothy died on December 9, 1666, in her early thirties. Both the cause of death and her place of burial are unknown (Gill; no date).

Jane Waugh (Whitehead) (nd). As pieced together from several entries in *The First Publishers of Truth* (Penney; 1907, ed.), Jane, along with William Simson, was "a faithful handmaid of the Lord [and] one of the first to preach in Warborough (Warbrow) in Oxfordshire, following Edward Burrough, Francis Howgill, Ambrose Rigge, and Thomas Roberson. In the Early Time of Truth, she came into Somersetshire to 'preach truth.'" She was at Banbury in

1654–55 with John and Anne Audland and "suffered imprisonment for her faithful testimony bearing to truth, and stood firm." Penney (1907) recorded that "on one occasion the jail being so damp that it sometimes would be over their shoes in water." Jane was whipped and imprisoned many times. Mack (1992) wrote that she was "ducked as a scold in York" (p. 248). At some point after her release, she married Thomas Whitehead (pp. 223, 255) and they supported each other's work. She died in 1674, leaving a husband and five children. Her burial site is unknown.

George Whitehead (1636–1723). Born at Sunbiggin, near Orton, Westmorland, the son of a poor farmer, George Whitehead became convinced of Quaker principles at the age of fourteen after hearing George Fox preach in Graygrigg. Listed as one of the Valiant Sixty, he was an active itinerant minister in 1652 at sixteen years of age, traveling through Yorkshire, Lincolnshire, East Anglia, and Kent, often as the companion of Richard Hubberthorne, but sometimes with George Fox. He championed women's equality.

George was first imprisoned in Norwich Castle in 1654 for eight weeks when but seventeen years of age for speaking out against baptism at the end of the service at St. Peter's Church in Norwich, England. When he appeared in court, he refused to remove his hat before the judge and was sent back to jail. He was arrested again in May of 1655 in Bures, Suffolk. No sooner released than he was imprisoned for three months at Bury St. Edmonds because he refused to pay an imposed fine. He was later released after he made a direct appeal to Oliver Cromwell. He was publicly whipped for vagrancy in London and jailed in both Norwich and East Anglia. George suffered harsh punishments in the stocks at Saffron Waldon and was whipped out of the town at Nayland.

George published his first book on Quakerism when he was eighteen years old, the beginning of an important Quaker publishing career. He reconciled with his parents when twenty years old, continuing to serve as an itinerant preacher in Northumberland, Newcastle, Berwick, Alnwick, and Holy Island.

When he was imprisoned for four months in Ipswich, George educated himself about the law. He caused a sensation in court by pointing out the illegality of the charges against him. Unfortunately, he was not released and was freed only after the death of Oliver Cromwell in September 1658 (so he wouldn't have been at the memorial in this novel). George became pivotal in showing Friends how to use the law to assert their rights. He spent much of the next decade in jail.

In 1657, he married Ann Dower in London only shortly before he was sent back to jail.

By 1660 Whitehead (twenty-nine years of age) had settled down, was preaching and jailed less frequently, and worked as a grocer in London to support his family. In 1661, he worked on legislation that was favorable to Quakers.

George Whitehead is remembered as a leading early Quaker preacher, author and lobbyist for religious freedom before three kings of England. He was buried in the Quaker Burying Ground at Bunhill Fields on March 13, 1724. [Sources: ODNB 29877, Whitehead, George Fox (1637–1724); Braithwaite 1 & 2; Quaker Burials, 1578–1841; London & Middlesex MM, Burials, RG6/673].

Martin Riley assisted with burial information. He wrote of his sources: "Most of the burial sites are well covered by either Quaker Burials listings (Archive set RG6 in British National Archives), and I also used two key reference books: *The Beginnings of Quakerism* by William C. Braithwaite and his second volume, *The Second Period of Quakerism*. Both are published by MacMillan, 1912 and 1919, respectively."

Queries for Book Clubs and Discussion Groups

1. What is something you learned from Elizabeth Fletcher's story?
2. How has the reading affected your First Day worship, if at all? How has it affected your private worship?
3. Describe the different ways that the characters in *The Kendal Sparrow* manifest their faith (e.g., George Fox and Edward Burrough use Christocentric language). Does one of their expressions speak to you more than another? How so?
4. Why do you think the story of Elizabeth Hooten, who was one of the first to deeply listen to George Fox, is included in the novel?
5. Name some of the specific Quaker terms that are described in the novel (e.g., a leading, convincement, etc.). Do you feel that you have a good sense of what they mean to the characters? If you are a convinced Friend, can you describe your convincement?
6. Are the tellings of martyred activists still relevant today?
7. Can you think of a Quaker woman in recent history who might have been "bridled" if the punishment still existed?
8. Have you been challenged to find "that of God in someone" as Elizabeth Fletcher was challenged in the novel by the Oxford students? How so? Can you describe a time when you lost one or more of the values underlying the Quaker testimonies for a time and how/if you regained it?

9. Do you think that Elizabeth Fletcher was able to find purpose for her life as she became increasingly sickly? How so? How can we find purpose as our energy lessens?
10. What can you compare about the lives of the young Quaker itinerant preachers as told in *The Kendal Sparrow* and young activists of today?

Sources

Richard Allen, Entries for Thomas Holme (and Elizabeth Leavens), Elizabeth Fletcher, and James Parnell in the *Oxford Dictionary of National Biography* (2008). www.oxforddnb.com.

Stephen W. Angell, "Preaching Truth and Listening for Truth: Early Quaker Mary Fisher and Prospects for Interreligious Dialogue" (Nov. 13, 2013). http://esrquaker.blogspot.com/2013/11/preaching-truth-and-listening-for-truth.html

Kristen Backstrom, "What Quality?" in *The Carillon*, 14 (4) (2016), 4–7.

Margaret Hope Bacon, *Mothers of Feminism: The Story of Quaker Women in America* (San Francisco: Harper and Row, 1986).

Hugh Barbour and J. William Frost, *The Quakers* (New York: Greenwood Press, 1988).

Joseph Besse, *A Collection of the Sufferings of the People called Quakers from 1650–1689*, 2 vols. (London: Luke Hinde 1753).

Black Lives Matter. https://en.wikipedia.org/wiki/Black_Lives_Matter. Wikipedia.

William C. Braithwaite, *The Beginnings of Quakerism to 1660* (London: Macmillan, 1912).

Mabel Brailsford, *Quaker Women: 1650–1690* (London: Duckworth, 1915).

Howard H. Brinton, *How They Became Friends* (Wallingford, PA: Pendle Hill, 1961).

Elizabeth Brockbank, *Edward Burrough of Underbarrow, 1634–1662* (London: Bannishdale, 1949).

Edwin Bronner, *William Penn, 17th Century Founding Father: Selections from His Political Writings* (Wallingford, PA: Pendle Hill, 1975).

Alice Clark, *The Working Life of Women in the Seventeenth Century* (London: George Routledge & Sons. New York: E.P. Dutton, 1919).

M. Coffin, "Acceptance," *The Carillon*, 14 (7) (2016), 4–5.

Ben Pink Dandelion and Frederick Martin, "Outcasts of Israel": The Apocalyptic Theology of Edward Burrough and Francis Howgill," *Early Quakers And Their Theological Thought*, Stephen Angell and Pink Dandelion, eds. (New York: Cambridge University, 2015).

Adrian Davies, "James Parnell," *Oxford Dictionary of National Biography* (2004). www.oxforddnb.com

John M. Douglas, *The Beginnings of Quakerism in 17th Century Ireland*. Address given at the Tercentenary Conference, 1954 (Friends School Lisburn: Historical Committee of the Religious Society of Friends in Ireland, 2004).

Marion Eames, *The Secret Room* (Swansea SAI: Christopher Davies, 1969).

Elizabeth Braithwaite Emmott, *The Story of Quakerism: 1855–1946* (London: Headley Brothers, 1916).

Elfrida Vipont Foulds, *The Birthplace of Quakerism: A Handbook from the 1662 Country* (1952).

Elfrida Vipont Foulds, *The Story of Quakerism, 1652–1952* (London: Bannishdale, 1954).

Antonia Fraser, *Cromwell: Our Chief of Men* (London: Weidenfeld & Nicolson, 1974).

Antonia Fraser, *The Weaker Vessel: Women's Lot in Seventeen-Century England* (Knopf Doubleday Publishing Group, 1984).

Judith Kegan Gardiner, *Renaissance Quarterly*: 59 (3), Fall, 2006 (pp. 950–52).

Catie Gill, *Women in the Seventeenth-Century Quaker Community: A Literary Study of Political Identities, 1650–1700* (Aldershot: Ashgate, 2005).

Amy Goodman, "From Keystone XL Pipeline to #DAPL: Jasilyn Charger, Water Protector from Cheyenne River Reservation" on "Democracy Now" (National Public Radio, January 4, 2017).

Amy Goodman, "A Violation of Tribal & Human Rights: Standing Rock Chair Slams Approval of Dakota Access Pipeline" on "Democracy Now" (National Public Radio, January 9, 2017).

Douglas Gwyn, *Seekers Found: Atonement in Early Quaker Experience* (Wallingford, PA: Pendle Hill Publications, 2000).

Douglas Gwyn, *The Covenant Crucified: Quakers and the Rise of Capitalism* (Wallingford, PA: Pendle Hill Publications, 2006).

Richard Harrison, *Dublin Quakers (1650–1900)* (Dublin: Historical Committee of the Religious Society of Friends in Ireland, 2018).

Lucy Violet Hodgkin, *A Book of Quaker Saints* (London: Friends Home Service Committee, 1968).

Charles Holder, *The Quakers in Great Britain and America: The Religious and Political History of the Society of Friends from the Seventeenth to the Twentieth Century* (New York: Neuner Co., 1913).

Larry Ingle, *First Among Friends: George Fox and the Creation of Quakerism* (Oxford: Oxford University Press, 1994).

Rufus Jones, *George Fox, Seeker and Friend* (New York and London: Harper and Bros., 1930).

Rosalind Johnson, "Quakers in Wessex: Through Much Reproach and Hard Travel: The Journeys of Ambrose Rigge and Thomas Robertson," a paper given at the Quaker Family History Society Regional Conference, Salisbury Quaker House, 28 April 2012, https://www.academia.edu/1723247/The_travels_of_Ambrose_Rigge_and_Thomas_Robertson

Barbara Luetke-Stahlman, *17th Century Remarkable Quaker Youth*. (Kansas City: Self-published under the care of Penn Valley Friends, 2001).

Phyllis Mack, "Feminine Behavior and Radical Action: Franciscans, Quakers, and the Followers of Gandhi," *Signs: Journal of Women in Culture and Society 11*, (3) (Spring, 1986), pp. 457–77.

Phyllis Mack, *Visionary Women: Ecstatic Prophecy in Seventeenth Century England* (Berkeley, CA: University of California, 1992).

James MacPherson, "Next Test for Pipeline Protesters: The North Dakota Winter," Associated Press: News Tribute (on the Internet). Photo in the article by James MacPherson (January 2017). http://amp.newstribune.com/news/national/story/2016/dec/02/next-test-pipeline-protesters-north-dakota-winter/651471/.

Marcelle Martin, *Our Life Is Love* (San Francisco: Inner Light Books, 2016).

Rosemary Anne Moore, *The Light in Their Consciences: The Early Quakers in Britain (1646–1666)* (University Park: The Pennsylvania State University, 2000).

Albert Cook Myers, *Immigration of the Irish Quakers into Pennsylvania (1682–1750): With Their Early History in Ireland* (Swarthmore, PA: author published, 1902).

Oxford Tour online: http://www.rpc.ox.ac.uk/downloadlibrary/Oxford_TourLJK.pdf-info

Norman Penney (Ed.) *The Frist Publishers of Truth: Being early records (now first printed) of the Introduction of Quakerism into the Counties of England and Wales* (London: Headley Brothers, 1907).

John Punshon, *Portrait in Gray: A Short History of the Quakers* (London: Quaker Home Services, 1984).

"Real Talk with Zeb." Jasiln Charher-Youth Speaking on the Dakota Access Pipeline (Sep 14, 2016). https://www.youtube.com/watch?v=pG1VVeLEHYM.

William Sewel, *The History of the Rise, Increase, and Progress of the Christian People called Quakers, Intermixed with several Remarkable Occurrences* (London: J. Sowle, 1722).

Gil Skidmore, *Dear Friends and Sisters* (Reading, England: Sowle, 1998).

E. Stevenson, "The Essence of the Quaker Faith - In the Experience of One Quaker," *The Carillon*, 13 (10) (2015), 4–9.

Carol Stoneburner and John Stoneburner, *The Influence of Quaker Women on American History* (Lewiston, Queenston: Edwin Mellen Press,1986).

Michele Lise Tarter and Catie Gill, editors, *New Critical Studies on Early Quaker Women, 1650–1800* (Oxford: Oxford University Press, 2018).

John Tomkins, *Piety Promoted, in a Collection of the Dying Sayings of Many of the People Call'd Quakers with a Brief Account of Some of Their Labours in the Gospel, and Sufferings for the Same*, 2nd ed. (London: T. Sowle, 1703).

Christine Trevett, *Women and Quakerism in the 17th Century* (York, England: The Ebor, 1991).

Christine Trevett, "Anne Camm and the Vanishing Quaker Prophet," *Quaker Studies*, 3(2), 82–110 (1998). George Fox University. http://digitalcommons.georgefox.edu/quakerstudies.

David Underdown, *Fire from Heaven: Life in an English Town in the Seventeenth Century* (London: Fontana, 1993).

William R. Wagstaff, *History of the Society of Friends: Compiled from Its Standard Records and Other Authentic Sources* (New York: Wiley and Putnam, 1845).

Judith Boulbie and Mary Waite, *The Oppression of Prophecy: Quaker Women in Late Seventeenth Century Yorkshire: Writings by Judith Boulbie and Mary Waite* (1669) (electronic edition). Edited with an introduction by Amy Enright. file:///Users/bluetke/Desktop/NOVEL%20Women%20Writers%20Resource%20Project%20:%20The%20Oppression%20of%20Prophecy:%20Quaker%20Women%20in%20Late%20Seventeenth%20.webarchive

Maurice J. Wigham, *The Irish Quakers* (Dublin: Historical Committee of the Religious Society of Friends in Ireland, 1992).

Jean Kinney Williams, *The Quakers* (Danbury, CT: Franklin Watts, 1998).

Thomas Wight and John Rutty, *History of the Rise and Progress of the People called Quakers in Ireland from the Year 1653 to 1700* (Dublin: I. Jackson,1751).

Background Material

Geraldine Brooks, *Year of Wonder* (New York: Penguin, 2001).

Geraldine Brooks, *March* (New York: Viking, 2005).

Geraldine Brooks, *Caleb's Crossing* (New York: Viking, 2011).

Jan de Hartog, *The Peaceable Kingdom* (London: Hamish Hamilton, 1972).

Sue Monk Kidd, *The Invention of Wings* (New York, Viking Penguin, 2004).

Ann Turnbull, *No Shame, No Fear (Quaker Trilogy #1)* (London: Walker Books, 2003).

Ann Turnbull, *Forged in the Fire* (London: Walker Books, 2006).

Ann Turnbull, *Seeking Eden* (London: Walker Books, 2011).

Acknowledgements

Nothing of importance that I have ever done was accomplished without the love and support of a tribe. This multi-year project is no exception. Thank you to you all, especially those who were so encouraging with first drafts and those who provided hospitality. I offer deep gratitude to my development editor, Julie Meadows, and the year she devoted to this project. Also to Meg Butterworth, a member of my Clearness Committee, who served with diligence and encouragement for four years, and Peggy Mayer, who sent encouragement (and editing suggestions) through to the project's end. I also appreciate the steadfast encouragement of Jim Ricks and his multiple times of editing throughout the process.

Many others assisted in various ways, including Rachel Bewley-Bateman, Mark and Sara Betnel, Richard Bloomfield and Denise Gabuzda, Karima and Steve Brooke, Meg Butterworth, Marcy Byrd, Max Carter, Jane Chattell and Roger Paddison, Justin Champion, Gunnel Tedin Clark, Susan Clark, Jaime Clausen, Bette Cox Gray-Fow, Angela Dahm (and the Committed to Get Fit team), Ben Dandelion, Tom and Carol Ewell, David K. Farkas, Val Fergunson, Sea Gabriel, Ginger Garner, Lucy Garnett, Iris Graville, Betty Hagglund, Tom Hamm, Wendy Hampton, Danise Heisey, Anna Higgins, Kate Holliday, Dáibhí Ingerson, Kendal Quaker Meeting, Mary Klein, Dvorah Kost, Charles and Marj Lamb, Peter Lamb, Martin Layton, David Lee, Piper Leigh, Jan Longfellow, Art Luetke, Charlie Luetke/Jen Rex, Hannah Luetke-Stahlman, Rachel MacNair, Edith Maxwell, Julie Meadows, Rick McClure, Stuart Masters, Peggy Mayer, Clare McCann, Ellen Michaud, Eric Moon, Rosemary Moore,

Christopher Moriarty (and the Irish Quaker Historical Library in Dublin), Northwest School for Deaf and Hard-of-Hearing Children, Roena Oesting, Penn Valley Friends Meeting, Kabian Rendel, Sara Reyerson, Breeze Richardson, Jim Ricks, Martin Riley, Judith Roads, Salmon Bay Friends Meeting, Paul Seaver, Gil Skidmore, Ellen Nickel Stone, Michelle Tarter, Ann Turnbull, Andrea Vanni, Cecilia Walsh, Roy Wilson and Susanne Ratcliffe Wilson, Mike Wold, and everyone at Woodbrooke Quaker Study Centre.

Finally, thank you to my readers. I am anxious to know of your reaction and thoughts about this, my first novel. You can find me on Facebook or contact me by e-mailing me at bluetke@ymail.com (which is ymail and not gmail). I am available to talk to your group about the research and writing processes, the facts, or the "telling."

About the Author

Barbara Schell Luetke is a member of Salmon Bay Meeting (Seattle, Washington) and North Pacific Yearly Meeting. She also attends Madison Temple Church of God in Christ, a Pentecostal church located in the heart of Seattle. Barbara is the mother of four adult daughters and was a professor in Deaf Education for fifty years. She has published eight books and over a hundred journal articles. This novel, her first, was written after a pilgrimage to 1652 Country and study at Woodbrooke Quaker Study Centre.

CPSIA information can be obtained
at www.ICGtesting.com
Printed in the USA
FSHW011113151119
64080FS